The Reluctant Republic

Malcolm Turnbull was born in Sydney in 1954 and was educated at Sydney University before winning a Rhodes Scholarship to Oxford University.

His first career was journalism. He wrote for *Nation Review* and the *Bulletin* and commented on state politics for radio while studying at Sydney University. He later wrote for the *Sunday Times* while at Oxford.

Returning to Sydney he was admitted to the NSW Bar in 1980. He established his reputation by defending Kerry Packer before the Costigan Royal Commission. In 1986 (and during appeals in 1987 and 1988) he successfully defended Peter Wright against the British Government in the famous Spycatcher Case.

Since its inception in 1987, he has been Managing Director of the investment bank Turnbull and Partners Ltd.

Malcolm Turnbull has been a prominent advocate of the need for Australia to become a republic. He was a Foundation Director and is the current Chairman of the Australian Republican Movement. In April 1993 the Prime Minister appointed him as Chairman of the Republic Advisory Committee. Their report was tabled in October 1993.

Malcolm Turnbull lives in Sydney with his wife, Lucy Hughes, and their two children, Alexander and Daisy.

Also by Malcolm Turnbull

The Spycatcher Trial

The Reluctant Republic

MALCOLM TURNBULL

William Heinemann Australia

Published 1993 by William Heinemann Australia
a part of Reed Books Australia
22 Salmon Street, Port Melbourne, Victoria 3207
a division of Reed International Books Australia Pty Limited

Typeset in 11/14 Palatino by J & M Typesetting
Printed and bound in Australia by Griffin Paperbacks

National Library of Australia
cataloguing-in-publication data:

Turnbull, Malcolm, 1954– .
The reluctant republic

ISBN 0 85561 372 6.

1. Republicanism – Australia. 2. Australia – Politics and
government – 1900– . I. Title.

321.860994

Dedication

It would be a long list indeed if I were to set out the names of all those who have worked tirelessly in the cause of the republic. I have had, as always, unstinting support in this endeavour from my wife, Lucy, and my two children, Alexander and Daisy. And while Alexander and Daisy have only given a few speeches in support of the republic, it is to them that I dedicate this book; for just as the republic is the cause of Australia, so is it the cause of the future. And the future, as always, belongs to the young.

Acknowledgements

It was the events of Australia Day 1988 which moved me to write this book and it is a tribute to the patience and good humour of my publisher and friend, Sandy Grant, that he has waited so long for it.

The Reluctant Republic was completed early in 1993, but when I was appointed Chairman of the Republic Advisory Committee we were obliged to postpone its publication until after the report had been completed. The book has since been updated, with help from Tony Pooley, to take account of events since April 1993 and, in particular, the Republic Advisory Committee's Report.

I am also indebted to the following people and organisations for their kind permission to reprint material included in this book: Mr Stephen Mills, Foreign Editor, *Australian Financial Review*; Newspoll and the *Australian*; Quadrant Research Services; the Roy Morgan Research Centre; Irving Saulwick and Associates; and the Australian Government Printing Service.

Contents

INTRODUCTION

by
Robert Hughes AO

I once saw the Queen up close, about eight feet away. With 23 other Riverview cadets, I was standing on the Figtree Bridge over the Lane Cove River, clutching a Lee-Enfield .303 at the 'present arms' position, when she drove by. We were sweating like young pigs in our battledress, and since (despite acute curiosity) we weren't allowed to swing our heads after her, the Monarch and her consort passed in a nanosecond; I retain a pink memory of something resembling a powder puff framed in the black gleam of the official Bentley, the disdainful beak of Philip, and a waving glove. We of the honour guard then shouldered arms, ordered arms, stood at ease, stood easy, shambled into the bus and were driven back to school. 'That's something you'll never forget', one of the priests said to us later — though his tone implied that it wasn't as though we had seen the Pope.

And of course I didn't forget it, but I can't claim — and I doubt if any of the other boys in the honour guard could either — that I felt any marked emotion at the sight of the Queen or at my own good luck in being allowed to salute her: certainly none that even faintly resembled the feelings which, on that royal tour of 1954, were convulsing the breasts of our elders, causing women of my mother's generation to faint in front of the Sydney Town Hall and be dragged away on stretchers, and making all the flower-clocks of the suburban railway stations run slightly fast in patriotic anticipation of the Second Gloriana. One may not have bought the line, created to console Britain for its post-war blues, that the coronation of Elizabeth II made us all 'new Elizabethans'. But at least one didn't think it automatically ridiculous, as such a claim would seem today.

In terms of monarchical enthusiasm, mine was a generation in transit. We who were born in or around 1938 grew up in an Australia whose attitudes to the Crown were almost inconceivably different from today's. The sacramental *mana* of royalty was still in place and wholly intact, not yet undermined by doubt or disfigured by scandal. The gravitational pull of the monarchy defied the inverse square law. It actually seemed to get stronger the further away from London you were.

The reasons for this, in the particular case of Australia, were no mystery. All through the nineteenth century, and well past the year of Federation, Australians had been troubled by their historical origins as citizens of England's dumping-ground, the criminal continent. Belief in the Convict Stain produced an obsession with respectability, while reinforcing the fear that we were actually second-rate. We rejoiced, insecurely, in being 'Britons', but the English themselves knew perfectly well what we were — colonials. Thus the fact that some of our ancestors had once been outcasts made us all extremely receptive to the rhetoric of Imperial unity. For at least half a century, from the 1880s to the 1930s, Australians felt forgiven for the Original Sin of our convict parents when England graciously allowed them to supply her with cheap wheat and wool, and permitted their sons to fight and die for her. Blood-sacrifice expunged the stain.

The working of this psychic device depended entirely on having a personification of Britishness — hence of our higher identity as 'Britons' — to look up to. Thus, the need for a monarch; Australians, by definition, could not 'look up to' another Australian, since that would have offended our own egalitarianism and put an impossible strain on our national sense of diminished self-worth. Having the Queen as Head of State exactly represented our colonial status in the nineteenth century; it therefore made sense. But by the 1950s the sense was withering and only the reflexes it had engendered remained. We needed an icon invulnerable to our own ironies, someone literally beyond them, and hence ourselves. Australians could point to the royal *mana*, and acquire some sort of power from doing so — the career of Robert Menzies, last of the full-scale Australian political royalists, illustrated that. But we could not reproduce that aura among ourselves, or imagine it credibly embodied in one of our own citizens. Hence it seemed entirely natural and inevitable that we should have a Head of State, with power to dissolve our governments and repeal our laws, who was not a citizen of our country and lived 14000 miles away. She was benign; she was 'above politics', transcending our often raucous factionalism; she had our true interests at heart. Her visits to Australia were epiphanies staged for a country whose own sense of civic ceremony had always been notoriously weak — pre-empted, in fact, by royal ritual. Australia's only binding secular ceremony in the 1950s, apart from royal visits, was Anzac Day. On one level, this annual rite of military remembrance celebrated the intrinsic bravery of Australians. But its basic imagery was loyalty — sacrifice, not to some idea of an Australian nation, but to England and the Crown. Through the institution of Anzac Day, Australia in the 1950s and the early 1960s remained one of the very few countries in the world to divert its imagery of sacrifice away from itself, from its own possible nature as a society moving in history, back towards its colonial origins in the subliminal stain. Hence the fiercely reactionary role played in the republican debate by spokesmen for the Returned Services League, from the moment the debate began to take form. It helped ensure that Australia's relationship to England, its sense of itself on a broad cultural level, would remain vassal-like and even childish — the Good Son among so many ungrateful prodigals — well into the 1960s.

The cause of republicanism was so feeble in 1954, so tied to old socialist dreams of the late nineteenth century, that it seemed to middle-class Australians merely an obsolete rhetorical idea, fatally contaminated by its left-wing origins. It belonged to the griping ratbags in the back of Henry Lawson's woolsheds, not to the new Australia of Holdens and TV. Hence the inversion — a perfect spectacle of the colonial double-bind. To be a monarchist was to be a 'real' Australian, speaking for 'really Australian' (that is, British) values. Whereas to be a republican, in favour of full Australian self-determination, was to be a Lefty, and hence, in the parlance of the day, a dupe of Moscow's imperial designs. The dead language of the dead Cold War. The force of this reflex was neatly represented in 1963 (can it really be 30 years ago? *Mais oui, citoyens*) when the writer Geoffrey Dutton, son of the grazing patriciate, great-grand nephew of a Premier of South Australia, created the first manifesto of modern Australian republicanism with an article published in *Nation* in 1963. 'The point is not to pick a quarrel with the English,' he wrote, 'but to reach an adult relationship with them ... The remedies I would advocate would lose me half my friends and provoke nothing more than a cynical smile from politicians of either side. They are simple: declare Australia a republic; elect our own Governors; abolish the use of the word British (in referring to ourselves) and substitute Australian. The Americans took much the same step in 1776.'

'SEND DUTTON BACK TO RUSSIA WHERE HE BELONGS' ran a headline in the Adelaide *News* a few days later. But thanks to Dutton's article, the cat was out of the bag. The first book to discuss republicanism as a practical Australian possibility was Donald Horne's *The Lucky Country*, published in 1964. By the beginning of the 1970s thousands of Australian kids, presently to be Australian voters, were reading in school the republican arguments of Horne — along with those of Dutton and Manning Clark, our Michelet. Many of these kids were the sons and daughters of post-war migrants: folk from places like Skópelos, Dubrovnik, Beirut, Montealegre, Ankara, Cracow or Budapest, people who, while indubitably Australian now, felt only a little more innate attachment to Queen Elizabeth II than we Anglo-Irish Australian schoolboys of the 1950s might have been expected to feel to King Farouk or King Zog. Thus by the mid-1970s the idea of republicanism had established a niche (a small and precarious one, but a niche all the same) in Australian political consciousness.

And then, in 1975, came John Kerr.

If Kerr's action, as Governor-General, in dismissing Whitlam in the Queen's name can be seen as a watershed of Australian republican sentiment, it wasn't for the reasons some adduce. It was a constitutional issue, not strictly a republican one — you could imagine (though in 1993 it would be a waste of time) a monarchist Australia with the Queen as Head of State, in which her Governor-General did not have the power to dissolve an elected government. In any case not all Australians, by any means, loved Whitlam; nor did they all see him as a charismatic figure, as some voters of the left still did when he was ejected from office. But the fact, suddenly made concrete, that any elected Prime Minister could be dismissed at the royal pleasure brought all Australians up with a sharp jerk, regardless of their political loyalties. *This*, when all was said and done, was the meaning of a clause in the Australian Constitution, a document unread by practically everyone except a few specialists — this old colonial bomb of a proviso, seemingly harmless, which had suddenly gone off and blown Whitlam out of Canberra. Notionally, it could do so again to someone else, left, right or centre. This, not nostalgia for Gough Whitlam, was what eventually stuck in the national craw. John Kerr's action unintentionally created the first tremor of *bipartisan* doubt about the monarchy's power in Australia. The Australian left, dazed by the toppling of Whitlam, talked about it in flat terms of angry and impotent *revanchism*, but below the turmoil Australian republicanism began in earnest to lift free of its left-wing origins.

This was a development no-one, and Kerr least of all, expected. But 20 years later, it is an accomplished fact, and if the Australian Republican Movement is to succeed — as it now seems bound to do, given the explosive recent growth of its support in the opinion polls (69 per cent according to one poll at the time of writing) before which most political opposition to republicanism has simply crumbled — it can only be as a bipartisan effort, created by the simplest minimum of constitutional change, representing a general consensus about who Australians are and how they want to stand in the world. Nothing else can carry the necessary referendum. In any case, republicanism, as Malcolm Turnbull eloquently argues in this book, must not be reduced to a party issue. It addresses Australian identity on a much deeper level.

Undoubtedly, the republican cause has been helped by TV — as much by the fact of its existence, as by the content of its programmes. My generation, which came of age without seeing a TV broadcast, couldn't have foreseen that TV would work against the political mystique of royalty. Nobody in the world imagined that, when I was 15. Indeed, nobody suspected it in the early 1960s, when I turned 25. Before TV, the monarch was remote, extraordinary, veiled. Australia got TV in 1956. After TV the monarch and her family started to become celebrities. The slow desacralisation of the Crown by the box began, by almost imperceptible degrees, in the late 1960s and gathered speed in the 1970s. Elizabeth II, the most genuinely popular monarch since Victoria, managed her relationship with TV and other mass media extremely well, but she was swimming against the current of exhibition and banalisation that TV and the tabloids set up. Her family, as all now know, have managed it very poorly. An earlier Prince of Wales, frolicking with the noted horizontals of the *belle epoque* in Maxim's and, as King, selling peerages for pocket-money, could get away with it because a loyal press did not report such things. But it is difficult to believe in the mystique of the Windsors when Fergie's toes are being sucked in front of a telephoto lens; and Camilla Parker-Bowles' tampon is to the future Charles III what the headsman's block was to Charles I. Monarchies can survive regicide, but not *that*.

But the need for an Australian republic is not contingent on what you think of the private or public behaviour of the royals. It lies beyond the scandals and transcends matters of celebrity. Real monarchists may loathe the behaviour of the younger royals, and feel betrayed by it; real republicans may have a genuine admiration for Elizabeth II. Both are irrelevant to the republican issue, which is one of self-governance and adulthood. The republic, when it is made, will enfold and make room for all shades of political opinion, all party issues. There is nothing contradictory about liking the Queen and not having her. The contradiction lies in being an Australian patriot who believes his Head of State should not be Australian. Whom should we 'look up to'? Ourselves. The republic cannot be put off. It is no longer a question of waiting until the emblematic year 2001. The republic will not wait. The importance of Malcolm Turnbull's text, I believe, is that of a practical manual, summarising the growth of this national desire, showing a coherent course of *political* action for realising it, analysing — clearly and incisively, in terms that any non-specialist can grasp — the constitutional issues involved, and showing how threadbare and even comic the monarchist opposition's case has turned out to be. He has written the republic's cookbook. We read Dutton, and hoped. We read Horne, and saw. Now we should read Turnbull, and act.

CHAPTER ONE

A Republican Roused

January 26, 1988. Sydney Harbour was glittering in the
bright sunshine. A million Australians crowded the foreshores. A fleet of tall ships, their sails full-bellied in the
wind, glided past hundreds of yachts and launches and surf
skis and sailboarders. It was Australia Day, the two hundredth anniversary of the day that Captain Arthur Phillip of
the royal navy founded the convict settlement at Sydney
Cove.

I watched all this from the top of a big building in the city,
towering above the spot where modern Australian history
began. Down below me, at the Opera House, a large crowd
of dignitaries had gathered to hear speeches from the Prime
Minister, the State Premier, religious leaders and others.
This was to be the most important day in a most important
year. It was a day that we would wish always to remember,
to tell our children and grandchildren about: the spectacle,

1

the fireworks ... but not the pride. This was not to be a day Australians would remember with the kind of pride such a day should inspire. The organisers could be proud that none of the sailing ships ran aground, and that the fireworks went off without setting the city alight. The police could be proud that nobody got hurt and that the crowds were good-natured and did not leave too much litter on the foreshore.

That day should have inspired a different sort of pride: a pride of nation, a pride of being Australian. There was every reason for Australians to be proud — the tangible evidence of their achievements was all around them. But the nation was not honoured on Australia Day, 1988. Instead of affirming our particular identity as Australians, we confirmed — or our leaders confirmed for us — that we were not a nation like other nations, that we were still something less. For at the Opera House I could see and hear the speeches. The most important one, the longest one, the one accorded the place of honour, was not uttered by an Australian. It was given by an Englishman, Prince Charles. He and his wife, Diana, were the focus of that morning's celebration. They arrived on an admiral's barge after all the other guests had assembled. At the last minute the Prince had decided he wished to speak for a little longer than had been originally planned, and of course the minor actors, including the Prime Minister of Australia, had to accommodate him. Our two hundredth national day was presided over by an Englishman. Our own national leaders were just warm-up acts for the Prince of Wales.

To his credit, Prince Charles seemed quite unsure why he had been asked at all. He referred to himself and his wife as 'visitors' who had been 'invited'. The heir to the Australian throne should not feel he is a visitor in his future realm. But of course Prince Charles understood, better than those who invited him, that Australia was not his country and that he was not an Australian.

I had always been a republican at least as long as I had thought about political matters. Like many Australians I had imagined the monarchy would just wither away. Its disappearance seemed too inevitable to justify a push. But 1988 convinced me that unless ordinary Australians spoke out against the monarchy and demanded that an *Australian* be our nation's Head of State, the change might never come about. That Bicentennial year was a year of shame. Every major event was presided over by a member of the British royal family. When the world was looking at Australia in a way it had never done before, we demonstrated to the world that we were not yet a nation. Billions of foreigners saw the woman they know as the Queen of England opening our new Commonwealth Parliament, the International Expo in Brisbane and the enormous Darling Harbour development in Sydney. They saw Prince Charles and Diana in centre stage on Australia Day. When the eyes of the world turned to Australia we showed them ... the royal family of another country.

Of course Australia was an independent nation in 1988, just as it is today in 1993 as I write these words. The British monarchy occupies no more than a symbolic position in Australia. True it is that a literal reading of the Constitution appears to confer immense power on the Queen and her appointed representative the Governor-General, but the Constitution is a quite misleading guide to the practice of Australian government. We are an independent nation. Our independence was as much forced upon us as claimed by us. The history of our relationship with Britain has been more a history of Britain pulling away from Australia than of Australia demanding its independence.

Yet so long as our Constitution provides that whoever sits on the throne of Great Britain is to be our Head of State, our progress to independence is incomplete. It is a sentence without a full stop. It is like a fence with all the palings painted but one. It is an unfinished work.

The cause of the Australian republic is more than just a patriotic ideal. It is not simply the legitimate national aspiration which demands that every office under our Constitution should be filled by Australian citizens who owe their first allegiance to this country and no other.

The republic is a challenge. It is a challenge to us today, and to all Australians in the years to come. It is a challenge to overcome those demeaning and diminishing sentiments of fear and despair which have often dogged our growth as a nation.

The republic is the cause of Australia. It asserts that this is the land we love the best. This is our home. This is the harbour of our destiny and of our children's destiny. It asserts that it is among our own citizens that we will find our best help and it is to our own citizens that we shall give our first assistance.

The republic says that this is Australia: a nation not defined by race or religion or colour or cultural background, but a nation defined by its citizens' commitment to this land above all others. A commitment to our own unique democracy and democratic institutions.

A nation defines itself by being different. Only colonies continue to borrow the monarchies of other lands.

But more importantly than all that, the republic is the cause which defines the attitudes we will take with us into the twenty-first century. It demands courage of us to overcome the fear born of ignorance. It demands a confidence in ourselves and our own capacity. It demands hope for the future instead of a despairing yearning for the past.

Are we really so uniquely incompetent as a people, so lacking in self-confidence, so frightened of change, that as the millennium approaches, we cannot agree to have an Australian Head of State, but instead will continue, for the centuries to come, to retain the most honoured place in our Constitution for the monarchy of another land? Are we to continue with a vacuum at the centre of our Constitution?

Fifty years ago the patriotic ideals of Australia were not distinct from those of Great Britain. Public and political meetings in those days would have seen the platform festooned with Union Jacks, there would have been a portrait of the King-Emperor on the wall and the meeting would have ended with *God Save the King*, *Rule Britannia* and other patriotic British airs.

History has seen Australia become its own nation, an

Australian nation, no longer defined by reference to the nationalities and cultures of other countries. We have established our own principles, our own ideals, and those ideals are affronted and offended by the British monarchy.

We live in a non-sectarian society; section 116 of our Constitution says in part 'no office or public trust under the Commonwealth shall be subject to any religious test'. Our Constitution says our monarch is whoever succeeds to Queen Victoria in the sovereignty of the United Kingdom. No one but an Anglican can be the King or Queen of England. Indeed, the King or Queen of England cannot even marry someone who is not a Protestant. Prince Michael of Kent had to renounce his succession to the throne when he married a Catholic, and an Australian one at that. So here we have a thoroughly sectarian monarchy presiding over our supposedly secular society. And yet the monarchists would have us believe that the monarchy is an Australian institution which represents our democratic ideals.

The monarchy does not represent my ideals, and I would be very sad to think that there were many Australians who idealise a sectarian nation. Rather, we believe that we live in a nation where all citizens are equal, and yet we have a monarchy constituting our office of Head of State to which only members of a particular, foreign family can succeed. We claim to live in a society which demands that there be no discrimination on the basis of sex, and yet the monarchy is the ultimate sexist institution because the youngest male child will take precedence over the eldest daughter. These traditions of vested privilege, of sectarianism and of sexism are traditions of Britain. They have no place in our country, Australia. For the monarchy is not only alien in Australia today in a sense that it is not Australian, but it affronts those fundamental democratic values which we hold dear and which define our nation.

Can we really inspire Australians to these democratic and egalitarian ideals, can we inspire young Australians to have pride in their nation by exhorting them to admire and love the Queen? Fifty years ago, when patriotism was encouraged in primary schools and high schools, they would talk about the King or the Queen and the Empire and Great Britain and the crimson thread of kinship which bound the British race together.

We would speak as Menzies did in 1948: 'the boundaries of Britain do not lie on the Kentish Coast, they are to be found at Cape York and Invercargill.'[1] Menzies saw Australia as part of Britain, as part of the British world. It is easy to satirise Menzies today, but I do not seek to satirise him at all. He was the most successful federal politician we have ever known, and he was successful because he represented the views and aspirations of many, often most, Australians. Those days have passed.

What does the Crown symbolise today? For Robert Menzies, or indeed Dr Evatt, in 1953, when the first Australian *Royal Style and Titles Act* was passed, the Crown meant Britain. That Act, for the first time, included a reference to Australia in the Queen's Australian title. Menzies said, when proposing that Bill, 'to us the Crown is the enduring symbol that wherever we are in the world we are one people'. 'We' did not mean the Australian people, nor did he mean the people of Victoria or Western Australia. Menzies meant the British people, the British race. We were part of one people populating all those lovely parts of the world which were coloured pink, rather than other, less edifying colours.

In 1901, when our Constitution was established, Australia was truly a colony. Far from being the birth certificate of a nation, our Constitution is rather the rule book for a colony.

What is the most fundamental principle of our democracy which we all hold dear? That the nation is ruled by a Government which must have the confidence of the House of Representatives elected by the people. That the Government is responsible to the House of Representatives, the people's House. This principle finds no reference in the Constitution. If you read the Constitution and took it literally you would be excused for believing that the Governor-General ran the country and that Parliament was an obscure debating society which had something to do with making laws and giving the Governor-General's Government the money it needed to govern.

And yet are we republicans to be vilified as radicals and revolutionaries betraying our country's history if we say that the principals of our democracy should be written down so that the people can read them? Or are our opponents rather like those old clerics in the Middle Ages who objected to the translation of the Bible into the vernacular because it would enable the laity to read God's word for themselves?

We have become weary of the hand-wringing anxiety of people who are afraid of the future, but lack the courage, or the energy, to play a part in shaping it. We are entitled, as Australians, to grow weary of the scare-mongering practised by those people who say: the republic is about abolishing the States, the republic is about abolishing the flag, the republic is about doing away with the Protestant churches, or, best of all, that it is an international conspiracy run by the Vatican and the Freemasons.

The republic is about nothing more than asserting our national identity. It is about having the courage to recognise who we are, and where we are, and that our destiny lies here. It is about creating meaningful symbols of nationhood. Do we doubt why there are so few pictures of the Queen in public offices and schools; why children no longer sing *God Save the Queen*; why, when students are exhorted to honour their country, they are not pointed to the Queen as a symbol of the nation?

The reason is that the Queen cannot symbolise the nation. When she visits an Australian city, do the people lining the route cry out, 'There goes Australia!'? Are they touched with the same kind of national sentiment that the people of France feel when they see their President lead the singing of the *Marseillaise*?

When other nations see their Head of State, they see through the mist the history of their nation. They see the battles and the sieges, the poets and the princes, they see the pride, the triumph, the shame and the despair that makes up the history of a nation. We have known those passions and those causes in our history. But when we see the Queen, what do we see but a nation not our own?

Are we to remain forever like adult children pathetically clutching the frayed ends of parted apron strings, no longer even connected to mother, because mother has gone away to Europe? Our development as an independent nation has been largely a phenomenon of Britain leaving Australia. This is the first time in our history that Australians have thought, as a people, of asserting their independence.

Since Federation, every step in the development of our independence has exclusively been the work of politicians and lawyers, often British, often from other British Dominions. In 1926 it was agreed at an Imperial Conference that the Governor-General would cease to be the representative of the Imperial Government. Prior to that date all communications between the Government of a Dominion, such as Australia, and the United Kingdom went through the Governor-General. That change in 1926 was not fought for by Australia. It was Canada and South Africa who demanded an increased level of independence.

In 1931 the *Statute of Westminster* incorporated those principles of Dominion autonomy into legislation and that Statute provided that the British Parliament would not legislate for any Dominion without the request and consent of the Dominion concerned.

Australia opposed these changes. Our fearful politicians decided that they smacked of independence and it was not until 1942, in the darkest days of the Second World War, that Australia reluctantly adopted the *Statute of Westminster*. More recently, the *Australia Act* of 1986 finally ended the colonial status of the Australian States and provided that when a Premier wished to appoint a Governor, he or she would communicate directly with the Queen rather than through the British Dominions Office. The *Australia Act* also finally abolished appeals from Australian courts to the British Privy Council.

The changes in 1926, 1931 and 1986 all amounted to substantial alterations to the way we are governed. We began this century as a colony with Governors-General supervising our governments and ensuring that no legislation was approved which did not meet London's requirements. Indeed section 59 of the Constitution enabled the British Government, via the Queen, to annul any Australian legislation (even though it had been signed by the Governor-General) within twelve months of its enactment. By 1986 the only colonial vestige was the Queen.

None of these changes was effected by the people, no section of the Constitution was altered by referendum. The people never had a say in that debate. All those changes were secured in Imperial conferences and meetings of prime ministers, premiers and attorneys-general. The republican referendum will be the first opportunity the Australian people have had to draw the line between the fearful hand-wringers clinging to the past, and those who have the courage to see the future and the hope to shape it, who have the courage to create national institutions that are meaningful for Australians.

We do not aspire to an American republic or a Latvian republic. We just aspire to have a Head of State chosen by Australians who would fulfil exactly the same role as the Governor-General does today. Now we are told by some that this will lead to dictatorship and if we lose the Queen our democracy will collapse. The Queen's ability to maintain democracy is not very evident in Northern Ireland, nor is it evident in Papua New Guinea, the Solomon Islands or in Fiji or many other realms.

Because the fact is that the republicans know that Australia's democracy and its political stability depend upon the goodwill and commonsense of Australians. It owes nothing to the Queen. The Queen is a symbol, a symbol without substance.

We look to the future and we see an independent Australia, we see Australians who define their nationhood by their commitment to the institutions and ideals of this country. That is the vision of the republic. It is a vision of patriotism. It is an Australian vision, a vision that in years to come will determine whether we have the courage to embrace the future or whether we are closed off by fear and despair that we will remain forever subject to a symbol that represents a childhood that has long passed us by.

The cause of the republic has come a long way since the Australian Republican Movement made its first public appearance in July 1991. A majority of Australians do favour a change and that majority is overwhelming among the younger generations and among those Australians who come from a non-English-speaking background. Time is on our side. But we cannot be complacent. It is important that this final seal on our nation's independence is placed there by the active and informed consent of the Australian people.

The republican debate is the most important constitutional debate in the history of our nation. It is engaging more people than any constitutional debate since the 1890s when the Constitution itself was drafted. More Australians are reading and discussing the Constitution than ever before. As they learn more about the Constitution and its history they are empowered. And they are not simply empowered to effect a change to the identity of the Head of State.

The single greatest obstacle to constitutional change in Australia is ignorance about the Constitution. Australian governments, both state and federal and of all political complexions, have failed to provide proper instruction about our system of government, our Constitution and its history. As the Republic Advisory Committee travelled around Australia listening to Australians' questions and ideas about the Constitution, it became apparent that most of our fellow citizens are more familiar with the American Constitution than they are with their own.

Widespread ignorance about the Constitution makes a meaningful discussion very difficult. All of us have perfect freedom to discuss quantum physics, but unless we are trained in that field of science the freedom is effectively valueless. So it is with the Constitution. The less people know about it the less they are able to participate in the debate and the more they can be successfully intimidated by scaremongering which seeks to prey on and promote that ignorance.

Some Australians are disappointed that the republican cause does not embrace a wider agenda for constitutional change. But they should not imagine that simply because republicans advocate a change to the identity of the Head of State that they support every other clause in the Constitution in its present form. The truth is that the identity of the Head of State is a separate and distinct issue. The role of the States, the powers of the Senate, the rights of indigenous people, the enactment of a constitutional Bill of Rights are all important and legitimate matters for constitutional debate. But they are logically separate issues from that of the identity of the Head of State. There are monarchists who favour the abolition of the States and republicans who favour a diminution of the power of the central government and an increase in the autonomy of the States. But all of these other important issues need to be advanced and debated on their own merits. If the republican bandwagon is overladen with other issues the axles will break and the wheels will fall off.

But as the republican debate increases the level of public awareness of the Constitution, so it empowers the Australian people to debate and consider other proposals for constitutional change. And that is the truly radical aspect of the republican cause. It is radical because it is genuinely democratic and because it is unprecedented in our society. Our opponents smugly observe that because Australians don't understand the Constitution, they will not be able to understand the republican cause. Our opponents will not only urge Australians not to vote for something they don't understand, they will do everything in their power to ensure that they never understand it. The defenders of the monarchy are advocates of ignorance.

The promotion of ignorance is the principal tactic left to the defenders of the monarchy. The Report of the Republic Advisory Committee which was released on 5 October 1993 was widely praised as a fair and informative contribution to the debate. The serious newspapers published extensive summaries of the report and urged their readers to obtain a copy and read it for themselves. Yet the response of Australians for Constitutional Monarchy, whose members include the Chancellor of Sydney University, Dame Leonie Kramer, was to dismiss the report as 'too long and complicated' and to discourage Australians from reading it. The spectacle of a group consisting of a University Chancellor, judges and senior members of the Bar urging Australians not to read a government report dealing with the constitution on the basis that it was 'too long and complex' was almost surreal.

It has often been said that a journey of a thousand miles begins with a single step. We have made many steps in our journey towards the republic, and perhaps are closer to our destination than we imagine. This book is but one step in that journey and if it assists other Australians in travelling with us it will have served its purpose.

CHAPTER TWO

A Dual Identity

The monarchy in Australia is a colonial institution. Its continued presence in our nation is testimony to Australians' reluctance to accept the reality, and responsibility, of nationhood.

Her Majesty is Queen of Australia simply because at the time our Constitution was enacted Australia was a colony of Great Britain. Australia was not an independent nation in 1901, nor did the vast majority of Australians wish it to be so. The Commonwealth Constitution is a Schedule to an Act of what was then called the Imperial (meaning United Kingdom) Parliament. The Preamble to that Act sums up the legislative intention quite nicely:

> Whereas the People of New South Wales, Victoria, South Australia, Queensland and Tasmania humbly relying on the blessing of Almighty God, have agreed to unite in one indissoluble Federal Commonwealth *under* the Crown of

the United Kingdom of Great Britain and Ireland, and under the Constitution hereby established … [emphasis added]

The first operative section of the Act (which precedes the Schedule), section 2, reads:

The provisions of this Act referring to the Queen shall extend to Her Majesty's heirs and successors *in the sovereignty of the United Kingdom*. [emphasis added]

Section 1 of the Constitution itself states that the legislative power of the Commonwealth is vested in a Federal Parliament which consists of 'the Queen, a Senate and a House of Representatives'. Section 2 states that the Queen's representative shall be a Governor-General appointed by the Queen 'during her pleasure'. It adds that the Governor-General shall have such 'powers and functions as the Queen may be pleased to assign to him'. The executive power itself of the Commonwealth is 'vested in the Queen' although 'exercisable by the Governor-General as the Queen's representative' (section 61).

Sections 58 and 59 confer extraordinary powers on the Queen. Section 58 provides that the Governor-General may give, or withhold, his assent to bills passed by both Houses of Parliament. It also provides that he may withhold such bills for the Queen's pleasure. If a bill is reserved for the monarch's approval she has two years to decide whether she wants to approve it (section 60). More disturbingly, however, under section 59 the monarch has the right to disallow, within 12 months of its enactment, legislation passed by Parliament and assented to by the Governor-General and such a disallowance 'will annul the law from the day when the disallowance is so made known'.

The purpose of this power of disallowance is succinctly described by those remarkably well-situated constitutional commentators, Quick and Garran, who wrote in 1901:

There can be no doubt that the reserved power of
disallowance will be wisely and sparingly exercised,
in accordance with the rule long established, that Her
Majesty's [Imperial] Government refrains from
interfering with any colonial legislation which is
consistent with colonial constitutional law, except in
cases involving Imperial and international relations.[1]

It was conventional at the time to refer to the United Kingdom or British Parliament as the Imperial Parliament. This
was not simply a vanity; it reflected the superiority of the
Parliament and Government in London over all the other
British (but inferior) Parliaments throughout the Empire.
Thus both the United Kingdom Parliament, and the Parliaments in Nova Scotia, Bermuda or New South Wales were
all 'British Parliaments' — but only one reigned supreme, at
the head of the Empire, and it was correctly termed Imperial.

The Power of the Monarch

How can one summarise the powers of the monarch (as
opposed to the viceroy) under our Constitution? First, she
has the power to appoint, instruct and remove the Governor-
General; second, she has the power to approve or disap-
prove legislation reserved by the Governor-General for her
pleasure; third, she has the power to override the approval
of the Governor-General and annul a law validly enacted up
to one year previously.

It is clear then that the Queen has considerable power
under our Constitution — power which extends well
beyond the limits already tested by her Viceroy, Sir John
Kerr, in 1975. Her power indeed appears to fly in the face of
parliamentary government. It is more extensive than that
which British constitutional convention allows a British
monarch. The Queen of Britain cannot disallow an Act of
the British Parliament.

So, as far as the Constitution is concerned, the monarch
appears to have powers which are almost dictatorial and

which are certainly anti-democratic. This would give rise to enough concern if the dictator were our own; but these powers were awarded to a foreigner — or more correctly, a foreign nation.

It is plain enough that at the time of the enactment of our Constitution, the Queen was not intended to be our Head of State in the sense that she was the Head of State of the United Kingdom acting solely on the advice of her elected government. Rather the Queen was:

- head of the executive government of Australia;
- her appointment was governed by laws and customs beyond the capacity of the Australian Parliament or people to influence or alter;
- she had considerable powers vested in her which included the right to disallow legislation validly enacted by the Australian Parliament.

It was intended that insofar as the Queen (as opposed to the Governor-General) would exercise her powers under the Constitution they would be exercised *on the advice of her United Kingdom ministers*. It is also true to say that it was intended that the Governor-General would act as an Imperial viceroy whose function included the protection of 'Imperial' interests (as opposed to local ones). Imperial in this context meant the protection of British interests in Australia — be they related to defence or commerce.

Thus for all practical purposes when the word 'Queen' was used in the Constitution it meant *not* the monarch of the United Kingdom for the time being, but rather the *Government* of the United Kingdom. This ultimate power of oversight or supervision was quite appropriate to Australia in 1900 since Australia neither was, nor sought to be, an independent nation. At the turn of the century Australia was no more than a self-governing federation of colonies whose scope of genuine autonomy was limited to those matters of such local importance that their disposition did not concern the British Government in London.

Australians were never obliged to fight for independence — or even self-government — in the way Americans were.

Indeed, the successful War of Independence waged by the American colonists ensured that the British Government in London would never again try to prevent white European British subjects from obtaining self-government. An interesting possibility to consider is that if the British Government in the late eighteenth century had taken the same approach to the North American colonies as it did to the Australian colonies a hundred years later, it is quite likely that America would have become a self-governing dominion of the British Empire much like Canada, Australia and New Zealand.

Responsible Government

The first British colony in Australia was, of course, the penal settlement established at Sydney Cove on 26 January 1788. The Governor was constituted as a despot. There was no popularly representative body established; the bulk of the inhabitants at the outset were either convicts or soldiers, and each of those groups was obliged to do as it was told.

As the proportion of free settlers in the British colonies grew, so did the requirement for more representative institutions. The transportation of convicts to the colony of New South Wales — which at that time included the whole of the eastern coast of Australia — ended in 1840. Twelve years later the last convicts were despatched to Tasmania, although transportation continued to Western Australia until 1868.

From 1856 to 1859 all of the Australian colonies, except for the tiny settlement in Western Australia, had obtained responsible government. Western Australia did not attain responsible government until 1890. They each boasted their own parliaments with two chambers: a Legislative Assembly and a Legislative Council. There were differences between the colonies' arrangements. Initially only South Australia's Legislative Assembly was elected on the basis of white adult male suffrage; the other colonies imposed property-owning conditions on the franchise. The legislative councils were differently elected also. In New South Wales, Queensland and Western Australia the Legislative Council was composed of members appointed by the Governor, whereas in Victoria, South Australia and Tasmania the Legislative Council was composed of members elected by inhabitants possessing property or educational qualifications. Over the following decades all of the legislative assemblies became elected by a universal white male adult franchise. The legislative councils remained either appointed by the Governor, or elected by the wealthier members of the community. This was a deliberate attempt to imitate the 'steadying' influence of the British House of Lords by creating in the legislative councils a more conservative chamber which would restrain the impetuosity of the popularly elected assemblies.

Uniting the Colonies

It is fair to say that in the course of the decades preceding and following the grant of responsible government in the late 1850s Australian politicians were preoccupied with agitating for, and then enjoying, a large measure of autonomy in their own colonies. The Australian colonists were only responsible for their own patches of dirt; it was the Imperial Government in London that concerned itself with defence, international trade and matters of principle. Statesmen in London were thinking about the big picture, while their counterparts in the colonies were concentrating on getting rich.

> Colonials had the same prerogatives as the harlot: they
> had power but not responsibility ... Politicians
> contended not over great questions of principle or
> matters of great moment, but rather over how to win
> 'the scramble for office' ... The minds of colonials were
> not called on to rise above the level of the parish pump.
> Every time a question of general interest was raised, a
> torpor descended on the proceedings of a colonial
> parliament. By contrast every time a question of local

interest was raised the proceedings deteriorated to that
point where they were 'unworthy of the dignity of a
parliament'. As soon as the question of a road or bridge
or school was raised the business of an Assembly
degenerated into a 'a scramble for a share in the
Government plunder.'[2]

So it should be no surprise that the first proposal that the
Australian colonies should be united came not from Australia, but from London. In July 1847, Earl Grey, the Secretary of State for the Colonies, announced his intention to
create a separate colony to be called Victoria, centred on the
new settlement at Port Phillip Bay. In his dispatch to the
Australian colonists he noted that it was appropriate for
matters bearing on the interests of the Empire to be dealt
with by the Imperial Parliament:

> But there are questions which, though local as it respects
> the British possessions in Australia collectively, are not
> merely local as it respects any one of those possessions.
> Considered as members of the same Empire, those
> colonies have many common interests, the regulation
> of which, in some uniform manner and by some single
> authority, may be essential to the welfare of them all.
> Yet in some cases such interests may be more promptly,
> effectively and satisfactorily decided by some authority
> within Australia itself than by the more remote, the less
> accessible and in truth the less competent authority of
> Parliament.[3]

The locals back in Australia — particularly those in New
South Wales — were most unimpressed by Earl Grey's help-
ful suggestions and nothing more was heard of them. The
authorities in London continued to be concerned that as the
Australian colonies acquired an increasing measure of self-
government they would impose different scales of tariffs
which would not only interfere with trade within the
Empire, but would also interfere with trade between the
colonies themselves. In 1849 a Committee of the Privy

Council was instructed to inquire into and report on the constitutional arrangements in the Australian colonies.

The Privy Council report supported Earl Grey's earlier recommendation that there be established a separate colony in Victoria. It also recommended that the Australian colonies of New South Wales, Victoria, South Australia and Van Diemen's Land have legislative councils one-third of whose members would be nominated by the Governor with the balance elected by the wealthier citizens of each colony. The Privy Council also recommended that one of the Governors of the Australian colonies should hold a commission constituting him Governor-General of Australia and that he should have the power to convene a 'General Assembly of Australia' which would be composed of delegates elected by the several legislatures of the colonies, with the larger colonies having greater representation. The Privy Council proposed that this General Assembly would have the power to legislate for all of Australia on inter-colonial trade, customs duties, management of beacons and lighthouses, a Court of Appeal and other matters referred to them by the colonies. In short, the Privy Council was proposing a form of federation. But the Privy Council proposed that representation on the General Assembly be based on population so that out of 25 delegates, New South Wales would have 12, Victoria four, Van Diemen's Land five and South Australia four. This proposal was included in the Australian Colonies Government Bill when it was presented to the British Parliament in 1849.

This far-sighted proposal was met with almost universal opposition in Australia. The Legislative Council of South Australia passed a resolution in December 1849 condemning the proposal for a General Assembly. The Governor of Van Diemen's Land wrote home to express his colony's opposition on the basis that a uniform tariff for all Australian colonies would be particularly harmful to Van Diemen's Land, the vast bulk of whose revenue came from customs duties.

Earl Grey, in the following year, attempted to make the General Assembly proposal more palatable. The Bill was amended to provide that each colony would have four representatives, with an additional representative for every 20 000 of population. This mollified the smaller colonies, but enraged New South Wales. The General Assembly was dropped from the Bill which became the *Australian Constitutions Act* of 1850 and which, nonetheless, established a degree of popular representation in the various legislative councils of the colonies.

A Governor-General

The British Government remained convinced, however, of the need for some form of federal government in Australia, and Earl Grey was clearly more than a little irritated by the provincial pettiness of the colonists. The British Government did, as an afterthought, establish the potential for some federal control by constituting the Governor of New South Wales as Governor-General of 'All Her Majesty's Australian possessions including the Colony of Western Australia' and granting him dormant commissions as Governor of each of the colonies which were administered by Lieutenant-Governors. The newly constituted Governor-General was entitled to visit any of the other colonies and by reason of his dormant commission take precedence over any of the Lieutenant-Governors who were instructed to report to him on any matter of overall Australian interest.

The Governor-Generalship turned out to be little more than a gesture. The experiment was not assisted by Governor FitzRoy being a notorious idler and lecher who made the daughter of the Berrima innkeeper pregnant, and after her father sued him for compensation for loss of the services of his child paid him off with 200 pounds. The visiting rights he enjoyed with the young women of the colony were not those envisaged by his appointment as Governor-General and John Dunmore Lang saw the depravity of the Governor as evidence of the need for independence.

It has been an ancient practice with the Colonial Office to send out men for the highest appointments in the colonies who have been bankrupt alike in character and

in purse; and if this practice has been continued to the
very latest period in New South Wales, it has doubtless
been because the people have hitherto had so little to say
in the management of their own affairs.[4]

In any event, the visiting rights were never exercised and
the last New South Wales Governor to bear the title of
Governor-General was Sir John Young in 1861.

The First Republicans

The history of the Australian colonies in the last half of the
nineteenth century is not particularly inspiring to an Australian nationalist, let alone a republican. While there were a
few radicals who advocated a republic as a means of obtaining complete independence from Britain — often through
the pages of the *Bulletin* — their voices were drowned out
by a chorus of Australian Britons whose love of England
and the Empire became almost a secular religion. In 1901
Quick and Garran published their commentary on the then
brand-new Australian Constitution. They were smugly, but
accurately, dismissive of republicanism:

> Some years ago a few ardent but irresponsible advocates
> of Australian federation indulged in predictions that the
> time would inevitably come when Australia would
> separate from the mother country and become an
> independent republic. Those ill-considered utterances
> caused, at the time, strong expressions of disapproval
> throughout the colonies, which effectually prevented
> the repetition of such suggestions, as being beyond the
> arena of serious contemplation and debate. Throughout
> the political campaign which preceded the election of
> the Federal Convention, not a solitary public writer or
> speaker seriously discussed the possibility, much less
> the probability, of separation.[5]

With a few radical exceptions, Australians — or at least the
white adult males among them — regarded themselves as

Britons who lived in Australia. Their Australianness was at best a sense of place, not a sense of nation. The desire to transplant English ways and manners in a different land is well summed up by the motto of the University of Sydney: *Sidere mens eadem mutato* — the same mind under different stars.

Not all of the colonists were of this mind however. There was always a radical, nationalistic element. John Dunmore Lang was a Presbyterian clergyman who arrived in Sydney in 1823. He was the first Presbyterian minister to come to Australia. In August 1824 he preached and dispensed the sacrament at the Presbyterian chapel at Ebenezer, the first Presbyterian church built in Australia, and the first church of any kind built by free labour.

Lang campaigned throughout his long life for complete independence for Australia. In 1850 he gave a lecture on this theme, called 'The Coming Event', to an enthusiastic crowd of supporters:

> Self-government is the inherent and indefeasible right
> of such communities as most of the British Colonies of
> the present day; and if that right is not conceded
> peacefully, those from whom it is unjustly withheld
> will only be acting in accordance with the great law of
> self-preservation, if they wrest it from their oppressors
> on the first favourable opportunity.[6]

In 1852 Lang published a manifesto of independence for the Australian colonies. Entitled *Freedom and Independence for the Golden Lands of Australia*, it was written during a sea voyage from Australia to England in 1851. Lang proposed a new federal nation be constituted consisting of what is now Queensland — divided into three provinces (from the north): Flindersland, Leichhardts Land and Cooksland — together with New South Wales, Victoria, Tasmania and South Australia. He proposed a House of Representatives with representation based on population, and a Senate with equal representation for the seven provinces. He also proposed there be a President with executive power and a

Vice-President who, like his American counterpart, would be speaker of the Senate.[7] He proposed that for 50 years, one-half of the revenues from the sale of land in the new nation would be used to pay the expenses of immigrants from Britain and, as a further encouragement to British support for his project, he also proposed there be no tariff imposed on any British goods for 50 years.

Lang wrote with the confidence of a man of God, asserting that both the law of nature and an Ordinance of God demanded that once colonies had reached their political majority, they should become free. Lang rejected what he described as 'municipal independence' by which the colony would be able to make its own laws for domestic matters, leaving the Imperial Parliament in London to oversee all matters of Imperial concern. He said that this arrangement, which was only another way of describing the system of responsible government eventually granted to the Australian colonies in the late 1850s, would not be acceptable to Australians who, he claimed, would not be 'abject and spiritless enough to accept such a constitution as this'.[8]

Lang was an unabashed republican:

As to the charge that the colonists who desire their freedom and independence are somewhat tinctured with republicanism, I fear it must be admitted. The fact is that there is no other form of government, either practicable or possible, in a British colony obtaining its freedom and independence than that of a republic.[9]

Lang's republicanism was never a majority view, and its appeal was heavily diminished following the grant of responsible government to the Australian colonies a few years later. One relevant factor in its favour, however, was the perception, in 1852, that Australia had no enemies in the Asian or Pacific region. Australia, he argued, had no need of the royal navy's walls of oak.

For who, I ask, are the enemies with whom the Australian colonies, if free and independent would have to contend?

Is it the wretched aborigines of their own territory? Alas! most of them have already disappeared from the face of the earth; the last man of the Sydney tribe or nation, once a comparatively numerous body of people, having died a few years ago. Is it the New Zealanders or the South Sea Islanders? The very idea is absurd. Is it the Malays of the Indian Archipelago or the adventurous subjects of the Emperors of China and Japan? These inoffensive and unwarlike people could never even find their way to the Australian colonies …

The fact is, the only chance we have of hearing of war in any shape in Australia for a century to come, lies in our connection with Great Britain as a group of her many dependencies. And considering the warlike propensities of our worthy mother, and the character she has so long sustained of being the prize fighter and pay-mistress of the world, our chance of peace under her wing is at best but very precarious.[10]

Lang's confidence that there were no enemies in the region was quickly dispelled over the following decades as Australians nervously observed the rise of militarism in Japan and clung closer still to Mother England as their only hope of salvation. Lang's robust desire for independence is full of echoes from the American revolution. He does not seek to be anything other than a Briton, and it is on behalf of a community of Britons in Australia that he demands the birthright of Britons — the right to independence, the right to be ruled by their own elected representatives, the right to nationhood.

And must the young Australian be debarred from the exercise of that generous and manly feeling, of which every rightly constituted mind is conscious, when he exclaims with deep emotion, *This is my own, my native land*.[11]

The dual identity — the sense of being British as well as Australian — is very hard for young Australians to understand in the 1990s. Yet it is the key to understanding why we have an English Queen as our Head of State and why our ancestors were so solicitous of things British. Today it all sounds like so much boot-licking, but to those past generations of Australians, praising Britain and things British to the heights was not much different from a Tasmanian praising Australia. The Tasmanian is an Australian; and 100 — even 50 — years ago, Australians believed they were British. This dual identity was even more weighted in the direction of being British in the late nineteenth century. The rivalries between protectionist Victoria and free-trading New South Wales (not to speak of the jealousies of the smaller colonies) precluded the development of any real national spirit.

CHAPTER THREE

The Reluctant Nation

As a result of continued pressure from London for the Australian colonies to establish some kind of federal government, a Federal Council of Australasia was established in 1883 in order to provide a means of legislating for certain extra-territorial matters. New South Wales and New Zealand stood aloof from it. The Federal Council rarely met and its single greatest achievement was to pass an Act in 1888 to regulate the Queensland pearl-shell and bêche-de-mer fisheries beyond territorial limits. South Australia dropped out in 1892 and it was, finally, decently interred by the establishment of the Commonwealth in 1901.

Greed and self-interest kept Australian colonists concentrating on their own patches. Why look for the big national vision when there were more tangible riches within reach? On the other hand, fear was an equally motivating emotion. Two potentially hostile powers started to grow in strength in the Pacific: Russia began to build up its Pacific Fleet based at Vladivostok and Japan had started its extraordinary industrialisation which, by 1904, saw it defeating the Russian navy.

The Australian colonists began to realise that they were a very long way from Mother England and that there were many enemies living much closer. John Dunmore Lang's 'inoffensive and unwarlike people' to the north were now seen as the crowded millions of alien, yellow hordes plotting to invade White Australia and pollute its British race. In 1887 the seven Australasian colonies (including New Zealand) agreed to contribute to the cost of an enlarged British fleet to be based in Australia. Two years later a British General was commissioned by the British Government to report on the land defence forces in Australia. Major-General Edwards recommended that the defence forces of the Australian colonies should be federated, that there should be uniform recruitment and administration, that there should be a uniform railway gauge and there should be federal small arms factories, gun wharves and ordnance stores.[1]

General Edwards's report was the spur the New South Wales Premier, Sir Henry Parkes, needed to push for a Federation. Parkes's efforts, supported by the Victorian Premier Duncan Gillies, resulted in a conference in Melbourne in 1890 at which representatives of all seven Australasian colonies resolved to convene a constitutional convention the following year. At the inevitable banquet Parkes spoke revealingly about his sense of identity when he replied to a toast to 'A United Australasia':

> The crimson thread of kinship runs through us all. Even the native-born Australians are Britons, as much as the men born within the cities of London and Glasgow. We know the value of their British origin. We know that we represent a race ... for the purposes of settling new colonies which never had its equal on the face of the earth.[2]

Drafting a Constitution

A Constitutional Convention was held in Sydney in 1891 with delegates appointed by the legislatures of all seven colonies. A draft Constitution was agreed upon, but the enthusiasm for Federation seemed to wane during the hard years of depression that followed. The next convention did not take place until 1897, and the stimulus for this new burst of Federation activity came from popular grassroots movements for Federation such as the Australian Natives' Association and the Federation Leagues, led by Edmund Barton, who later became Australia's first Prime Minister.

The 1897 Convention in Sydney and the 1898 Convention in Melbourne finalised a draft Constitution. Most of the discussion was taken up with matters of trade and commerce, the composition and powers of the Senate, and above all, the vexed question of tariffs. The colonial governments had derived most of their revenues from tariffs and the power to levy tariffs was being ceded to the new Federal Government.

It is remarkable to note the way in which the delegates freely and unashamedly disavowed any aspiration to independence. In the 1897 session in Sydney, Edmund Barton and Sir George Reid (later our fourth Prime Minister) agreed that it was inappropriate to refer to any treaty-making power on the part of the Commonwealth. Mr Barton observed:

> ... inasmuch as the treaty-making power will be in the Imperial Government, we should omit any reference to the making of treaties by the commonwealth; in other words, while they concede that we should make certain trade arrangements, which would have enough force if ratified by the Imperial Government, the sole treaty-making power is in the Crown of the United Kingdom.[3]

Sir George Reid concurred:

This [the reference to treaties] is an expression which
would be more in place in the United States Constitution,
where treaties are dealt with by the President and the
Senate, than in the Constitution of a colony within the
Empire.[4]

Following the Constitutional Conventions, a draft Constitution was put to the people of the Australian colonies in referenda. The only colony in which there was substantial anti-Federation feeling was New South Wales. The 'anti-Billites', as they were called, criticised the proposed Constitution on a number of grounds, principally because it accorded equal representation to the States, regardless of size, in the Senate — and because the new Commonwealth Government would be financed by customs duties, of which free-trading New South Wales believed it would have to bear the lion's share.

Finally, the several colonies approved the Constitution Bill in referenda, although by a narrower margin in New South Wales than elsewhere. The Imperial Government in London, while very supportive of Federation generally, was troubled by some aspects of the Constitution Bill which was proposed to be enacted in the United Kingdom Parliament. Joseph Chamberlain, the Secretary of State for the Colonies, was particularly concerned about two matters. First, he wanted it to be made absolutely clear that the *Colonial Laws Validity Act* applied to Commonwealth legislation in the same way that it applied to the legislation of the Australian colonies. The effect of this British law was that any colonial law which conflicted with a British law that was intended to apply in the colony was invalid. Chamberlain was concerned to ensure that the Imperial Parliament should have the power when it chose to overrule Australian legislation and that important British laws, such as the *Merchant Shipping Act*, which were intended to apply across the Empire, could not be varied by a subordinate legislature such as the Australian Commonwealth Parliament.

The Privy Council

Chamberlain's second concern related to the Privy Council. The Privy Council was, and remains, a body of persons appointed to advise the Queen. Its members are styled 'Right Honourable' and they are the successors of the medieval *concilium regis* which provided confidential advice to the monarch. Over the centuries membership of the Privy Council became increasingly honorific, and by the end of the nineteenth century, the only Privy Councillors who provided advice to the monarch were those who happened to be members of the British cabinet. The only other function it performed was through the Judicial Committee of the Privy Council, known colloquially as 'the Privy Council'. The Privy Council traditionally heard appeals from colonial courts, including those of India, and was composed of English (and occasionally Scottish) judges and senior lawyers.

There was widespread support in the Federation debates for the abolition of almost all appeals from Australian courts to the Privy Council, on the simple ground that Australian judges were of equal calibre to those in England and that, because of their better understanding of Australian conditions, they were better equipped to deal with Australian disputes.

Chamberlain was vehemently opposed to any limitation on appeals to the Privy Council and invited the Australian colonies to send a delegation to London in 1900 to discuss this issue.[5] He urged that appeals to the Privy Council had been:

> ... a link effectively binding together every part of Her Majesty's dominions; the weakening of this tie would seriously lessen the value of even so great and beneficent a result as the Federation of Australia. If the Bill were passed in its present form, while it would mark a step in advance as far as the Federation of Australia is concerned, it would be a retrograde measure so far as it affects the larger question of Imperial Federation.[6]

Moreover, he noted:

> In the interests of Australia, the final decision in
> important questions as to the boundaries of Federal
> and State powers should lie with the highest court of
> the Empire, beyond suspicion of local bias.

and added:

> Banks and other institutions having large interests in
> Australia are strongly against the limitation and weighty
> representations on the subject have been made to the
> Imperial Government.[7]

The members of the Australian delegation dug their toes in.
The Constitution Bill as presented to Chamberlain had
reserved the right to appeal to the Privy Council in any con-
stitutional matter if 'the public interests of some part of Her
Majesty's Dominions, other than the Commonwealth or a
State are involved'.[8] They rejected the suggestion that Privy
Council appeals were an important link of Empire.

> The consciousness of kinship, the consciousness of a
> common blood and a common sense of duty, the pride of
> their race and history — these are the links of Empire;
> bands which attach, not bonds which chafe. When the
> Australian fights for the Empire, he is inspired by these
> sentiments; but no patriotism was ever inspired or
> sustained by the thought of the Privy Council.[9]

The Bill was introduced into the House of Commons with
the Privy Council appeal section 74 left blank. The Leader
of the Opposition, Sir Henry Campbell-Bannerman, criticised the Government for flouting the wishes of the
Australian colonies. Under considerable pressure from
Chamberlain, and uncertain of the extent to which the Australian population would support their local leaders against
the better judgment of London, the Australian delegation,

with the support of the colonial governments, compromised, and section 74 of the Constitution was enacted so as to prohibit appeals from the High Court to the Privy Council in matters involving disputes as to the respective powers of the States and the Commonwealth. It permitted the Commonwealth Parliament to enact legislation limiting other rights of appeal from the High Court to the Privy Council, but it provided that any such law 'shall be reserved by the Governor-General for Her Majesty's pleasure', thereby ensuring that the British Government would have the final say.

Federation

In 1901, the Commonwealth of Australia consisted of a Federation of six colonies, the Federation itself being a colony. The sovereign power was, for all practical purposes, the British Government. The sovereign's viceroy, the Governor-General, acted partly as Head of State and partly as the local representative of the British Government. Australian cabinet ministers communicated with London via the Governor-General who in turn dealt with the Colonial Office.

If the British Government's representative, the Governor-General, considered that proposed legislation was inimical to British Imperial interests, he could refer it to London for consideration. If he made some slip, and approved something London did not favour, the British Government had 12 months in which to have the monarch disallow it.[10] Any Australian law which conflicted with British legislation intended to apply in the colonies was automatically invalid because of the *Colonial Laws Validity Act*, and any Australian judges who reached decisions unattractive to British interests would have their judgments scrutinised by a British court, the Privy Council, back in London. The Australian Constitution, far from being the birth certificate of a nation, was no more than a rule book for a self-governing colony — but a colony in the affairs of which the British Government reserved the right to interfere as and when it saw fit.

It is easy to look back at the founding fathers (they were

all men) in 1900 and regard them as forelock-tugging courtiers to the British. The truth is that they not only thought they were British, they probably were. Australia was not entirely, in Metternich's acid comment on Italy, a geographic expression, but it was not a nation. Australians then, and for at least another 50 years, regarded themselves as Britons living in Australia.

But the times were changing rapidly, and the years that followed Federation and its essentially colonial Constitution saw the gradual disappearance of the political reality of colonialism, if not its forms and symbols.

The extraordinary powers of royal disallowance were never in fact implemented. It is no credit to Australians that the issues over which royal disallowance fell into practical disuse were racist ones. Throughout the late nineteenth and early twentieth century there was continued tension between Australian governments at state, and later federal, level on the one hand and British governments on the other over the vexed question of Asian immigration into Australia. Britain had forged a military and naval alliance with Japan, and the Japanese, seeing themselves as the champion of equality for Asians, objected strongly to the white settler society in Australia trying to limit or prohibit Asian (predominantly Chinese) immigration. Indeed in 1905 the Colonial Office in London instructed all Australian State Governors and the Governor-General to reserve for royal (that is British) assent any legislation designed to restrict Asian immigration. Alfred Deakin, the Australian Prime Minister, objected at this interference and the instruction was withdrawn.

Loyalty to Empire

The Australians and the New Zealanders were always ready to characterise their loyalty to the Empire as being built on a common race. But the British Government in London regarded India, rather than the white-settler dominions, as the brightest jewel in the Crown of Empire and

insisted that any immigration legislation enacted by the
dominions be colour-blind. The Australians complied with
the letter of this requirement by enacting an *Immigration Act*
which required all would-be immigrants to pass an examination in any of a number of nominated European lan-
guages. An English-speaking Indian who sought admission
was asked to sit an examination in, for example, Spanish or
German, and upon failure, was not admitted.

The Australian Prime Minister, Alfred Deakin, writing in
1908 for a London newspaper as its anonymous Australian
correspondent was quite open about his country's attitude:

> In fact and in effect our colourless laws are administered
> so as to draw a deep colour line of demarcation between
> Caucasians and all other races. No white men are
> stopped at our ports for language or any other tests. On
> the contrary, they are welcomed and encouraged to settle
> among us. On the other hand all coloured men are
> stopped unless they come merely as visitors ... the
> Empire ... though united in one whole is, nevertheless,
> divided broadly into two parts, one occupied wholly or
> mainly by a white ruling race, the other principally
> occupied by coloured races who are ruled. Australia and
> New Zealand are determined to keep their place in the
> first class, and in order to secure that pride of place agree
> in putting racial purity before economic gain."

At the same time, English politicians — Joseph Chamberlain
being the best example — were fond of describing Britain
and the settler dominions of Canada, New Zealand, South
Africa and Canada as 'sister states'. But rhetoric was not
always matched by reality. The Commonwealth Government opened its mission in London at Australia House in
1910, but the High Commissioner was compelled, at White-
hall's insistence, to act only as a conduit for relatively trivial
inter-governmental communications. The principal means
of communication between Australia and London was still
to be by way of the Governor-General and the Colonial

Office. Australia House, which still graces the Strand with its imposing façade, was the largest — and in real terms, most expensive — building erected by the Commonwealth Government until the completion of the new Commonwealth Parliament in 1988. Impressing the English in the heart of the Empire's capital was more important than the edification of Australians.

Hudson and Sharp describe a typical example of the relationship between Federation and the First World War:

> While in London for the colonial conference of 1907, Deakin was disturbed by French press reports that French convicts were to be sent to New Caledonia. Had he been the prime minister of an independent state, Deakin could have taken up the matter with the French ambassador in London, gone to Paris to speak to French ministers or sent an Australian official to Paris to confer with French officials. As the prime minister of a dependency he could do none of these things.
>
> Instead he had one of his officials write to an official at the Colonial Office to inquire about the veracity of the French press reports; the Colonial Office referred Deakin's inquiry to the Foreign Office; the Foreign Office asked the United Kingdom ambassador in Paris to look into the matter; the ambassador in Paris reported back to the Foreign Office that the press reports were without foundation; the Foreign Office passed this information on to the Colonial Office; the Colonial Office in turn passed the information on to the Governor-General in Melbourne, Lord Northcote, and he passed it on to Deakin who by now was back in Melbourne ... The Australian official's note had gone to the Colonial Office on 20 April and Deakin got his reply through the Governor-General on 15 July.[12]

Another example of British insistence on maintaining the colonial status occurred in 1908 when Deakin directly invited the United States Government to send its 'Great

White Fleet' to Australia for a visit. The Foreign Secretary in London, Sir Edward Grey, demanded that Deakin be reminded that 'invitations to foreign governments should not be given except through us'.[13]

To Sir Edward Grey, best remembered for observing on 3 August 1914 that 'the lamps are going out all over Europe, we shall not see them lit again in our lifetime', Deakin's presumption seemed ridiculous.

The Empire

The First World War itself saw no change in the colonial status of Australia. War was declared by the British Government in London, the dominions, including Australia, were not consulted. The Governor-General was advised of the declaration and instructed to inform his Ministers. It was not a question of a jingoistic Australia deciding to throw in its lot with Britain; Australia was part of the Empire, and its participation was as automatic as that of any part of Great Britain itself.

Already, however, there were developing signs that wholehearted adherence to Empire was not everyone's cup of tea. When Britain called on Australia for yet more troops, the Australian Government led by William ('Billy') Hughes reluctantly agreed to support a national referendum to approve conscription. That referendum was defeated in 1916 and again in 1917. The trade union movement, and the majority of Labor Party members of federal and state parliaments, opposed conscription. Hughes left the Labor Party with his small band of supporters, forming a new Government with the support of the Liberals, whom he ultimately joined in a new National Party in 1917.

Hughes was an unusual species of Austral-Briton. Born in Wales, he had come to Australia in 1884 at the age of 20 and had quickly made a mark for himself in the growing trade union movement. He became a Labor member of the New South Wales Legislative Assembly in 1894, moving to the Federal House of Representatives in 1901. He served in a variety of ministries under Andrew Fisher whom he succeeded as Prime Minister in 1915, a position he held until 1923.

Hughes was a noisy, eloquent advocate of the Empire. During the First World War, when Britain had been in desperate need of reinforcements from the Empire, the governments of the various white-settler dominions — Australia, South Africa, New Zealand and Canada — had been admitted into the councils of the Empire in a way they had never been before. At the Peace Conference in Paris after the First World War, the dominions were represented — albeit as part of the British delegation — and Hughes was able to secure some important victories for Australia. In particular he was successful in forcing the British Empire delegation to oppose Japan's attempt to have a statement supporting racial equality inserted into the Covenant of the League of Nations.

After the war, he was scathing in his criticism of those who advocated greater legal autonomy for the dominions. He believed in the Empire and wanted the dominions to continue to collaborate in the formation of Imperial policies. He was much less inclined to take the lead from Britain than either his predecessors or successors were. He had no doubt that the Empire belonged to the British race and that the British race living in Australia had as much right to a say in its destiny as did those living in England itself.

This fantasy, of dominion participation in Imperial (that is British) foreign policy, was encouraged when Britain needed dominion troops during the First World War, and for a short time after the war. In December 1921 Lloyd George told the House of Commons that the dominions would join with Great Britain in deciding Imperial foreign policy.

> The advantage to us is that joint control means joint responsibility, and when the burden of Empire has become so vast it is well that we should have the shoulders of these young giants to help us along. It

introduces a broad and calmer view into foreign policy. It restrains rash Ministers and will stimulate timorous ones. It widens the prospect.[14]

Lloyd George's vision was quickly proved a mirage in events which also put Hughes's loyalty to Britain to the test in 1922. The Treaty of Sèvres, signed in 1920, had inflicted a punishing peace settlement on the Ottoman Empire. All its possessions outside Turkey were lost; that part of Turkey in Europe, across the Bosphorus, was ceded to Greece — as were all of the Aegean islands and the important coastal city of Smyrna — and Constantinople was constituted an international city occupied by allied troops.

Kemal Atatürk, leading his own Young Turk Party in Anatolia, overthrew the Ottoman regime and seized power. The Greeks intervened, invading Turkey. By August 1922, however, the Turks had turned the tables on the Greeks, who were driven into the sea. The eviction of hundreds of thousands of Greeks from the Asia Minor seaboard, where they had lived for millennia, is still regarded by Greeks everywhere simply as 'the catastrophe'.

The Turkish army swept on towards Constantinople and encountered a small British outpost at Chanak. The British cabinet on 15 September 1922, influenced by Lloyd George and Winston Churchill, decided to fight — and immediately cabled the Dominion Prime Ministers, including Hughes, asking for military support. Churchill released the text of this request the following day.

Hughes was furious. Australia had not been kept up-to-date by the British about the events in Turkey. Instead, Britain had decided on war and had then, publicly, asked Australia to support it. Hughes had no choice but to respond that Australia would be prepared to support Britain.

Privately, he responded rather differently. In a long cable to Lloyd George he stressed how important it was for Britain to consult the dominions before taking important steps in foreign policy:

The point that the Commonwealth Government desires
to most strongly emphasise is this — that the Dominions
ought to be consulted before any action is taken or
irrevocable decision made by Britain, then and only then
can our voices be heard and our counsels heeded. The
Empire is one and indivisible or it is nothing. If the
Empire is only another name for Britain and the
Dominions are to be told that things are done after they
have been done, that Britain has decided upon war, and
asking whether they wish to associate with her and to
stand by her side, when in fact they have no other
alternative, then the relations between the Dominions
being what they are it is perfectly clear that all talk about
the Dominions having a real share in deciding for an
Imperial policy is empty air.[15]

Apart from Australia, only New Zealand felt bound to offer
immediate support. Canada and South Africa made no
response other than that they would place the matter before
their parliaments. On this occasion, as on others, Canada
and South Africa acted like independent countries. Australia and New Zealand, albeit with private protests, fell
into line like dutiful colonies.

A truce was signed with the Turks on 29 September, so
the military crisis passed. But it was decided to reconsider
the harsh Treaty of Sèvres at a conference to be held at Lausanne. Despite Hughes's repeated requests, Australia was
not invited to attend the conference. The British Foreign Secretary, Lord Curzon, tried to mollify Hughes by telling him
that if the dominions were invited, the French would insist
on Tunisia and Morocco (two French colonies) being represented also. To someone with Hughes's views about race,
the shame of white Australia being compared with two
African colonies would have been almost too much to bear.
The British offered to keep Australia informed of what was
going on at Lausanne. But not even reference to the thousands of Anzac graves along the Gallipoli peninsula could
persuade London that Australia had a right to be present.

Hughes could only console himself with another long telegraphic tirade. He repeated his concerns about Empire unity:

> Plain speaking between friends and blood relations is best. What you suggest may be, probably will be, quite satisfactory to Canada and South Africa; they were not prepared to fight. We were and it is most emphatically not satisfactory to Australia ... This habit of asking Australia to agree to things when they are done and cannot be undone, and when in practice there is only one course open to us — and that is to support Britain — is one which, if persisted in, will wreck the Empire.[16]

It is not difficult to understand the British position. Why would a world power like Britain, ruling over the largest Empire ever known to man, accept the relatively tiny and remote white communities in Australia and New Zealand as its equals in the councils of Empire? Australians' endless harping on blood relationships and ties of race were all very fine for after-dinner rhetoric, but the bulk of Britain's Imperial subjects were coloured people in India and Africa. If white Australia was to be given the privileges of equality and independence, how could they be denied to India?

Independence for the Dominions

In the years that followed, profound changes took place in the relationship between Britain and Australia, as well as the other dominions. The impetus for these changes, which culminated in the *Statute of Westminster* in 1931, came largely from dominions other than Australia, in particular South Africa and Canada — with Ireland pushing further and faster on its way to complete separation from the Empire and the Commonwealth.

Canada and South Africa, of course, share two distinct characteristics which Australia lacked. First, their populations were not wholly British; large and influential sections of each had grave reservations about the desirability of being associated with Britain at all. Second, because of their geography they did not perceive any real threat of invasion. Australia, on the other hand, had an almost entirely British population. More importantly, however, it saw the Empire as the only possible source of defence in the event — some would have said inevitable event — of an invasion from Japan. This explains Australia's reflexive, docile obedience to British wishes throughout the first half of the century. Like the little child who will

... always keep a-hold of Nurse
For fear of finding something worse[17]

Australia clung to Mother England as its only protector from the growing military and industrial might of Asia.

So, during the 1920s, while Canada and South Africa endeavoured to loosen the bonds of Empire into what became the Commonwealth, Australia, often led by Billy Hughes, wanted to move in two different, but complementary directions. Hughes had no patience for British interference in Australian domestic matters — and it is fair to say that by this time the British had no appetite for it either — but at the same time he wanted to increase the amount of consultation and involvement Australia had in formulating Empire foreign and defence policy.

This difference in approach was particularly apparent at the 1923 Imperial Conference in London when Australia, represented by Stanley Melbourne Bruce, argued vigorously for an Empire — as opposed to a British — defence policy. In practical terms Bruce was most concerned that Britain continue with its plans to establish the new naval base at Singapore. On the other hand, Mackenzie King, from Canada, was quite uninterested in such matters and the Conference, overall, had the effect of increasing the devolution of power to the dominions by confirming that dominion governments were entirely independent in matters of foreign policy and could conclude agreements and treaties with foreign powers as they saw fit.

The next Imperial Conference in 1926 saw another change. At the express request of Canada, the British Government agreed that Governors-General (but not State Governors) should cease forthwith to act in the dual role of Head of State and local representative of the British Government. The report of that conference summed up the new, autonomous status that had been thrust on a reluctant Australia and New Zealand:

> We refer to the group of self-governing communities composed of Great Britain and the Dominions. Their position and mutual relation may be readily defined. They are autonomous communities within the British Empire, equal in status, in no way subordinate one to another in any aspect of their domestic or external affairs, though united by a common allegiance to the Crown and freely associated as members of the British Commonwealth of Nations.[18]

The cessation of the Governor-General acting as representative of the Imperial Government left a gap, and British High Commissioners were sent to Ottawa in 1927 and Pretoria in 1930, although Canberra had to wait until 1936.

This change in 1926 was of immense constitutional significance. If 'Queen' and 'Governor-General' in the Constitution in 1901 meant, in truth, 'the British Government', then this development effectively created Australia — at least in terms of its executive government — as an independent nation. It was an example of our Constitution being dramatically changed without either a constitutional amendment approved in a referendum or even an Act of the Australian Parliament. Far from being an assertion of Australian independence or identity, it was yet another example of the United Kingdom, supported by Canada and South Africa, forcing a change on Australians they did not want. Put another way, it was more like the adult child being told to find his or her own apartment, rather than boldly moving out of home. This is not to say Australians were aware of the significance of the change — or if aware, welcomed it. Sir John Latham, in 1928 the Attorney General and subsequently Chief Justice, denied that Australia was independent:

> ... few Australians have the illusion that Australia could maintain her existence as a completely independent State. Alone Australia is weak ... As a member of the British Commonwealth, Australia is strong.[19]

In 1932 Sir John went to a League of Nations disarmament conference and advocated the prohibition of bombers, despite his belief that they represented the best defence for Australia. He felt, however, that London could not survive a bombing raid, and:

> ... we regarded the preservation of London as the nerve centre of the Empire as of greater value to Australia than the advantages which Australia would derive locally if bombing ... were to be continued.[20]

Latham's attitude was not atypical; in 1929, the New South Wales Premier, Thomas Bavin, could write about Australians being 'citizens of the British Empire':

> When an Australian leaves his country for the first time to visit Great Britain and other Dominions, the fact that strikes him with a new significance is that Australia is part of a great Empire, and he himself a citizen of it.
>
> London, the heart of the Empire, whose very stones are instinct with history, reminds him, as no other city in the world can do, of a heritage which he shares and of traditions which still mould and govern the life of the British race in whatever quarter of the globe it is found.
>
> He finds among British public men of every part a keen interest in and knowledge of Empire problems, and it gradually begins to dawn on him that perhaps they are even more alive to the significance of those problems than the Dominions themselves. It is brought home to him as never before that he is more than Australian — he

is a Britisher, and more than a Britisher, for he is a citizen of the Empire, and he gets a more vivid conception of the fact that such citizenship carries with it obligations as well as privileges.[21]

The trend to devolution of the dominions found its culmination in the 1930 Imperial Conference which recommended the enactment of what became known as the *Statute of Westminster*. The effect of the *Statute of Westminster* was to surrender any right of the Imperial Parliament to legislate for the various dominions, being Canada, Australia, New Zealand, South Africa, Ireland and Newfoundland, unless the dominion concerned had expressly requested the United Kingdom Parliament so to do. The *Statute of Westminster* also created a 'divisible Crown'. While the King of Great Britain was the Head of State of all of the dominions, the King acted, in respect of Australian affairs for example, only on the advice of his Australian ministers. This meant in practical terms that Canada, for example, ceased to be a Federation under the 'Crown of the United Kingdom of Great Britain and Northern Ireland', but was largely independent, with a Head of State who acted as his or her local advisers directed, although the identity of the Head of State was, as before, the same as that of the King or Queen of the United Kingdom.

Australia did not just drag its feet in the face of these changes, it dug in its heels and begged to be excused. Sir John Latham, as Leader of the Opposition, created sufficient public concern at the prospects of independence that it was expressly agreed that the Statute would not apply to Australia until it was adopted by the Federal Parliament (which did not occur until 1942). He also ensured that the abdication of Britain's legislative jurisdiction over the States would not be effected — and as a result, one may argue that if Australia became independent in 1931 (or alternatively in 1942) the States of Australia remained colonies until the passage of the *Australia Act* in 1986.

Australia was still slow to show real signs of independence. Australians entertained an utterly mistaken view of themselves, Britain and the world. Australians saw themselves as being British, first and foremost. They saw London as the centre of the Empire that would protect their interests as fiercely as it protected the interests of the British Isles. But this touching loyalty from Australia to Britain was not shared by the British. Australian historian David Day observes:

> A large part of the continued Australian confidence in British power was based on a firm but unspoken conviction that Australia was as important in British minds as Britain was in Australian minds. If Britain was the mother country to most Australians the implicit corollary in most antipodean minds was that the Pacific Dominions stood as sturdy sons to most Britons. Countless cartoons of the period portrayed just such a relationship … It was inconceivable that Britain could have extra-Imperial interests that would outrank in priority her responsibility for Australia and, within the Empire, that Britain would feel more protective of India than she did of Australia.[22]

The 'security blanket' afforded by membership of the British Empire was a critical element in Australian neglect of its own defences prior to the Second World War. That neglect resulted in Australia being defenceless in the face of the Japanese attack. While Britain rearmed during the 1930s, Australia slept on. Despite Australia's greater per capita wealth, her per capita expenditure on defence was a little more than one-half of Britain's. When war was declared in September 1939, Australia had a tiny regular army of a few thousand soldiers and an inexperienced volunteer militia which spent 12 days in camp each year. Its air force was practically non-existent, its most modern planes being Wirraways. These Australian-made planes were in fact American-designed trainers and were no match for modern fighters, particularly the Japanese Zero. The navy was probably the best equipped of the services, although most of its small fleet was outdated.

The truth was that Australian governments, both Labor and conservative, gave precious little thought to defending Australia at all. They assumed that the British Empire would defend Australia if it were ever attacked, and that Australia would provide the raw material of men and materials to help defend the Empire. The idea that Australia might have to defend itself was almost unthinkable.

CHAPTER FOUR

Menzies and Beyond

At 8 p.m. on 3 September 1939 Prime Minister Robert Menzies heard the wireless announcement of Chamberlain's declaration of war. At 9.15 p.m. Menzies broadcast his own announcement:

> It is my melancholy duty to inform you officially that in consequence of a persistence by Germany in her invasion of Poland, Great Britain has declared war upon her, and that, as a result, Australia is at war. No harder task can fall to the lot of a democratic leader than to make such an announcement.[1]

Unlike the Prime Ministers of Canada and South Africa, Menzies did not consult his Parliament before announcing that Australia was at war. He later justified this automatic response in his memoirs, writing:

> ... those were the days when the Commonwealth was a
> Crown Commonwealth, its constituent nations, Great
> Britain, Canada, Australia, South Africa and New
> Zealand bound together by a common allegiance to a
> common Crown ... How could the King be at war and
> at peace at the same time in relation to Germany?[2]

Menzies had been anxious, in the pre-war years, about the
possibilities of another war and had promoted appeasement
of both Germany and Japan. He was much more attracted to
the policies of Chamberlain than he was to the warmonger-
ing rhetoric of Churchill. His enthusiasm for a negotiated
settlement continued after the declaration of war. Menzies,
in his private correspondence to Australia's High Commissioner in London, Stanley Melbourne Bruce, foresaw a possible need for:

> ... a new alignment of nations in which not only Great
> Britain and France, but Germany and Italy, combined to
> resist Bolshevism.[3]

A War in the Pacific

While Japan did not enter the war until December 1941, it
had been clear for many years that a war in the Pacific was
possible. Japan was an aggressive, expansionist military
power that was already at war with China and was publicly
threatening to create an 'East Asian Co-Prosperity Sphere'
that would drive the European colonial powers out of Asia,
which would henceforth be reserved for the Asians — by
which the Japanese simply meant they would replace European rule with their own.

Despite this potential threat, Australia's response to the
rigours of war was dutifully to fall into line with British
requirements. Three new army divisions were raised and
despatched to the Middle East. The navy was sent to the
Mediterranean; instead of building up a viable new air force
of its own, it was decided that Australia should support an

Empire Air Training Scheme which 'had the effect of turning the RAAF into an organisation devoted to the recruitment and basic training of aircrew destined for operations in Europe'.⁴ All three arms of the military forces were headed by British officers at the outset of war.

While Australia had stripped itself of the means of self-defence, Britain pursued policies in the Pacific which were positively dangerous for Australia. From the outbreak of the war until the Japanese attack on Pearl Harbor on 7 December 1941, the principal object of British policy was to bring the Americans into the war on the British side. The British therefore supported the use of economic sanctions against Japan, as a protest against Japan's invasion of China. Menzies protested this could provoke war in the Pacific, and both he and Bruce proposed schemes for appeasing Japan and ensuring peace in the Pacific. Churchill had no time for such ideas. He knew that Roosevelt could not persuade an isolationist America to go to war against Germany. But he also knew that if Japan went to war in the Pacific it would have to fight America, and he had been assured that if war began in the Pacific America would join in the war against Germany as well.

When war did come, Britain's inability to defend Australia was quickly revealed. The impregnable fortress of Singapore fell on 15 February 1942. It fell for one reason: Britain had not provided sufficient air support to defend the island. This lack of air support also resulted in the loss of two British battleships, the *Prince of Wales* and the *Repulse*, which were sunk by Japanese torpedo bombers on 10 December, only three days after Pearl Harbor.

It is perfectly clear why Britain did not provide sufficient air cover to defend Singapore. Singapore and Australia were well down on the list of British priorities. Every nation is entitled to determine its own strategic priorities, and there can be no criticism of Britain for having done just that.

Historians will debate forever the extent to which Australia's lack of preparedness was the result of Britain misleading Australian governments about its capacity to defend Australia, or of Australia not wishing to face up to the considerable cost of establishing a proper defence force. While Britain was always confident about the strength of Singapore and the ability of the royal navy to protect all the Empire's possessions, it must have been blindingly obvious to any intelligent Australian that if Britain became embroiled in a European war with Germany, it would have very little ability to defend Australia in a war with Japan.

Indeed, as early as 1910, Lord Kitchener of Khartoum, in a report commissioned by the Australian Government, had recognised that Australia might have to fight alone if Britain was engaged in Europe — and that it could be some considerable time before Britain would be able to establish superiority of sea power in the face of enemies in Europe and the Pacific. Accordingly he had recommended that at least 80 000 fighting troops would be required to defend Australia from invasion.[5]

On the other hand, in the years preceding the Second World War and in the period before Japan entered it, British leaders, including Churchill, went to considerable lengths to persuade Australian leaders that Australia had nothing to fear from Japan, that Singapore was impregnable and that if Japan did attack help would not be long in coming. The only criticism of Britain in this period, therefore, which Australians are entitled to raise is that Britain misled Australians about its ability to defend Australia and the Far East and did so with the purpose of ensuring Australia remained no more than a provider of men and materials for use by British generals in theatres far from Australia.

The result of all this was that Britain was much better defended than Australia. In January 1941, for example, Britain had 36 army divisions, of which only four were abroad. One was in Iceland, and three were in Egypt, together with three Australian divisions. Britain's air force was still intact, having won the Battle of Britain, and the royal navy's domination of the Atlantic and the Mediterranean was secure. Australia had not one division of trained troops in Australia. Its air force was non-existent and its navy was under the command of the British navy in the Mediterranean. So while Australia's enemy was further away than was Britain's, she had virtually no ability to defend herself.

Far from regarding Australians as the sturdy sons of Empire Australians believed themselves to be, the attitude of leading British figures was frequently disparaging. When John Curtin protested against Churchill's strategy of beating Hitler first and leaving the Pacific to be cleaned up later, Churchill observed that 'the Australians came of bad stock'.[6] Churchill later, falsely, ascribed much of the blame for the collapse of Singapore on the cowardliness of Australian soldiers.

Curtin became Prime Minister on 4 October 1941 after the short-lived Fadden Government was defeated in the House of Representatives. Curtin pursued a much more independent approach to the war, and to defence policy generally, than Menzies had done. He had every reason to do so; within two months of taking office the Japanese had entered the war. He engaged in many bitter fights with Churchill as he successfully pressed for Australia's two divisions in the Middle East to be returned to defend Australia. Both he and his Minister for External Affairs, Dr H. V. ('Doc') Evatt stridently lobbied both London and Washington for more military equipment and aircraft.

When Britain declared war on Japan, Curtin insisted on making a separate Australian declaration, departing from Menzies' view of the indivisibility of the Crown. But while he was more aggressively Australian than the Anglophile Menzies, Curtin was still a Britisher first.

Those holding Curtin up as an Australian nationalist cite his famous call for the help of the United States. The following passage from a newspaper article written by the Australian Prime Minister is often quoted:

> Without any inhibitions of any kind, I make it quite clear
> that Australia looks to America free of any pangs as to
> our traditional links or kinship with the United Kingdom.

> We know the problems that the United Kingdom faces,
> we know the constant threat of invasion, we know the
> dangers of dispersal of strength, but we know, too, that
> Australia can go and Britain can still hold on.[7]

Curtin's remarks were little more than a recognition of the
simple fact that Britain did not have the capacity to defend
Australia in 1942 and that the only nation which had that
capacity was the United States. When these remarks were
criticised by loyal Austral-Britons, Curtin observed:

> I did not mean that Australia regarded itself as anything
> but an integral part of the British Empire. No part of the
> British Commonwealth is more steadfast in its devotion
> to the British way of life and to British institutions than
> Australia. Our loyalty to the King goes to the very core of
> our national life.[8]

In the grim war years Britain's attempt to defend Australia
had failed miserably at Singapore and Australia had turned
to the United States for help. Despite this in 1943 Curtin told
a Labor Party Conference that the full expression of our
responsibilities in a post-war world was to be 'a good Australian, a good British subject and a good world citizen'. The
following year he gave a speech to MPs in the House of
Commons and said:

> We carry on out there as a British community in the South
> Seas and we regard ourselves as the trustees for the
> British way of life in a part of the world where it is of the
> utmost significance to the British Commonwealth and to
> the British Nation and to the British Empire — call it by
> any name that you will — that this land should have in
> the Antipodes a people and a territory corresponding in
> purpose and in outlook and in race to the Motherland
> itself.[9]

The Statute of Westminster

In October 1942 the bleak realities of war finally encouraged the Australian Parliament to adopt the *Statute of Westminster*. Dr Evatt, in moving the adoption, was at pains to explain to the House of Representatives that the Statute of Westminster Adoption Bill was only designed to remove some doubts and difficulties relating to the ability of the laws of the Commonwealth Parliament to apply to Australia's servicemen outside of Australia. He stressed that no change was being made to the relationship between Britain and Australia.

> Another question which has been asked, arising, no doubt from motives of pure patriotism, is: 'Will the adoption of the statute weaken the Imperial tie?' My answer is unhesitatingly, 'No'. I go further. I say that the tie between Britain and Australia will be confirmed and strengthened. It would be a sorry day if the Australian people were told that their relationship with the people of Britain might be weakened merely because Australians desired that legislation on Australian affairs, passed by their own representatives in their own Parliament should no longer run the risk of invalidation and annihilation by means of a British Act of Parliament which was quite suited to the colonial conditions of 1865 but is quite unsuited to the needs of Australia today — nearly eighty years afterwards. In my submission the passage of this bill will give further emphasis to the undoubted fact that the real link between Britain and Australia is not the legal subordination of the Parliament of this great Dominion to the Parliament of the United Kingdom at Westminster but the unity of the Crown throughout the Empire, our common allegiance to the King and the indissoluble tie of tradition and kinship which binds the two people ...
> For the truth is: the relationship between Britain and Australia has never been closer or more intimate than it is

today. I recall a phrase of the present Prime Minister of Britain which I heard him use during my recent mission to Britain, and which is relevant to our discussion. He said, 'I have always found this about you Australians — the better an Australian a man is, the better a Britisher'.[10]

'Doc' Evatt was later to become leader of the Labor Party. He was regarded as a relatively radical and assertively Australian politician. Yet, he speaks of adherence to Britain in the same breath as patriotism. Despite his left-wing politics, Evatt saw no conflict in being both Australian and British. In that sense, even to Evatt, Australia was not a nation like France, or America or Japan. Australia was part of the British nation, and proud to be so.

A Changing Relationship

The Second World War was the great watershed in Australia's relationship with the United Kingdom. From that moment on, the substance of our involvement with Britain declined in every field. Our courts became less deferential to English precedents, our admirals and generals looked to Washington rather than London, our cultural interest became more American. Finally in the 1960s we found ourselves, for the first time, fighting a war in Vietnam in which Britain was not even involved, and if anything, was mildly opposed to.

Nonetheless these changes were gradual; in 1950, Australian Minister for External Affairs Percy Spender — who was much less of an Anglophile than his Prime Minister Mr Menzies — stressed the need for Australia to work closely with the United Kingdom in international affairs. He warned against Commonwealth members developing independent views on foreign policy: 'Unanimity freely reached should always be our aim.'[11]

By the mid-1950s, Australia was certainly an independent nation. The only substantive constitutional links with the United Kingdom were the appeals to the Privy Council in

London and, of course, the Queen herself. Australia had the ability to act independently in world affairs, but generally it did not.

The Suez Crisis

A humiliating example of Australia's continuing willingness to do Mother England's bidding was the Suez Crisis of 1956. The Australian Government, led by Menzies, backed British aggression in the face of worldwide opposition led by the United States, the super power upon whose military might depended the independence of Australia.

In 1869 a French-financed company completed the construction of the Suez Canal, linking the Mediterranean and Red seas. Six years later, the Egyptian Government sold its shares in the canal company to the British Government. The British regarded the canal as a vital link between England and India, and to a lesser extent its Pacific possessions. Britain ruled Egypt as a protectorate until 1922 and exerted considerable influence there until 1954, when a nationalist Egyptian Government insisted that all British troops be removed from Egypt, including the canal zone.

On 26 July 1956, the Egyptian Government, led by President Gamal Nasser, nationalised the canal company. The nationalisation was legal. The company was incorporated in Egypt and subject to Egyptian law. Western governments had been busily nationalising all manner of enterprises in the years following the Second World War. The only legitimate matters for concern were whether Egypt could manage and maintain the canal, and whether it would continue to abide by an 1888 Convention which guaranteed freedom of access to the canal by all nations. Nasser undertook to ensure that Egypt satisfied both concerns.

At the time of the nationalisation Menzies was in North America; having attended a Prime Ministers' Conference in London in May, he was taking a leisurely trip back to Australia. The Acting Prime Minister, Arthur Fadden, the Minister for External Affairs, Mr Richard Casey, and the Defence Minister, Mr Philip McBride, sent a joint telegram to Menzies on 1 August which expressed opposition to any use of

force by the United Kingdom and France (the two dispos-
sessed former owners of the canal company) even if the
United States were to support them. They noted that the
taking of military action of this sort, without United Nations
endorsement, would be likely to alienate many friendly
countries, especially Asian ones. They also observed that
any military interdiction which did not occupy all of Egypt
— a huge step likely to plunge the entire Middle East into
war — would probably be ineffective as the Egyptians
would have the continuing capacity to attack and harass the
canal zone occupation force.[12]

Over the next 10 weeks, the British and French governments planned an invasion of Egypt. A sub-committee of
the British cabinet had, on 30 July, resolved to bring down
the Nasser Government by use of force. The British Government did not, at any time, take Australia's Government, or
even its 'British to the bootstraps' Prime Minister, into its
confidence. Britain (and France) lied publicly to the world,
and privately to their allies. It was in fact the American Secretary of State, John Foster Dulles, who was responsible for
telling Menzies that he had reason to believe the British and
French were planning an invasion and that the United
States regarded such a step as unjustifiable and calculated to
lead to world war.

The Menzies cabinet, with Casey as a sole voice of cau-
tion, nonetheless decided to give its full support to Britain
in whatever course it chose to take. As Fadden cabled to
Menzies on 7 August following a cabinet meeting:

> There was unanimous agreement that we should
> maintain our traditional support for the United Kingdom
> ... and every effort should be made to get the utmost
> American support for the British cause.[13]

Menzies went to great lengths to show his enthusiasm for the
British cause. On 13 August, at the request of British Prime
Minister Anthony Eden, he went on British television to
denounce the nationalisation of the canal. He said it would be
'suicidal' to leave 'our vital interests to the whim of one man'

and concluded by saying, 'we in Australia ... cannot accept either the legality or the morality of what Nasser has done'.[14]

A conference of those countries using the canal, including Australia (represented by Menzies), was held in London in mid-August. The Americans, led by Dulles, succeeded in producing a compromise proposal for consideration by Nasser which would have recognised Egypt's sovereignty over the canal, but nonetheless placed its operations under the control of an international board. The British went along with this proposal, as was later admitted, because they expected it to be rejected by Nasser and that his rejection would provide some justification for themselves and the French to invade.

Following the conference Menzies led a mission to Egypt to present the Dulles proposal to Nasser. It was, as the British had hoped, a failure. Over the next month world opinion moved further against the use of force. The Americans were quite explicit in their opposition to an invasion, as indeed were the Canadians. Of Britain's allies, only Australia and New Zealand were doggedly supportive. On 25 September, Menzies gave an extremely aggressive speech in the House of Representatives describing Nasser as a tyrant and assuring members that the British race would never surrender to tyranny.[15]

War broke out on 29 October. The British and French had secretly conspired with the Israelis, who had agreed to attack Egypt across the Sinai Desert. It was agreed that the British and French would immediately ask both the Israelis and the Egyptians to withdraw 10 miles from the canal zone so that they could occupy the zone in order to protect the canal. For the British and French an Israeli attack would provide a *casus belli*. For the Israelis, the war offered the prospect of having Anglo-French assistance to pre-emptively destroy Egypt's military capacity, particularly its air force. The Israelis attacked as planned, the ultimatum was given as planned and, as expected, the Israelis accepted the ultimatum while the Egyptians did not. After all the Egyptians were being asked to withdraw from their own territory and to cease defending it from an unprovoked invader.

The following day the American representative on the United Nations Security Council proposed a resolution calling on the Israelis to withdraw from Egyptian soil and further calling on all United Nations members to refrain from intervening themselves or providing military assistance to Israel. The Australian representative on the Security Council abstained rather than run the risk of being seen to vote in a manner which was contrary to the wishes of the British. Britain and France, being permanent members, were able to exercise their vetoes and the resolution was not carried. The British Government lied to the House of Commons, as it did to Australia and the rest of the world, when it denied any advance knowledge of Israel's intentions.

In the face of world opposition, and despite his having been lied to by the British, Menzies remained loyal, cabling Eden on 1 November that Australia supported the British use of force and noting, 'you must never entertain any doubts about the British quality of this country'.[16]

As British and French planes bombed Egypt, largely destroying its air force as the Israelis had wanted, the UN General Assembly again tried to bring the fighting to a stop. An American-sponsored resolution calling for a cease-fire and withdrawal of Israeli forces was carried by 64 votes to five. The five votes against were the United Kingdom, France and Israel (the three belligerents) supported by Australia and New Zealand. Over the next four days Australia continued to support the United Kingdom in every vote at the UN, even voting against a cease-fire resolution sponsored by Canada.

When, on 6 November, Menzies was advised that British commandos were about to land at, and capture, Port Said, the Australian Prime Minister was still supportive, assuring Eden that 'our support remains undiminished'.[17]

The invasion ended almost as soon as it began. The British pound had come under considerable pressure and when intervention from the International Monetary Fund was sought, the Americans advised the British that they would not allow any IMF assistance for Britain unless there was an immediate cease-fire. The British succumbed to the American pressure, and the French followed suit. Suddenly Menzies found the team he had been barracking for had walked off the field.

Menzies' uncritical support of Britain did not have the same political consequences for him as it did for Anthony Eden, who was quickly replaced by Harold Macmillan. But it did result in Egypt breaking off diplomatic relations with Australia, and it did reinforce Australia's image as a dutiful colony of Britain. It did no good for Australian–American relations. On 18 November, Casey was refused an audience with President Eisenhower as a sign of American displeasure.

Menzies, Lord Warden of the Cinque Ports

Menzies is widely portrayed as the classic Austral-Briton. He was of the generation that had been brought up in the Victorian and Edwardian eras. Menzies was often the subject of mockery on account of his love of all things English and it is convenient for the modern, nationalistic Australian to classify him as an eccentric, rather than accept that his attitudes were typical of those held by a large number of Australians.

It needs to be remembered that Menzies is the most successful politician ever to be seen in federal politics. His run of election victories, from 1949 until his retirement in 1965, could never have been achieved had his attitudes been totally out of kilter with the people that voted for him.

Menzies, like Henry Parkes before him, saw himself as a member of the 'British race'. In 1948, during his time as Opposition Leader, Menzies wrote about the need for there to be a 'redistribution of Empire population' from the overcrowded slums of England to Australia and New Zealand. He argued that immigration from Britain to Australia is not a loss to Britain.

> ... the boundaries of Great Britain are not on the Kentish coast, but at Cape York and Invercargill.[18] If our great Empire is only a thing of fragments, then we must

discuss migration quite differently. If it is in reality a living and breathing and everlasting unity, then we will no more question the movement of people from England to Australia than we would question a movement of people from Yorkshire to Somerset or from Melbourne to Perth.[19]

To Menzies, England was the centre of his world, and of Australia's. Everything in Australia was somewhat second-rate compared to England. Menzies despised Australian politics and yearned for a seat in the House of Commons. During his long visit to London in 1941 he spent most of his time intriguing to obtain a seat in Parliament from whence he believed he could challenge the uncertain leadership of Churchill.

It is churlish to mock the memory of a man as great as Robert Menzies and it is far too simplistic to describe him as a 'boot licker' and 'groveller'. Menzies believed he lived in the provinces of a great Empire the centre of which was London. His aspiration to be recognised and admired in that metropolis was no different from a talented South Dakotan aspiring to fame and fortune in Washington or New York. He did not regard Australia as an independent nation in the same way that France, or Germany or the United States were. Nonetheless, despite his adoration for things British, particularly if they were royal, Menzies had a clearer view of the monarchy's role in Australia than any of our latter-day royalists.

In 1953 the Federal Parliament enacted a *Royal Style and Titles Act*, the purpose of which was to change the monarch's title, for use in Australia, to include (for the first time) reference to Australia. The new title was to be 'Elizabeth the Second, by the Grace of God, of the United Kingdom, Australia and Her other Realms and Territories, Queen, Head of the Commonwealth, Defender of the Faith'.

Menzies, in his second reading speech, anticipated the question as to why the reference to the United Kingdom was retained. He said:

In the first place I think juristically speaking it would be
fantastic to eliminate a reference to the United Kingdom,
because the plain truth is that Her Majesty Queen
Elizabeth the Second sits on the throne not because of
some law of Australia, but because of the law of the
United Kingdom ...

Menzies goes on to state that because all of our political
institutions (and those of the other Commonwealth countries) had been inherited from Britain it was to deny our history to remove the reference to the United Kingdom in the
title. He concluded his speech, hoping that in two hundred
years we would still feel:

... the Crown is the defender of our faith, still feel that of
all our nations and ourselves in particular he, or she, is
the enduring monarch, the monarch who dies as an
individual, but who passes on a crown that will always
be the sign and proof that wherever we may be in the
world we are one people.[20]

So to Menzies, the monarch, or the Crown, was a symbol of
the Britishness that was our heritage and which united the
British Commonwealth nations. In other words, even to that
old royalist, the Queen was not an Australian symbol. She
was an international symbol.

Dr Evatt, the Leader of the Opposition, endorsed Menzies' remarks. As he concluded his speech he expressed
regret that to satisfy the demands of India (which had joined
the Commonwealth as a republic) the word 'British' had
been dropped from Commonwealth.

In this country no such difficulty could ever arise because
the word British means to us as much as it does to the
people of the United Kingdom itself and of New Zealand
and Canada. To all of us it means the British tradition of
government under which every member of this Parliament
pledges his faith and allegiance to the monarch.[21]

The Royal Visits

In many respects, the 1954 royal visit was the last hurrah of the monarchy in Australia. Subsequent royal visits have been lower key affairs, reflecting both a lessening commitment to the British connection and the decreasing public interest in the Queen herself as time transformed her from the fairy-tale princess to the serious-looking grandmother of today. The first visit by Queen Elizabeth in 1954 was an event which no Australians who witnessed it would ever forget. There was none of the contemporary nonsense that the Queen was a representative of the Australian nation. She was the crowned head of the British peoples, and when Her Majesty opened the Federal Parliament on 15 February 1954, she addressed the assembled members, not so much about Australia, but about the Commonwealth.

It is, I think, fitting that I should, speaking to you today, recall to mind those elements of unity which combine in the fabric of the British Commonwealth. The great institutions of parliamentary sovereignty, a democratically controlled executive, the just and impartial administration of the law; these exist and flourish in each of the great realms which call me Queen.

Already in my journeys through the Commonwealth, I have been made even more vividly conscious of the true brotherhood of my peoples, even prouder of their services to civilisation, and more richly confident of their future destiny.

To play their part in the achievement and preservation of peace, my Australian ministers will continue the closest co-operation with my Governments in the other Commonwealth nations. Only last month my Finance Ministers conferred in Sydney with the frankness and friendliness which always mark discussions between the Commonwealth countries. This was one of a long and continuing series of such conferences. Their immediate objective is to strengthen the British Commonwealth; but their ultimate benefit will flow to other nations and the great world community of people everywhere.[22]

Moving Apart

In the post-war years, Australia and Britain moved further apart. The story is a familiar one to all of us. In 1950, 38.7 per cent of all Australian exports went to Britain. In 1990 that figure was 3.5 per cent. In 1950, 35.7 per cent of all imports into Australia came from Britain. In 1990 that figure was 7.3 per cent.[23] In the same period, trade with Asian countries exploded from 15.6 per cent of exports and 21.0 per cent of imports to 49.1 per cent and 37.6 per cent respectively.

Figure 4.1: Destination of Australia's Exports by Country, 1900–1990

	1900	1920	1950	1985	1990
UK	52.8	56.3	38.7	11.9	3.5
Europe	19.4	10.4	26.6	15.5	15.2
USA & Canada	2.8	7.6	9.6	16.3	13.0
Asia	5.6	11.1	15.6	41.5	49.1
NZ	2.8	5.6	3.5	4.8	5.1
Others	16.7	9.0	5.9	10.0	14.1

Note: Numbers are expressed in percentages.
Sources: Wray Vamplev (ed.), *Australian Historical Statistics*, Fairfax, Syme and Weldon, 1987, Table 107–121 and 221–237; Australian Bureau of Statistics, *Yearbook 1990*, Dec. 1990.

Figure 4.2: Origin of Australia's Imports by Country, 1900–1990

	1900	1920	1950	1985	1990
UK	57.3	38.5	35.7	21.8	7.3
Europe	10.3	6.6	16.7	18.4	20.4
USA & Canada	15.0	26.4	19.4	28.8	23.8
Asia	5.0	16.5	21.0	24.2	37.6
NZ	2.5	2.2	1.7	2.2	4.2
Others	10.0	9.9	5.5	4.6	6.7

Note: Numbers are expressed in percentages.
Sources: Wray Vamplev (ed.), *Australian Historical Statistics*, Fairfax, Syme and Weldon, 1987, Table 152–166 and 265–281; Australian Bureau of Statistics, *Yearbook 1990*, Dec. 1990.

The population mix also changed rapidly. In 1947, 9.8 per cent of the total Australian population was born outside of Australia, and 7.2 per cent of the Australian population had been born in the United Kingdom. By 1991, however, 22.7 per cent of the Australian population had been born outside Australia and only 6.9 per cent had been born in the United Kingdom. The lesson is clear: in 1947 almost all foreign-born Australians had come from the United Kingdom; in 1991, less than a third had. So while the United Kingdom was still the largest single source of immigration, Australia was no longer an exclusively British destination. The biggest element in the change had been the number of Australians who had been born in Asia. In 1947 those persons amounted to 0.1 per cent of the population; by 1991 it had increased to 4.7 per cent.

Self-perception was slow to change, however. In the 1910 Commonwealth *Yearbook* the Australian people were described as 'fundamentally British':

The Australian at present is little other than a transplanted Briton with the essential characteristics of his British forebears, the desire for freedom from restraint however, being perhaps more strongly accentuated. The greater opportunity for an open-air existence, and the absence of the restrictions of older civilisations, may be held to be in the main responsible for this.[24]

This description was only slightly amended over the succeeding years, and even in 1954 the *Yearbook's* comment was: 'The non-indigenous population of Australia is fundamentally British in race and nationality'.[25]

The British Isles continued, however, to provide the largest single source of immigrants to Australia, and it is only in the last years that Hong Kong overtook Britain as a source of migrants.

The monarchy was not an issue during the 1960s. Australians still saw London as the centre of their world. Some Australian writers and artists emigrated, never to return;

Figure 4.3: Birthplace of the Australian Population by Percentage, 1901–1991

	1901	1911	1921	1933	1947	1954	1961	1971	1981	1991
UK	18.2	13.5	12.5	10.8	7.2	7.4	7.2	8.5	7.9	7.0
Europe	2.0	1.6	1.3	1.4	1.4	5.5	8.1	8.8	7.8	6.9
USA & Canada	0.3	0.2	0.2	0.2	0.1	0.1	0.2	0.3	0.4	0.5
Asia	1.0	0.6	0.4	0.2	0.1	0.3	0.4	0.5	1.3	4.1
NZ	0.7	0.7	0.7	0.7	0.6	0.5	0.4	0.6	1.2	1.7
Others	0.6	0.4	0.4	0.3	0.3	0.5	0.7	1.4	2.3	2.6
Total Foreign Born	22.8	17.1	15.5	13.6	9.8	14.3	16.9	20.2	20.9	22.7
Australian Born	77.2	82.9	84.5	86.4	90.2	85.7	83.1	79.8	79.1	77.3

Sources: Wray Vamplev (ed.), *Australian Historical Statistics*, Fairfax, Syme and Weldon, 1987, Table 45–54; Australian Bureau of Statistics, *Estimated Resident Population by Country of Birth, Age & Sex*, Catalogue 3221.0, June 1990.

almost all attempted to make it in Britain. One of them, Barry Humphries, made his fortune out of denigrating his own country to appreciative audiences in London. The young heir to the throne, Prince Charles, spent two terms at Timbertop, a kind of Outward Bound school for the boys (and now girls) of Geelong Grammar. Speaking to Jonathan Aitken in 1970 the Prince was dismissive of republicanism:

> He jokes about the poet chap who leads the campaign for the overthrow of the monarchy (Geoffrey Dutton of Adelaide) and believes that a majority of the young Australians still have the feeling that Britain is 'home'.[26]

The Queen of Australia

The most significant political event after the resignation of Sir Robert Menzies was the election of the Whitlam Labor Government in 1972. Whitlam was an enthusiastic Australian nationalist. In 1973 Whitlam introduced legislation to change the Queen's title for use in Australia. The references to the United Kingdom and to Defender of the Faith were dropped. The Queen's title became simply; Elizabeth, by the Grace of God, Queen of Australia and her other Realms and Territories, Head of the Commonwealth.

The proponents of this legislation no doubt congratulated themselves on their Australian nationalism. Yet, in truth, they no less than their conservative predecessors, had continued to perpetrate a confidence trick on the Australian public. For by changing the label they hoped to obscure the real legal and constitutional fact that the Queen was no more an Australian institution than the House of Lords or the College of Heralds. They had created Elizabeth, a Queen of Australia, but they had not, and could not, make her an Australian Queen.

Whitlam's *Royal Style & Titles Act* of 1973 lacked the integrity of Menzies' Act of 1953. Menzies acknowledged that the Queen sat on her throne because of British laws. He knew that our Constitution decreed that whoever sat on that British throne was to be the King or Queen of Australia. He knew that the monarchy was a thoroughly British institution. So did Whitlam. It is one of the supreme ironies of political history that today the successors to Menzies on the conservative side of politics who are trying to defend the monarchy point to the Queen's title as 'Queen of Australia' and cite that title as evidence that the monarchy is now an Australian institution.

The sacking of the Whitlam Government by Governor-General Sir John Kerr in November 1975 (discussed at length in Chapter 5) revived the thoroughly dormant republican movement for a few years. But it was clear that whatever had gone wrong in 1975, it had nothing to do with the Queen. A republican President with the same powers as the Governor-General could do exactly the same thing again. Those who wanted to prevent a repetition of 1975 had to amend those sections of the Constitution which dealt with the powers of the Governor-General.

The Australia Act

The year 1986 saw the passage of the *Australia Act* by both the United Kingdom Parliament and the Australian Parliament. Her Majesty the Queen assented to the first in her capacity as Queen of the United Kingdom and to the second in her capacity as Queen of Australia.

The *Australia Act* (United Kingdom) was passed by the United Kingdom Parliament at the request of the Australian Parliament and the Australian States. While the *Statute of Westminster* in 1931 had liberated the Commonwealth from the operation of British laws, the States had been unaffected. For that reason, state laws were invalid insofar as they conflicted with any British law which had been intended to apply to those states. This was not a mere academic matter. In a series of cases in the 1970s the High Court, by a majority (with Justice Murphy dissenting), had held that the 1894 (British) *Merchant Shipping Act* applied to limit the liability of ship owners for accidents occurring to seamen in Australian ports.

Prior to the passage of the *Australia Act*, the appointment of State Governors was made by the Queen acting on the advice of the British Government. It was true that since the Second World War the practice had developed of the British Government acting merely as a conduit for the views of the relevant Premier; but nonetheless the procedure was still a colonial one. As a result of the *Australia Act*, all advice to the Queen in respect of a State is given directly by the Premier concerned.

The most important substantive change effected by the *Australia Act*, however, was the final abolition of appeals to the Privy Council from all state courts. This ended the bizarre arrangement by which an unsuccessful litigant before the Court of Appeal of a State could elect to take an appeal either to the Privy Council in London or the High Court in Canberra. Appeals to the Privy Council from the High Court had been abolished — except with the leave of the High Court, which will never be granted — in 1975. As a result, judges of the state Supreme Courts were under the legal jurisdiction of two different ultimate appellate courts.

Matters of national dignity aside, the Privy Council had become a severe embarrassment to the legal profession and the judiciary. In 1976 in a case called *Oteri v. The Queen*[27] the Privy Council had, inexplicably, observed that the legislative power of the Commonwealth of Australia does not extend to criminal law, which, their Lordships stated, was within the competence of the States only. This remarkably mistaken throwaway line was, although plainly wrong, a powerful weapon in the hands of those determined to end appeals to London.

The *Australia Act* was the penultimate point in the achievement of independence for Australia. Most historians would regard Australia as having achieved its independence well before 1986, and in many respects they would be right. But a country which does not control its own judicial system and which cedes the right of final judgment to the courts of another country cannot be called fully independent.

The last fetter of colonialism is the monarchy itself. It is true that the fetter does not chafe as much as it did — just as it is true that the Queen's only substantive function in Australia is to appoint as Governor-General the person nominated by the Australian Prime Minister. But insubstantial though her functions may be, her removal from our Constitution will be a great moment in our history. It will be a point of finality, and a point of definition. It will be the finish of our two centuries of colonialism and subordination, and it will define our nationhood for the centuries to come.

CHAPTER FIVE

The Office of the President

If you took the Constitution literally you would be excused for believing that the Governor-General is an all-powerful dictator who picks advisers to suit himself or herself. You would imagine that Parliament is almost an obscure debating society somewhere on the outskirts of the real power at Yarralumla.

Of course that is not the way things really work. One of the quaint, and very British, aspects of our Constitution is that most of the important things about the way Australia is governed are not in the Constitution at all. There is no mention of the Prime Minister, there is no mention of the cabinet, there is no mention of the fact that the Ministers of State whom the Governor-General appoints to advise him or her have to be able to command a majority in the House of Representatives, although they do not have to be able to command one in the Senate.

According to the *Oxford English Dictionary*, a 'constitution' is 'the system or body of fundamental principles according to which a nation, state or body politic is constituted or governed'. That being so, it is fair to say that most of the important parts of the 'small c' constitution are not in the 'large c' Constitution. Many lawyers, particularly those teaching at the universities, complain that not enough Australians read the Constitution. In some respects it is just as well they do not, as they would be well and truly confused if they thought it contained the full story.

In some countries, such as the United States, the Head of State is also the Head of Government. In that sense Bill Clinton is the Queen and Prime Minister rolled into one. In Australia (and most other countries) the Head of Government is the person who leads the party or parties that control a majority of the seats in the House of Representatives (or its equivalent). That person is often called the Prime Minister. The Head of State is the formal leader of the nation and it is in his or her name that the Government is conducted, but such heads of state have no real political power on a day-to-day basis.

Our system of democracy is representative democracy. We elect other people, the members of parliament, to make decisions for us. In days gone by, before the development of modern political parties, members of parliament were often elected because of their personal talents or characteristics or because of their connections with a certain area, but not because they were the nominated candidates of any political party. They did not commit themselves always to vote one way or the other and they were expected to use their judgment.

Nowadays almost all members of parliament are members of either the Australian Labor Party, the Liberal Party, the National Party or the Australian Democrats. Most of these members would have not the slightest chance of winning their seats without the endorsement of that particular political party. Most Australians who vote in elections are aware of the party leaders and a few of the leading lights on each side, but that is all. They will go to the polling place and vote 'Liberal' or 'Labor'. They may be doing so because they like 'Hewson' or 'Keating', but the chances are they will neither know nor care who the particular individuals are who are standing for the major parties in their electorate.

That generalisation is not always correct, of course, particularly in electorates which are closely contested. Where the numbers of supporters of each party are roughly equal, a well-known local identity or an unusually talented candidate may be able to swing sufficient votes to tip the scales in his or her favour and win the seat. Nonetheless, Sir Joseph Porter's description of how he rose to be First Lord of the Admiralty[1] in Gilbert and Sullivan's *HMS Pinafore* is still fairly accurate:

> I always voted at my party's call
> And never thought of thinking for myself at all.[2]

Under our federal system of government, we have a Parliament with two Houses; the House of Representatives and the Senate. The House of Representatives has 147 members, each of whom is elected to represent an electorate. Each electorate is a geographical area with about 80 000 people in it. While the electorates are kept approximately equal in terms of population, there are huge differences in the size of the electorates. A densely populated inner-city electorate may be only a few square kilometres. The electorate of Kalgoorlie, however, consists of three-quarters of Western Australia. Because the Constitution requires members of the House of Representatives to be chosen from States 'in proportion to the respective number of their people', there are 50 members from New South Wales, 38 from Victoria, 25 from Queensland, 13 from each of South Australia and Western Australia, five from Tasmania, two from the Australian Capital Territory and one from the Northern Territory. Tiny Tasmania would only have four seats in the House of Representatives were it not for section 24 of the Constitution, which guarantees every original State at least five seats.

The Senate is differently composed. There are 12 Senators

elected from each State and two from each of the federal Territories — the Australian Capital Territory and the Northern Territory. The Territory Senators have a term of three years only. Senators are elected by the voters of their State or Territory at large. So all 12 Senators from New South Wales, for example, represent the whole of that State.

The Senate is elected by a system of proportional representation. Senators' terms are a maximum of six years, so that every three years one-half of the Senate is up for re-election, except that the term for Senators representing the Territories is three years. In the event of a double dissolution of both Houses of Parliament all of the Senate is up for re-election. Because of the proportional representation system minor parties and some Independents have been able to secure seats in the Senate, whereas it is relatively rare for Independents or smaller parties to secure seats in the House of Representatives. Indeed, ever since 1980 the balance of power in the Senate has been held by Independents and minor parties. At present there are 36 Coalition Senators, 30 ALP Senators, seven Democrats, two Greens and one Independent (Senator Harradine).

In strict demographic terms, the Senate therefore is thoroughly undemocratic. Fewer than 400 000 Tasmanians elect as many Senators as five million New South Welshmen (and women). Equal representation for the States in the Senate was, however, the factor that persuaded the smaller colonies to join the Federation in the first place. Prior to Federation they were in charge of their own affairs. As a consequence of Federation they ceded important fields of government to a new Federal Parliament. If its representation had been entirely based on population the smaller States would have been completely swamped and would effectively have surrendered control of much of their affairs to New South Wales and Victoria. So equal representation for the States in the Senate was the big trade-off. Many federations have a similar arrangement. In the United States of America each State sends two Senators to the United States Senate — so that Wyoming with 540 000 people has as many

Senators as California with 30 million and New York with 20 million.

The Senate and the House of Representatives have exactly the same powers over legislation, and for any law to be passed it has to be approved by a majority vote in both Houses of Parliament. The only (small) exception to this is that 'money bills' may not originate in the Senate and may not be amended by the Senate. But they can be rejected.

Money bills are the one form of legislation that every government needs every year. Most of the legislation which goes through the Parliament is not absolutely critical. It may be highly desirable that the *Broadcasting Services Act*, for example, be amended this year, but the Government will not fall if it is not. However, the Government is not permitted by the Constitution to spend any public money without the approval of Parliament given in an appropriation or 'supply' Bill.

Most Commonwealth expenditure is 'permanently' authorised by special appropriation laws relating, for example, to the payment of social security benefits. However, all of the salaries of public servants are covered by annual appropriation legislation. So every year each House of Parliament has the opportunity to turn off the supply of money to the Government with the inevitable consequence that that Government will fall.

The power of Parliament to control the purse strings was established more than three hundred years ago in England and, because Parliament could deny the King the money to pay for his wars, frolics and other governmental activities, Parliament developed the right to determine who his advisers would be. By the time the Commonwealth Constitution was enacted in 1901 it was accepted in Great Britain that the Queen was purely a ceremonial Head of State and that the party who controlled a majority in the House of Commons was entitled to form a government. The Government was administered in the name of the Queen, but all the decisions were taken by the politicians who had the numbers in the House of Commons.

As Walter Bagehot wrote in his work *The English Constitution* in 1867:

> The Queen … must sign her own death warrant if the two Houses unanimously send it up to her. It is a fiction of the past to ascribe to her legislative power. She has long ceased to have any.[3]

In Britain there are two Houses of Parliament. The House of Commons is composed of members elected to represent individual electorates, much the same as they are in the House of Representatives in Australia. Unlike the Australian Senate, the other 'upper' House of Parliament, however, is not democratic in any way at all. The House of Lords is composed of people who hold noble titles — and none of them is elected at all. Not all of the 'Lords' in the House of Lords inherited their titles. The bishops of the Church of England sit in the House of Lords and nowadays there are numerous life peers who are given the title of Baron or Baroness for their lifetime, in much the same way as knights are addressed as 'Sir' during their lifetime, but cannot pass the knighthood on to their children.

The House of Lords does not have the power to block any money bill whatsoever. Nor can it block any other form of legislation for more than 12 months. Compared with the Australian Senate it is a very weak House of Parliament. In practical terms, therefore, Britain's Parliament is closer to unicameral parliaments like that of Queensland and New Zealand where there is only one, popularly elected, chamber.

In considering the history of our Australian parliamentary institutions it is important to bear in mind that the differences between our system and Britain's are at least as important as the similarities. A British Prime Minister who (by definition) controls a majority in the House of Commons is able to govern Britain with few restraints. The upper house has no power, there are no States and there is no written constitution. Lord Hailsham, the former Lord

Chancellor, once described Britain as having an 'elective dictatorship' because of the remarkable absence of constitutional checks and balances on the power of the executive government.

When the Australian Constitution was being drafted in the 1890s there was much anxiety that an Australian Government would need to command not only a majority in the House of Representatives but in the Senate as well. People from the larger States of New South Wales and Victoria feared that while they would have the majority in the House of Representatives, the smaller States would control the Senate and use their majority in the Senate to extract all manner of concessions from the larger States. The Senators for Tasmania, South Australia, Queensland and Western Australia, representing one-third of the population but two-thirds of the votes in the Senate, could say to the Government: 'Unless you support billions of dollars of extra federal spending in our States, we will not pass your legislation, nor will we vote you any money to administer the Government.'

This nightmare did not occur for one very simple reason. Almost all members of the House of Representatives and Senators have been elected as representatives of the major political parties. The major political parties are controlled by people in Victoria and New South Wales because in those States are found the bulk of the population and the bulk of the money. The dream that the Senate would be a States' House where the separate interests of the smaller States would be given full recognition was never realised. The Labor Senator from Tasmania has to comply with the directions of his party just as much as if he had been elected from New South Wales.

Paul Keating is the Prime Minister because, at the last federal election, the Labor Party won a majority of the seats in the House of Representatives. Mr Keating is the Head of Government of Australia, but he is not the Head of State. That position is filled by the Queen and her representative, the Governor-General. Only half of the Senate seats were up for election on this occasion and following the election neither Labor nor the Liberal–National Party Coalition controls a majority in the Senate.

Legislation is validly enacted once it is passed by the House of Representatives and the Senate and then 'assented to' by the Governor-General. There is nothing in the Constitution which says the Governor-General has to sign whatever legislation is put in front of him, but the constitutional 'convention' is that he does.

These conventions are a confusing aspect of Australia's 'small c' constitution. Despite the fact that the Governor-General is described as having considerable political power under the Constitution, in reality he has very little. Over the years conventions — which is another way of saying customs — have developed about the way power is exercised in our system of government. The Governor-General is described in section 68 of the Constitution as being the Commander-in-Chief of the naval and military forces of the Commonwealth. Theoretically, therefore, he could call out the troops and instruct them to arrest the Prime Minister and machine-gun his ministers. The generals commanding the army, however, would be most unlikely to take any instructions from the Governor-General on this, or any other, matter. They know that their real boss is the Minister for Defence, as set out in the *Defence Act*. In other words, they know the Constitution is, if read in isolation, quite misleading.

Under section 58 of the Constitution, for example, the Governor-General may return to the House in which it originated any proposed law so presented to him, and may transmit therewith any amendments which he may recommend, and the Houses may deal with the recommendation.

A Governor-General who took this provision literally could receive, for example, a new law relating to firearms and, drawing on recent experience as a kangaroo hunter, suggest a few changes and improvements and send it back to Parliament for consideration. If Parliament did not approve of the proposals, the Governor-General could refuse to sign it — and if you took the Constitution literally, would be quite entitled to do so.

Because of the constitutional conventions, Governors-General act only on the advice of their ministers, so Mr Hayden would not do either of these things. He is entitled to be fully informed about the legislation and he can ask questions and give his own advice. But if the Prime Minister says 'Sign', the Governor-General has to sign it. The Queen is in exactly the same position in Britain.

The Constitution therefore is unquestionably deficient in that it does not accurately describe the way the Government works. Unwritten conventions, the content of which are not always entirely clear, are quite unsatisfactory. While the system works reasonably well, it is important that an Australian be able to pick up the Constitution and in reading it obtain a reasonably accurate description of how the Commonwealth Government operates. At present the description is utterly misleading. As we will see this deficiency can be remedied very readily and we should take that opportunity when Australia's Constitution is amended to establish the republic.

If Australia becomes a republic we will have a President instead of a Governor-General, and the President will not be the representative of anyone (other than the people of Australia). The Australian Republican Movement has proposed that the President should have exactly the same powers and duties as the Governor-General. Those powers, as we have seen, are governed both by the Constitution itself and by constitutional conventions which require the Governor-General to do as he or she is told by the ministers who constitute the Government.

What, one may ask, is the point of having a President (or a Governor-General) if all the Governor-General does is sign documents whenever told to do so by the Prime Minister? It is a perfectly good question. What does the Head of State do?

The Ceremonial Duties of the Head of State

The duties of the Governor-General (in common with State Governors) can be divided into three parts. The largest part of the Governor-General's work is almost entirely ceremonial or community work. This appears to occupy about 80 per cent of the Governor-General's time. The balance of the time is taken up with governmental functions where the Governor-General acts on the advice of the Government of the day. Apart from the important, but few, 'reserve powers' in the exercise of which he or she may act contrary to the wishes of the Prime Minister, all of the Governor-General's duties in the administration of the Government of the Common-wealth are undertaken on the advice (which means at the direction) of the Ministers of State who are nominated by the leader of the party or parties which has a majority in the House of Representatives.

The Governor-General assents to legislation as advised by the Prime Minister; formally dissolves Parliament; calls elections; opens the new Parliament and so on. As Head of State the Governor-General acts as the official representative of the Australian Commonwealth. He or she receives ambassadors and visiting dignitaries, is invited to open art festivals, cattle shows, learned conferences and so on. Because the Governor-General does not have the same punishing workload as a Prime Minister (who actually has to run the country) the Governor-General can do a great deal more in the area of good works, ribbon-cutting and speech-making to worthy gatherings.

One of the State Governors consulted by the Republic Advisory Committee described the community role of the Governor, and his comments would be equally applicable to the role of the Governor-General:

> Speaking on behalf of the community the Governor is
> able in speeches to recognise and pay tribute to volunteers
> who contribute much to the quality of community life,
> those who excel in doing what is in the community
> interest and people who give other commendable
> service to the community. The Governor acknowledges
> those who donate to good community organisations or
> causes. The Governor and Governor's wife encourage

good community organisations, indicating public
encouragement of their activities and raising their profiles
by becoming their patrons ... Community recognition
and gratitude to volunteers giving outstanding
community service, those who in their occupations serve
the community well beyond the call of duty, the brave
and others of conspicuous good conduct, is expressed by
the Governor investing them with their awards at
Government House in the presence of friends and
families.[4]

Do we actually need a Head of State to do all this? In Britain
the Queen performs exactly the same functions, but at least
her defenders can claim that she is a tourist attraction
because of all the attendant pomp and ceremony.

The Governor-General is not cheap to run. The cost of
paying his (tax-free) salary, maintaining grand residences in
Canberra and Sydney and paying for his staff, travel, enter-
tainment and security will be $9.5 million in 1993–94. When
you add to that the $20 million cost of the six State Gover-
nors, it is clear that Australia pays a very high price for its
ceremonial heads of state.

Do we need to have a Head of State who does not actually
run the country? Or is it just an expensive and superfluous
indulgence? The principal function of a non-executive Head
of State (by which is meant a Head of State like the Queen or
our Governor-General — one who is not also the Head of
Government) is to act as a non-political representative of the
nation. Political figures (such as a Prime Minister) are
inevitably contentious and rarely command the support of
much more than 50 per cent of the population. Often a
Prime Minister is profoundly contentious and unpopular.
When the former Prime Minister of Canada, Brian Mul-
roney, announced his resignation earlier this year his popularity, according to the opinion polls, was just 12 per cent.
Even the recently elected Paul Keating, basking in the glow
of post-triumph celebrity, could only muster, in late April
1993, a 36 per cent approval rating.

The Head of Government will always have strong opponents in the community because it is impossible to please all of the people all of the time. Especially in difficult economic times, such as those we face at the moment, political leaders have to take tough decisions which will cause short-term pain, in the hope of long-term benefits. The Premier of Victoria, Mr Kennett, is a good example of this. Mr Kennett inherited, from the previous Labor Government, an almost bankrupt State Government. He has taken some very harsh measures to reduce spending with the stated aim of eliminating the State's deficit by 1996. Whether Mr Kennett's measures are the right ones or not, there can be no question that some very hard decisions had to be taken by whoever was responsible for the Government of Victoria. So Mr Kennett is hoping that by the time he next faces a general election Victoria will have seen the benefit of his spending cuts and a grateful public will re-elect him.

The Head of State, however, can rise above all that necessary strife. The Head of State is not responsible for making political decisions. As a non-political representative of the nation, the Head of State should be the person who can speak for all of those things that we have in common. And despite the enormous heat which political controversies generate from time to time, we agree on many more things than we differ on. A non-executive Head of State is capable of providing a degree of national leadership which politicians cannot. The Head of State should be an ambassador of the nation, both within and without its boundaries. Our Australian President will not be obliged to steer away from controversial subjects for fear of treading on political toes. There are many important issues confronting Australia which can be addressed passionately and cogently by a Head of State who stands above party politics. Social inequality, the degradation of the environment, the promotion of Australian literature and arts, the reconciliation with the indigenous people of this land — these are just some of the important issues in respect of which a President can provide real leadership. Clearly the more able the man or woman who fulfils that role, the more ably it will be discharged. But there is a platform there which can fruitfully be employed to promote discussion and awareness of those things all Australians have in common.

It is that very Australianness which is so important to the cause of the republic. We have so much diversity in our society. Multiculturalism is a relatively new term which means no more than that diverse cultures and backgrounds are entitled to equal respect and legitimacy. This respect for diversity does, however, have a centrifugal effect on our society unless there is also a respect and advancement of those things which all Australians have in common. This does not mean that all Australians have to look the same, worship at the same altar or maintain the same standards of personal morality. But simply because our life, our family and our fortunes are tied to this land and our Australian society, more than any other, we have a great deal in common. Because the republic is an affirmation of our identity as Australians, it is a celebration of that Australianness which should be encouraged and developed as the cement that holds our very tolerant and diverse society together.

One of the alienating aspects of Australia to many people of non-British backgrounds is that all the public symbols of the nation have been so very British. Much of that has changed and become distinctively Australian. But as long as the British monarch is our Head of State, Australians who come from non-British backgrounds will inevitably feel that their presence in Australia lacks the same kind of legitimacy as those whose ethnic background is the same as the Queen herself. While an Australian President may well be a white Anglo-Saxon Protestant, the fact that any Australian citizen can be the President (and over a period of time there will no doubt be a considerable diversity in the background of our Presidents) means that the Presidency itself becomes an affirmation that all Australian citizens reside in this country with equal legitimacy.

The international role of a Head of State is little understood in Australia, and that is hardly surprising since our

Head of State, the Queen, has never represented Australia. We have her face on our coins, our banknotes and in our public buildings. We swear allegiance to the Queen and the business of our governments is conducted in her name. But when she travels to the United States, or to Japan, or to the Middle East she does so only in her capacity as the British Queen. She goes to International Trade Fairs and promotes the sale of British goods, she has travelled to the Middle East and assisted in selling British weapons. She has even been to Strasbourg and praised the further integration of the European Community, a trading bloc of which Great Britain is a member and one which, in its efforts to protect the hopelessly inefficient, but politically powerful, farmers of France, has destroyed the livelihoods of thousands of efficient Australian farmers.

When Australia becomes a republic, we will have a President as our Head of State and unlike the Governor-General, the President will be no-one else's deputy or representative. We will no longer be humiliated by the world seeing our Head of State, the Queen, travelling abroad to advance and promote the interests of those who do us harm. Our President will be able to represent Australia as its Head of State, and will be able to promote the interests of Australia in just the same way the Queen promotes the interests of Great Britain.

This ability to project a distinct international identity is particularly important in our own region. Memories of colonialism are still strong in our part of the world. An Australian President, visiting our neighbours, will be a tangible demonstration of our independent identity and of our commitment to this region. The President will not go to Jakarta, or Kuala Lumpur or Tokyo as the representative of a person the whole world knows and recognises as the Queen of Great Britain. Our President will represent the people of Australia. Few of our Asian neighbours will publicly criticise the monarchy in Australia, any more than we will publicly criticise their constitutional arrangements. But those few Australians who have spent a lot of time with our neighbours, and more importantly have spent a lot of time listening to them, report that our current Head of State is an embarrassment. For that reason, our neighbours are intensely interested in the republican debate in Australia. It seems to them to demonstrate that Australians want to establish a distinct identity for themselves and have come to terms with Australia not being, at least in cultural and economic terms, moored somewhere in the North Atlantic comfortably close to Mother England and Big Brother America.

Frank Ching, writing in the *Far Eastern Economic Review*, recently described the ridiculous scene at an Australia Day reception in Hong Kong:

> The high point ... is when the Australian diplomat and the governor toast each other's sovereign. First the consul-general raises her glass and proposes a toast to 'Her Britannic Majesty, Queen Elizabeth II'. After the guests dutifully raise their glasses and murmur 'the Queen' before sipping their champagne, it is the governor's turn to toast 'Her Australian Majesty, Queen Elizabeth II'. This always elicits a few chuckles.[5]

Ching goes on to describe how the advent of an Australian republic would be viewed in Asia:

> The time is drawing near for Australia to take concrete action to make this commitment to Asia unambiguous. This does not mean that Australia must ... deny its cultural heritage. To remain true to themselves, Australians must assert, not reject, the values they hold dear, such as democracy, rule of law and individual rights and freedoms ... In Asia, a republican Australia will not be viewed with suspicion as a stalking horse for British — or American — interests. Australians can then make it clear that they represent nobody's interests but their own, and that Australia's interests are similar to those of its neighbours in the region.

Some monarchists contend that the Governor-General is an adequately Australian Head of State. They point to the fact that Governors-General have travelled abroad. But they have difficulty explaining why it is that these overseas visits, or indeed most of the domestic visits, of the Governor-General go almost unnoticed. It is an interesting feature of our Governors-General and State Governors that they seem to be almost invisible. The Governor-General is rarely written about in the press or portrayed on television and the vast majority of Australians would not even know the names of their State Governors. There are two possible reasons for this.

First, there is no doubt that power is a most alluring quality and people who wield real power attract the interest and attention of others. If given the choice of listening to a speech by the Prime Minister or one by the Governor-General, most people would prefer to listen to the Prime Minister. The Governor-General's speech will be uncontentious and may be inspiring and eloquent. But because he wields no real political power he will not be able to promise anything. Because he has no political opponents he will not be engaging in colourful criticism of the 'scumbags' (to pick a word out of the air) on the other side of the House. The Prime Minister, on the other hand, wields more real power than any other person in Australia. He may be announcing a tax reduction (or worse an increase). He may be announcing a reshuffle of his Ministry, or he may simply be laying into the unfortunate Opposition. This first factor is inescapable and it applies to some extent in every country where the Head of State is not also the Head of Government.

Second, the Governor-General, and the State Governors, are not perceived as being Heads of State in their own right. They are representatives of the Queen. Another term for a Governor-General or Governor is 'Viceroy', from which derives the adjective 'viceregal'. Viceroy is a French term which means, literally, 'deputy King'. The British official who headed the Government of India before Indian Independence was known as the Viceroy of India because he was the deputy of the King-Emperor or Queen-Empress.

This diminution in status because the Governor-General is a mere deputy is exacerbated in modern times by the ability of the Queen, and other members of her family, to visit Australia regularly.

In the days before jet travel, royal visits were very rare and no reigning monarch visited Australia before the Queen's first visit here in 1954. The bicentennial celebrations in 1988 are a good example of the problem. In that year every major bicentennial event was presided over by either the Queen or another member of her family. The Queen opened the new Federal Parliament House, the Darling Harbour development in Sydney, the new State Library in Sydney and the Expo in Brisbane (among many other things). The single most spectacular event of the bicentennial year was the Australia Day celebration on 26 January at Sydney Harbour. An estimated one million Australians crowded the foreshores of the Harbour to see a fleet of tall (sailing) ships enter the Harbour in a re-enactment of the First Fleet's arrival 200 years before. This magnificent day was presided over, not by an Australian, but by Prince Charles, who gave the keynote speech at the Opera House.

In this respect, the Bicentenary was not so much a 'celebration of a nation' as it was claimed to be, but rather a *denial* of a nation. Rather than asserting our distinct identity as Australians, which is what any other country would do on such an anniversary, we imported members of the royal family from Britain to officiate at every significant event and ceremony. One is reminded of the elephant who is bigger and stronger than any other animal, but is scared of a tiny mouse. Confidence is everything, and yet in 1988 our Australian nation — which has achieved so much materially and has created a society which is fairer and kinder than most — nonetheless did not have sufficient confidence in its own identity to provide, from the ranks of its own citizens, the leading actors in what was meant to be a celebration of *this* nation, and no other.

So desperate was the Bicentennial Authority to avoid any substantive discussion of national identity that it refused to publish, in its own newsletter, an article by Franca Arena advocating the establishment of an Australian republic. In a 'celebration of a nation', we were not permitted to talk about nationhood. What should have been a year of pride was just a party, a celebration of hedonism and directionless sentiment.

The Governor-General was almost invisible during that year, confirming the constitutional fact that far from being the Head of State, the Governor-General was just a stand-in who represented the Queen when she could not be here. An Australian President would not suffer from this phenomenon of being overshadowed by the Queen. If we chose to invite the Queen of Great Britain (who is also the Head of the Commonwealth) to visit Australia, she would be greeted by the Australian President as an equal in the same way that she is greeted by the President of Germany or Italy or by the Queen of Denmark or the Netherlands.

It is, however, unlikely that an Australian President will ever command the same kind of public interest and attention that the Queen does in Great Britain. An Australian President will (it is hoped) not have the same kind of luridly fascinating goings-on in his or her own family. Indeed, because the President's children will not be on the public payroll and will not inherit the Presidency it is doubtful whether the public will take any interest in them at all. The Queen is surrounded by a great deal of very colourful (and expensive) pomp and ceremony which makes for a wonderful spectacle and excellent television. The Queen on horseback reviewing the Coldstream Guards with breastplates glinting and plumed helmets waving in the breeze is much more interesting to watch than an Australian President (or Governor-General) dressed in a lounge suit inspecting some khaki-clad Australian soldiers. But do we want to have a President (or even a Governor-General) marching around in feathered hats and dripping with gold braid, epaulettes and medals?

The pomp and ceremony, and public interest, that attends the British royal family is not typical of modern monarchies. In the other European countries which maintain monarchies

(Sweden, Norway, Denmark, Spain, the Netherlands, Belgium and Luxembourg) the monarchy is a much more low-key affair. Typically only the monarch, his or her spouse and the heir apparent are on the public payroll and there is much less spent on grand palaces. Queen Margaret of Denmark, for example, mixes easily with her people, with minimal security, and is widely respected for her considerable skill as an artist and illustrator. If the British monarchy is to survive in any form, it is likely that it will move towards this European style, although it is doubtfulwhether the British monarchy could ever be quite as low key as the monarchy in Scandinavian countries — if only because of the much greater security threat posed to a British monarch by terrorist organisations, the IRA in particular.

It is interesting to consider, in passing, what might have happened had Australia become genuinely independent in 1901. The conventional nineteenth-century practice for newly independent countries in Europe was to import some down-at-heel German Prince to be installed as their new King. The Kings of Greece, Bulgaria and Romania were all imports. That is why the Duke of Edinburgh, Prince Philip, is of German and Danish descent rather than Greek, despite the fact that he is a nephew of a King of Greece. So it is Phil the Hun, rather than Phil the Greek.

An Australian royal dynasty might have been established by a junior member of the British royal family. Had this new line of Aussie Kings and Queens survived our Australian cynical good humour we may now have our own indigenous monarchy: King Bruce and Queen Sheila. On reflection, perhaps not. The idea has echoes of William Charles Wentworth's efforts in the mid-nineteenth century to constitute a local aristocracy so that the Upper House of the New South Wales Parliament, the Legislative Council, could become a hereditary chamber of nobles like its British counterpart, the House of Lords. This preposterous idea was hooted down with gales of laughter led by John Dunmore Lang and Daniel Deniehy who speculated on the appropriate titles for the would-be colonial aristocrats. One could almost regret the lost opportunity to have the Baron of

Woolloomooloo, the Earl of Emu Holes, the Count of Ku-ring-gai and the Marquis of Murwillumbah.

An Australian President will have a higher profile and a more respected role in Australian society than a Governor-General, and the same can be said for State Governors, assuming the States continue to maintain their own heads of state. However, in an egalitarian, democratic society like our own a non-executive Head of State will never have the same glamour that attaches to the British royal family. Nor would many Australians be happy with an Australian President who sought to create that kind of pomp and ceremony.

One very useful role fulfilled by non-executive heads of state is to represent their countries abroad. When the (non-executive) President of Ireland, Mary Robinson, visited Australia last year she charmed everyone she met with her dignity and eloquence and with the passionate way she spoke about Ireland, its people and its role in the world. It is doubtful whether a politician, constantly on the lookout for the barbs of his opponents, could have spoken that way.

I heard Mary Robinson speak at a state dinner hosted by the New South Wales Premier, John Fahey. Mr Fahey and his wife Colleen are of Irish extraction and it was clearly a special moment for them to welcome the President of the land of their forebears. As was appropriate on such an occasion, the Premier proposed a toast to 'The President of Ireland'. Mary Robinson then rose to her feet and with more than a faint flicker of a grin proposed a toast to 'The Queen of Australia'. I may have been transferring my own feelings to the rest of the gathering, but I could feel a sort of inward groan from all the Australians present as they rose to toast, not their Queen, but the Queen of another country. I was seated at a table with some Liberal members of the State Parliament. One leant across the table to me and said, 'If you can guarantee me a President like Mary Robinson, I'll become a republican'. Without detracting from any of Mrs Robinson's elegance or eloquence, no Australian could fail to yearn for a genuinely Australian Head of State after seeing what a genuinely Irish one could do for her country.

These ceremonial or formal functions of the Head of State are not, of course, the only ones a President has to perform. Under our Constitution the Governor-General retains important powers which he or she is entitled to exercise without, or contrary to, the advice of the Prime Minister.

As we have seen, the Government of the Commonwealth of Australia is administered in the name of the Queen via her representative the Governor-General. Thus when you are charged with speeding the case is called *Regina v. John Smith*. Neither the Queen, nor the Governor-General, has the slightest interest in whether you were driving at 100 km/h in a 60 km/h area, but somebody who works for the Government in the Police Department does. Similarly, if you receive a letter from the Government marked 'OHMS' or 'On Her Majesty's Service' it is most unlikely to contain an invitation to lunch at Buckingham Palace, but will almost certainly contain some dreary bureaucratic correspondence, probably demanding money with menaces.

All the functions of government in Australia, and in the individual States, are administered in the Queen's name. But the real decisions are made by the various ministers who constitute the Government, and it is they who are responsible for the actions of the many public servants who actually do the work. On the face of it, all of our laws can be blamed on the members of the House of Representatives and Senators who voted for them and on the Governor-General who assented to them. But we know that the Governor-General has to sign where he or she is told to sign. That is why people throw eggs at the Prime Minister when he puts up our taxes, but spare the Governor-General from such abuse even though he signs the new *Tax Act* into law.

There are very few occasions when the Governor-General is entitled to act other than in accordance with the advice of the Prime Minister. His right, and duty, to do so is referred to by the mysterious term 'the reserve powers'. It makes these powers sound as though they are like a miniature revolver a cowboy keeps in his hat to pull out at the critical moment when his enemies least expect it. Gough Whitlam, who ran foul of one of these reserve powers in 1975, would probably agree with that description.

This element of mystery surrounding the reserve powers is precisely what is wrong with them. They are not spelt out in the Constitution, nor indeed in any other law of the Commonwealth. Being the subject of 'convention', which as we have seen is only another way of saying practice and habit, they are capable of differing interpretation.

Figure 5.1: The Role of the President

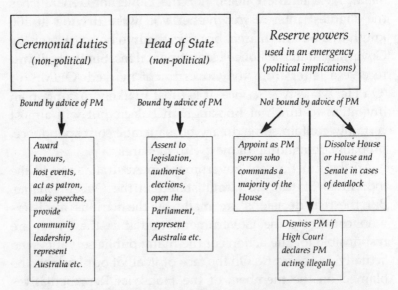

The best thing we can do about the reserve powers is to codify them in some way, thereby eliminating all uncertainty and mystery. Some lawyers will argue this is a difficult task. They may find the task difficult, but that would be a comment on their own lack of imagination rather than on the inherent complexity of the task. Very few modern democracies have so much of their constitution in the form of unwritten conventions as we do. Other countries have spelt out the powers and responsibilities of their legislatures, their heads of state and their judiciary. We can surely do the same.

The first task is to ascertain what those reserve powers are. They relate only to two heads of power: first the appointment or dismissal of the Prime Minister, and second the dissolution of the House of Representatives (which can be done at any time up to but not after its three-year term) and/or the Senate (which can only be done in special circumstances).

Appointment and Dismissal of the Prime Minister

It is clear that the Governor-General should appoint as Prime Minister that person who can command a majority in the House of Representatives. (A republican Constitution should put this matter of convention into black and white, and state simply that the Head of Government is the Prime Minister who is that person commanding a majority in the House of Representatives.) Normally the Prime Minister will be the leader of the parliamentary Labor Party or the leader of the parliamentary Liberal Party. The formal procedure for this appointment is that the outgoing Prime Minister will advise the Governor-General to appoint the new Prime Minister in accordance with these principles. If, just after the Labor Party had won an election with a majority of members in the House of Representatives, the outgoing Liberal Prime Minister were to advise the Governor-General to appoint, say, the leader of the National Party, the Governor-General would ignore the advice and appoint the leader of the Labor Party.

In most cases it is perfectly clear who should be Prime Minister. Sometimes it is not so clear. What if the Prime Minister dies in office and no successor has been appointed? What if the Government's majority in the House of Representatives disintegrates because some of its supporters cross the floor to join the Opposition, or because some of its supporters die or resign and are replaced at by-elections with members who support the Opposition?

When Prime Minister Harold Holt vanished in the surf on 17 December 1967 there was a brief moment of uncertainty about who should be appointed to replace him. Was it to be the deputy leader of the Liberal Party, William McMahon, or was it to be the Deputy Prime Minister, and leader of the Country Party, John McEwen? McMahon tried to persuade the Governor-General that he should become Prime Minister. He was, so he argued, the leader of the larger and hence senior party in the Coalition Government and it was appropriate that he should be Prime Minister. On the other hand, it was pointed out that while McMahon had been elected deputy leader of the Liberal Party, he had not been elected leader, and the appropriate course of action was to appoint John McEwen Prime Minister pending a vote by Liberal Party members of parliament to elect a new leader and hence a new Prime Minister.

Figure 5.2: Dismissing a Prime Minister

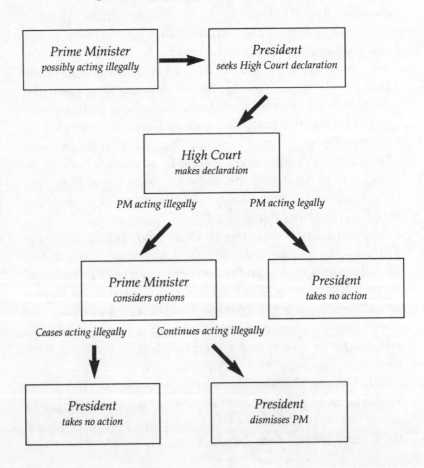

The Governor-General, Lord Casey, took the second course of action and appointed McEwen as Prime Minister. Shortly afterwards the Liberal Party elected Senator John Gorton as their new leader, McEwen resigned and Gorton became Prime Minister.

Lord Casey has been criticised for taking too active a role in ascertaining whether McMahon or McEwen would be the appropriate choice. Nonetheless it seems that the appropriate course of action nowadays is that in the event of a Prime Minister dying in office the Governor-General should appoint the Deputy Prime Minister as Prime Minister unless he or she has reason to believe that the Deputy Prime Minister does not enjoy the support of a majority in the House of Representatives and another person does. The fundamental principle is that the Prime Minister should always be that person who enjoys the support of the House of Representatives.

But what happens if that support is lost? The New South Wales Liberal–National Government, led by Premier John Fahey, does not have a majority in the Legislative Assembly in its own right and survives thanks to the support of four Independent members. These Independents have not agreed to support the Government on every item of legislation but they have agreed, for the time being, to support the Government on 'money bills' and motions of no confidence.

What should the Governor-General (or in the case of New South Wales, the Governor) do if a government loses its control of the House of Representatives in the way John Fahey would lose control of the Legislative Assembly if the Independents decided to vote with the Labor Party on a motion of no confidence in the Premier?

The fundamental principle is that the House of Representatives (or its state equivalent) is entitled to choose the Prime Minister or Premier. Accordingly, if the House of Representatives resolved that it had no confidence in a Prime Minister, that Prime Minister should resign and advise the Governor-General (or President) to appoint as Prime Minister that person in whom the House of Representatives does have confidence. If another person does enjoy the confidence of the House and is able to obtain the support of the Senate for the passage of those appropriation bills necessary to fund the operations of Government, then there is no problem in the transfer of power. The difficulty arises when no other person can gather sufficient support. In those circumstances, when nobody can command a majority in the House, the Prime Minister would not resign but would advise the Governor-General to call an election. This approach, just stated, is in accordance with established constitutional convention.

A slightly different approach would be to say that a Prime Minister who had lost the support of the House could nonetheless properly advise the Governor-General to call an election. This course of action could only be justified by deciding that changes of Government other than as a result of a general election were not desirable. It is an affront to democracy, some would say, that a few members of parliament who were elected as Liberals, for example, could change their spots, cross the floor and put the Labor Party into government. There is a tension therefore between the democratic tradition of modern elections, where people vote for 'Labor' or 'Liberal', and the representative tradition of parliament, where people elect individuals to represent them and those individuals are entitled to give their support to whichever leader they prefer. In a sense it is a tension between the late twentieth-century political tradition and that of the early nineteenth century.

Many would argue that in the 1990s most Australians would take the view that it was they who decided which party was to govern them and that if a particular party lost the support of a majority of the House, for whatever reason, the appropriate course of action would be to have a general election to let the people decide. If one took this more modern approach, the Constitution could be amended simply to say that elections for the House of Representatives could be called at any time by the President, acting on the advice of the Prime Minister, subject always to the House not overrunning its prescribed maximum term.

This would eliminate any discretion on the part of the President and would ensure that if a Prime Minister lost control of the House because of a by-election or because Independents changed their support, that Prime Minister could quickly call an election.

On the other hand, it could produce the unfortunate situation that a Prime Minister who has lost the support of his or her own party could call an election out of spite — or threaten to do so — and thereby intimidate the party into continuing to support the Prime Minister.

Apart from changes in Prime Minister caused by the results of elections, the most usual change arises from the Prime Minister's own supporters sacking the Prime Minister and replacing him or her with another person. Thus in December 1991 the parliamentary Labor Party voted to replace Bob Hawke as leader with Paul Keating. Mr Hawke advised Governor-General Hayden of this fact and advised him to appoint Mr Keating as Prime Minister.

The Hawke sacking poses some interesting hypothetical situations. What should Governor-General Hayden have done if Mr Hawke had not resigned and advised him to appoint Mr Keating as Prime Minister, but instead had advised the Governor-General to dissolve Parliament and call an election? Should the Governor-General have taken Mr Hawke's advice? Common sense would suggest not. But on the other hand, if some of Mr Hawke's supporters had crossed the floor and joined the Liberal Party so that Dr Hewson commanded a majority in the House of Representatives, there is a strong argument for saying that the Governor-General should not have appointed Dr Hewson Prime Minister if Mr Hawke had advised him to dissolve Parliament and call an election.

What is the difference between the two situations? In the first, Mr Hawke has lost the support of his parliamentary colleagues and thus cannot command a majority in the Parliament. Mr Keating has won that support and can command the majority. It seems ludicrous to suggest the Governor-General should follow Mr Hawke's advice that an election be called, rather than appointing Mr Keating Prime

Minister. In the second, Mr Hawke has lost the support of sufficient of his supporters (and Dr Hewson has gained it) so that he cannot command a majority in the House, but Dr Hewson can. Why does it seem appropriate in that circumstance for the Governor-General to follow Mr Hawke's advice to dissolve Parliament and call an election?

A reason may be that in the first case the Governor-General knows that the Labor Party won the last election and that a stable Labor Government can be maintained subject to the change of leader. In the second case, making Dr Hewson leader would cause the Liberal Party (which had not won the last election) to completely replace the Government. The question for determination then is whether we should favour the more modern democratic tradition which says that governing parties are chosen at elections, or the older representative tradition which says that the governing party is whichever one has the support of the majority in the House.

Most Australians would be likely to prefer the democratic tradition as it gives the electorate the right to determine changes of government. In support of that position it can be said that 'baton changes' as a result of members changing their party or, if Independents, withdrawing their support, are inherently unstable.

We could adopt either of two alternatives. For the representative tradition, we could formulate the principle that if a Prime Minister lost the support of a majority in the House of Representatives and advised an election, the President would not call the election if he was satisfied another person did command a majority in the House. For the democratic tradition, we could formulate the principle that any Prime Minister is entitled to advise the President to call an election for the House of Representatives and that the President is bound to act on that advice. The unlikely case of a Prime Minister losing the support of his own party and seeking to call an election out of spite could be resolved by stating that the advice to the President must be that of the Executive Council, which is another way of saying the cabinet, thereby ensuring that an unwanted party leader could not call an election as a frolic of his own.

However, it must be acknowledged that what we have described as the 'representative tradition', which requires that whoever commands a majority in the House will be Prime Minister, is more consistent with the principle of parliamentary sovereignty.

The Republic Advisory Committee prepared a full codification of the powers of the Head of State which deals with these issues. That codification is set out and discussed in Chapter 8 and is incorporated in the revised Constitution at the end of this book.

The Government Breaks the Law

Another circumstance in which the Governor-General or the President in a republican Australia could be justified in sacking a Prime Minister would be if the Prime Minister, or his or her Government, were persistently breaking the law. Governments break the law all the time; after all, a government is not infallible and is made up of ordinary people who are just as fallible, and in some cases venal, as the rest of us. Every day the courts are hearing cases in which citizens are alleging that the Government has acted contrary to the law. Sometimes one government, that of a State for example, will allege that another government — usually the Commonwealth, more rarely the government of another State — is breaking the law. The courts hear these cases, make a decision, and the governments concerned abide by the decision.

But what happens if a government quite deliberately sets out to break the law and then, when it is caught out, takes no notice and continues to act illegally? If that were allowed to go on it would undermine our whole system of democratic government which depends on everybody, citizens and governments alike, obeying the laws of the land and the orders of the courts charged with administering those laws.

An example of this kind of problem occurred in 1932 in New South Wales. That year found Australia, and the world, in the grip of the Great Depression. Nearly a third of Australian men were out of work (women were not counted) and the political atmosphere was fiercely charged with anxiety. Nowhere more so than in New South Wales, headed by Premier J. T. Lang. 'The Big Fella', as Jack Lang was known, was a powerful orator who had secured total control of the New South Wales Labor Party. Many countries in the 1930s were either completely repudiating, or postponing, the payment of interest on their public borrowings. Lang believed that the meagre revenues of New South Wales would be better spent on aiding the unemployed and destitute than paying interest to the (largely British) bondholders who had lent money to the State in the past. Others argued that if New South Wales defaulted on its loans it would never be able to borrow again and the consequent suffering of working people would be even worse.

The conservative Federal Government, led by Joseph Lyons, was determined that Australia should continue to pay its debts. The Federal Parliament passed legislation which authorised the Commonwealth Government to seize revenues of New South Wales and to apply them to the payment of that State's loans. Lang challenged the validity of the legislation but the High Court on 6 April, 1932 upheld it.[6] On 12 April, Lang issued a circular ordering the public service of New South Wales not to bank any moneys collected in State fees and taxes but to forward them in cash to the Treasury. My great-uncle was working for the State Government in that exciting time and often described how he carried sacks of 'threepences and sixpences' down to the State Treasury.

Lang was trying to avoid the operation of the new Commonwealth law. The Commonwealth, having established the validity of its 'garnishee' legislation, would have had little difficulty in persuading a court to order the surrender of the money held in the State Treasury. But the Commonwealth did not move.

On 12 May, the State Governor, a highly decorated English Air Vice-Marshal called Sir Philip Game, asked

Lang either to withdraw the circular or demonstrate its legality. Lang refused to do either and on the following day the Governor dismissed him and appointed the Leader of the Opposition, Mr Bertram Stevens, as Premier. The Legislative Assembly in which Lang held 55 out of 90 seats was dissolved and an election was called. The election was held on 11 June. It was a disaster for Labor, which lost 31 seats.

Subsequent criticism of Governor Game's action has focused on the fact that the legality of the circular was not something the Governor should be entitled to form his own view upon. Had events not moved as quickly as they had, Game would have received a dispatch from the Colonial Office in London advising him not to dismiss Lang. Part of that dispatch read:

> So long as the courts have not settled the issue, and the possibility of raising the issue in the courts still remains, it could not, I think, be said to be unconstitutional if a Governor refrained from taking the initiative in restraining his ministers from action alleged to be illegal. If the courts had pronounced against the legality of any particular action and the ministers still persisted in continuing to perform such action, the position would of course require further consideration.[7]

It is not possible to support the continuation in office of a government which persists in breaking the law. But it should not be open to a Governor-General, or President, to make his or her own decision as to the legality of the Government's conduct. That should be decided in the courts. Normally those people affected by the Government's conduct are only too ready to assert its illegality, and Governor Game would have been well advised to wait for the Commonwealth Government to seek the appropriate orders from the courts that Lang's circular was unlawful. Had Lang disobeyed a court order nobody could have rationally defended his continuance in office.

There can also be no doubt that a Governor-General is

entitled to seek confirmation from the Government, via the Attorney-General, that particular Government action is lawful. But what should the Governor-General, or President, do if he or she believes that advice is wrong? There seems to be a gap in both the letter and practice of the law here. In my view the gap can be filled very simply by providing in our coming republican Constitution that if the President believes the Government is not acting in a lawful fashion, the President can seek a declaration from the High Court of Australia on the matter. If the High Court declares that the Government's action is unlawful, and if the Government persists, then the President should be entitled to dissolve the House of Representatives and/or dismiss the Prime Minister and appoint another person Prime Minister. That other person would presumably be the Leader of the Opposition who, faced with an election, would be obliged to govern the nation in a caretaker fashion only.

I appeared on 19 April, 1993 on the ABC current affairs programme, *Four Corners*, to debate the republican issue. I canvassed the problem of governments breaking the law, much as I have done above, and suggested there be a constitutional amendment allowing the President to seek a declaration from the High Court to settle any concern that the Government's actions were unlawful. This proposal is now incorporated in the Republic Advisory Committee's full codification model for the reserve powers.

The following day, Mr John Howard, the former Liberal Opposition Leader and now Shadow Minister for Industrial Relations, issued a press release criticising this proposal. He wrote:

> This is no minor change. It would open up a rich area of potential conflict between President and Prime Minister in a republican Australia, greatly politicising the role of the Head of State and dramatically altering the approach of Australian governments towards High Court appointments.
> It could well compromise the independence of the

High Court which, for almost a hundred years, has been a cornerstone of Australia's constitutional and political stability.

Mr Howard went on to accuse republicans of seeking to advance radical plans for constitutional reform, including the abolition of the States, and repeated his charge that the republic was no more than a Trojan horse.

Mr Howard's remarks were, unfortunately, quite typical of his determination to avoid playing any constructive role in the republican debate. There is no doubt that the Governor-General or the State Governors are entitled to dismiss a Prime Minister or Premier who is persistently breaking the law. My proposal recognises that power and suggests an orderly mechanism which allows the appropriate court to determine authoritatively the question of whether the law is being broken. I cannot imagine that Mr Howard believes the Governor-General should sit idly by while governments break the law, and so it is difficult to understand why he would object to the proposal made by me. The alternative is to leave the constitutional situation as it is, with all of its uncertainties.

His suggestion that this would politicise the High Court is laughable. The High Court's principal function is to determine highly political questions involving the powers of the Federal Government, the rights of the States and so on. Is it possible to imagine any decision more political than the High Court's decision in the *Mabo Case* which dramatically altered the legal standing of indigenous people in Australia? The High Court is constantly deciding whether government actions are lawful, or government legislation is constitutionally valid. It is the institution especially established to determine matters of constitutional law, all of which are intensely political. It is the appropriate institution to determine whether the Government is breaking the law.

In practice, of course, the President would never need to rely on the constitutional provision allowing him or her to instruct the Attorney-General to seek a High Court opinion.

The President would only need to say to the Prime Minister, 'I am concerned at the legality of such-and-such an action. I have read the opinion offered me by the Attorney General, but I am not sure it is right. I think it might be wise to seek a declaration from the court'. The Prime Minister would take the hint and seek the declaration.

The Senate's Power to Block Supply

As we have seen, the Senate has the same power to reject or approve legislation as the House of Representatives. In 1975 the Senate exercised its power and precipitated a chain of events that resulted in the Labor Government of Gough Whitlam being dismissed by the Governor-General. Those events remain the most controversial in Australian political history. Few Australians alive at that time will ever forget the drama of 11 November 1975. (I have a particularly strong recollection of those events. I was 21 years of age and was writing about politics for the *Nation Review*. The previous week I had sagely assured my readers that those people who were predicting the Governor-General would sack the Government were reckless alarmists and that a dismissal of that kind was unthinkable!)

In late 1975 the Labor Government was under fierce attack from both the Opposition and the press. The second half of the year had been turbulent in the extreme. Attempts by the Government to borrow large sums of money through a mysterious Middle Eastern financier called Tirath Khemlani gave the Opposition the justification, so it asserted, to try to force an election.

The Senate was controlled by the Opposition and on 15 October 1975 the Senate resolved not to consider the Appropriation Bills until the Government agreed to a dissolution of the House of Representatives and a general election. A furious debate ensued about the rights and wrongs of the Senate's attitude. It was speculated in some quarters that the Governor-General, Sir John Kerr, would intervene and dismiss the Prime Minister and install in his place the Opposition Leader, Malcolm Fraser, who would thereupon call an election.

Kerr gave no inkling to Whitlam that he would dismiss him. Moreover, by 11 November cracks were starting to appear in the Opposition's senatorial ranks. Two Victorian Liberal Senators, Alan Missen and Eric Bessell, were on the point of crossing the floor and supporting the passage of the Appropriation Bills. Their consciences were troubled by the fact that the Senate was forcing a Government to an election while it held a majority in the House of Representatives, a majority it had secured at a general election only 18 months before.

There was a general feeling that Fraser had over-played his hand and that the Senate would back down. Rather than waiting for the events to play out, on 11 November Kerr intervened and dismissed Whitlam. He appointed Fraser Prime Minister on condition that he obtain passage of the Appropriation Bills, which was done, and that he advise the Governor-General to dissolve both the Senate and the House of Representatives and call elections for both.

Normally only half of the Senators are up for election every three years, but if the Senate has twice rejected legislation passed by the House of Representatives the Governor-General may, on the advice of the Prime Minister, dissolve both Houses and cause elections to be held for all Members of the House of Representatives and all Senators. The Liberals in the Senate had rejected a number of Whitlam's Bills and it was in response to these rejections that the newly appointed Liberal Prime Minister advised the Governor-General to dissolve both Houses.

The upshot of Kerr's dismissal was a political furore which polarised the entire nation. The office of Governor-General was discredited in a way almost unimaginable. Kerr was pelted with eggs by angry crowds. Whitlam encouraged the hatred of the Governor-General. As the proclamation dissolving Parliament was read from the steps of Parliament House, an angry crowd of protesters had gathered below. At the conclusion of the proclamation the clerk intoned the inevitable phrase 'God Save the Queen'. Whitlam, towering above him, stepped forward and uttered the most unforgettable words in Australian political history:

> Well may they say 'God Save the Queen', because
> nothing will save the Governor-General.

Whitlam lost the election. The Labor defeat was almost as overwhelming as that of Jack Lang in 1932. The Australian public may have been unhappy about Kerr's dismissal of a recently elected Prime Minister, but the people did not manifest their displeasure at the ballot box.

There are a great many conspiracy theories about Kerr's conduct. It has been alleged that he was plotting with the Opposition and even that he was acting on the direction of the American Central Intelligence Agency. Certainly there were some unusual features to his conduct. First, he was utterly lacking in candour. Both Kerr and Whitlam would have recognised that no government can continue indefinitely without money. Kerr should have ascertained from Whitlam when the money was likely to run out and told him that if the Appropriation Bills had not been passed by a certain date he would have to dismiss the Government unless it secured their passage — which it could only have done by calling an election. This assumes the Liberals would have remained solidly and unanimously committed to their strategy of not passing the Bills. Second, Kerr should have kept this advice to the Prime Minister utterly confidential between himself and Whitlam. He should not have sought advice from third parties. The day before Kerr sacked Whitlam he sought legal advice, informally, from the Chief Justice of the High Court, Sir Garfield Barwick. Both of these men should have recognised that it is no part of a judge's duty to give legal advice anywhere other than in his court. Kerr had been Chief Justice of New South Wales and knew the proprieties as well as Barwick did. Kerr also knew that Barwick was a former Liberal member of parliament and was personally very hostile to the Labor Government.

Some writers have suggested that Kerr should not have acted until the money had completely dried up. No-one would criticise as being over-hasty a Governor-General who intervened at the point when all the public servants were going without their pay and the administration of the Commonwealth had ground to a halt. There would, however, be a very good case that such a Governor-General should have acted sooner. The problem with the 1975 events is that there were no rules to guide the actors. It is likely that Kerr failed to consult candidly with Whitlam because he feared that once Whitlam knew he was considering dismissal, the Prime Minister would advise the Queen to dismiss him and replace him with another more pliable Governor-General. If that is so, it is still no excuse. Public officers are bound to do their duty regardless of the consequences. Better to act honourably and be sacked than act dishonourably in order to maintain your job.

A straightforward way of resolving this issue is to amend the Constitution to remove the Senate's right to block Appropriation Bills. This would never obtain the support of either the conservative political parties or, in my view, majorities in the smaller States. After all, equality in power between the Senate and the House of Representatives was one of the fundamental elements in the bargain between the larger and smaller States that allowed Federation to occur.

Another straightforward way of solving the problem would be to lay down some procedures which can be followed. In that way we would recognise that the Senate has the power to reject an Appropriation Bill and thereby force the Government to an election, but we would set out some rules to ensure that there would never be a repetition of the confusion and uncertainty that attended the dismissal of Whitlam in 1975.

Sir Charles Court[8] suggested an approach of this kind to a meeting of the Australian Constitutional Convention in 1976. His proposed amendment provided that if the Senate failed to pass an Appropriation Bill within 30 days of its having been transmitted to the Senate after passage through the House, the Governor-General must forthwith dissolve both Houses of Parliament. He proposed that if after the dissolution the House of Representatives passes the proposed Appropriation Bill it shall be taken to have been duly passed and be presented to the Governor-General for the Queen's assent.

Sir Charles' proposal has the considerable advantage of ensuring that a double dissolution follows a rejection of Supply by the Senate. As the Constitution currently stands the Senate has the ability to reject an Appropriation Bill and force the Government to dissolve the House of Representatives and call an election for that House. But there is no necessary requirement for the whole of the Senate to be dissolved at the same time. The only reason a double dissolution followed the 1975 dismissal was that the Senate had rejected sufficient legislation within the terms of section 57 of the Constitution.

Section 57 is designed to resolve deadlocks between the two Houses. If the House of Representatives passes a law and the Senate fails to pass it, or passes it with amendments the House of Representatives does not agree with, and if, after three months, the same law is passed by the House of Representatives and again the Senate fails to pass it, then the Governor-General may dissolve both the Senate and the House of Representatives. After the election, if the House of Representatives again passes the law and if the Senate again rejects it, then a joint sitting of both Houses is held and the matter is determined in that way. Given that there are twice as many members of the House of Representatives as there are Senators it is highly likely that at the joint sitting the House of Representatives will have its way.

While there have been five double dissolutions under section 57, on only one occasion has the Joint Sitting been convened. That was in 1974, after the Senate forced the Whitlam Government to the polls. After the 1974 double dissolution and election the Labor Party had control of the House of Representatives but not of the Senate. Nonetheless, in a joint sitting Labor members had a small majority and the six Bills which had been the subject of the double dissolution were duly approved.[9]

It is quite possible for there to have been no Bills rejected by the Senate within the meaning of section 57 and for the Senate nonetheless to reject an Appropriation Bill. It would seem quite unjust for the Senate to force the House of Representatives to a general election and not have to go to the polls itself. The Government whose money supply has been cut off should, in my view, be given the chance of securing a majority in the Senate in its own right.

But the Court proposal was opposed by the Labor Party when it was raised and the ALP's attitude is unlikely to change. Labor's concern is that if an amendment of that kind is made to the Constitution it will be seen as legitimising the ability of the Senate to force the Government to an early election. Moreover, if there is a double dissolution that means that all 76 Senators will be up for re-election. As a consequence the 'quota' or minimum number of votes required to elect a Senator from any State will be one half of what it is for the purposes of the normal 'half-Senate' election. The smaller quota means that it is easier for small parties and Independents to get elected. Accordingly, it will be argued, the Democrats, Greens and other Independents would have a vested interest in rejecting Supply because their prospects of being re-elected would, all other things being equal, be enhanced. It is this latter factor which may give today's coalition parties cause for concern. Given the voting system used for the Senate it is unlikely any government will control a Senate majority. Moreover, since the demise of the DLP the smaller parties represented in the Senate have tended to be ideologically closer to the ALP than the coalition parties. The Court proposal, were it adopted, could come back to haunt a future Liberal Government.

The Republic Advisory Committee canvassed two other approaches to the problem of the Senate blocking Supply. One option would simply be to leave things exactly as they are. Their report neatly describes the merits of that approach:

A future Head of State would have no more guidance on the issue than did Sir John Kerr — a prospect which to some extent defeats the purpose of codification. On the other hand, it needs to be acknowledged that while the blocking of Supply by the Senate is often discussed, in 93

years of federal parliamentary experience it has only
occurred on one occasion. Leaving the situation as it
stands may not be the most elegant solution, but in light
of the political sensitivity of the issue it may turn out to
be the most practicable one.[10]

Another approach to the problem arose, almost by accident,
from the Republic Advisory Committee's full codification
model (which is set out in full in Chapter 8). The effect of
the full codification is that the President would not be able
to dismiss a Prime Minister who commanded a majority in
the House of Representatives unless that Prime Minister's
Government was persisting in a breach of the Constitution
or a refusal to comply with a court order. In my view, most
Australians would regard that as a sensible approach. A
law-abiding Prime Minister with a majority in the House
should be entitled to govern. The full codification model
makes no change to the powers of the Senate which could
block the Supply Bills. If the Government refused to back
down and comply with whatever demands the Senate had
made as its price of passing the Supply Bills, in due course
the Government would run out of lawfully appropriated
funds and any attempt to spend money which had not been
lawfully appropriated would be a breach of section 83 of the
Constitution. The consequence would be that the President
would not be able to dismiss the Prime Minister and dissolve the House of Representatives until such time as the
money had, literally, run out. The only change to the status
quo would be that the President would not be able to launch
a pre-emptive strike against the Prime Minister as Sir John
Kerr did against Gough Whitlam.

We have now canvassed all of the reserve powers. They
are extremely important, but it is more likely than not that a
Governor-General, or a President, will serve his term without ever having to consider the exercise of them. If we make
some minor amendments to the Constitution to clarify the
operation of these reserve powers we will eliminate all of
the uncertainty, and almost all of the controversy, relating to
their exercise.

It is important to bear in mind that the uncertainty of the scope of the reserve powers, and the consequent need to define them, is not something that is created by Australia becoming a republic. The problem exists in our Constitution as it stands today, and a devoted monarchist could make precisely the same arguments for greater clarification as have been made above.

An ultra-minimalist approach to the reserve powers, and the powers of the President generally, would be to amend the Constitution to say words to this effect:

> The Head of State shall exercise his or her powers and perform his or her functions in accordance with the constitutional conventions which related to the exercise of the powers and performance of the functions of the Governor-General, but nothing in this section shall have the effect of converting constitutional conventions into rules of law or of preventing the further development of these conventions.[11]

That would serve to import all the conventions into the Constitution and ensure there was no hiatus between the monarchy and the republic whereby the conventions were lost. It would, of course, leave the question as to the precise scope of the reserve powers unanswered.

Should the President have Greater Powers than the Governor-General?

It is a relatively straightforward matter to amend the Constitution to replace the Queen and the Governor-General with a President and to provide that the President would exercise the same powers as the Governor-General. It is similarly straightforward to form a view about the scope of the reserve powers and then draft the relevant amendments to incorporate a clear definition of those reserve powers in the Constitution. But should we take the opportunity to give the President greater powers? Should we have a President who is the Head of Government as well as the Head of State and whose powers are closer to those of, say, the President of the United States?

No two countries have a constitutional framework absolutely identical to the other, and there is certainly no harm in examining the constitutional arrangements of other countries. Much can be learned from the experiences of others. But we should not lose sight of the fact that Australia is a distinct country with its own unique history. We have nearly 100 years' experience of operating our federal system, which is considerably more than most countries' experience of any form of democracy, and we should not be afraid of developing our own, Australian, systems of government. If they correspond with other nations' experience, so be it. But a gram of Australian experience is worth, in my view at least, a tonne of experience in other countries.

Nonetheless, one option for change is to invest the Head of State with the powers of the Head of Government. The best example of this kind of republic is the United States. It has lived under its present form of government for more than 200 years and its constitutional arrangements are much easier to understand than, for example, the arrangements in France where executive power is shared between the President and the Prime Minister. Indeed it can be said of France, that while it is clear that the President is the Head of State, it is far from clear which of the President and the Prime Minister is the Head of Government. France, in fact, has two Heads of Government — which is fine if they are both of the same mind and the same party. In the April 1993 French parliamentary elections the conservatives won control of the Parliament. So now there is a conservative Prime Minister, M. Balladur, who must work with the Socialist President, M. Mitterrand. It will be an experience in cohabitation that few French men and women look forward to.

The founders of the American republic were concerned to establish a clear separation between the three branches of government. The executive power was vested in the President, who was elected by the people; the legislative power was vested in the Congress, consisting of a Senate with equal representation for each of the States and a House of Representatives composed of members elected on the basis of population; and the judicial power was vested in a Supreme Court with the power to interpret the Constitution and to determine whether laws, be they enacted by the Federal Congress or the various State legislatures, complied with it.

It will be seen that our Constitution relied heavily on American precedent. The principal difference is that our Head of Government is not the Head of State, but rather the Prime Minister, who holds office for so long as he or she commands a majority in the House of Representatives. The essential difference between the Australian Head of Government (the Prime Minister) and the American Head of both State and Government (the President) is that the Prime Minister, by definition, controls at least the House of Representatives.

The main consequence of this difference is that an Australian Prime Minister can be reasonably sure of being able to get parliamentary support for his or her own legislative programme. An American President has no such assurance. Over the last 20 years the Congress, both House of Representatives and Senate, has been controlled by the Democrats. It should be noted that the American political parties (Democrats and Republicans) do not have anything like the same degree of control over their congressional members and there are Democrats (from the South for example) who would, on some matters, be considerably more conservative than many Republicans. The consequence, however, of a Republican President (as we had with Nixon, Ford, Reagan and Bush) and a Democrat Congress is that the President may have enormous difficulty obtaining congressional support for his political programme. Indeed, while the President may have been elected by the people on the basis of a particular legislative mandate, the majority in Congress may have been elected by the people on the basis that they will do everything in their power to stop him implementing it. It remains to be seen whether Democrat President Bill Clinton will be able to persuade Congress to support his own legislative programme.

An Australian Prime Minister must select his or her own ministry from the ranks of supporters in the Parliament. Indeed, under section 64 of the Constitution no minister can hold office for more than three months without being a member of the House of Representatives or the Senate. In the United States the reverse is true. The President appoints a cabinet of ministers (called 'Secretaries'), but if they are members of the Congress they must resign. Thus in Australia, our ministry is sitting in Parliament every day and participating in the business of Parliament. In the United States the President has the whole population of the United States to draw upon in filling his cabinet. Theoretically he should be able to find more talented people to fill his cabinet than an Australian Prime Minister can, but there is little evidence that the calibre of American cabinets is any greater, or less, than Australian ones.

In both America and Australia, the Parliament is expected to act as a watchdog on the activities of government. Critics of the Australian system point out that an Australian Government, by definition, controls at least the House of Representatives and is therefore able to prevent that House from setting up committees to inquire into the activities of the Government. The American Congress is not under that kind of discipline and it is fair to say that the Congress has been a much more vigilant investigator of governmental wrongdoing in America than the Federal Parliament has been in Australia. On other hand, the Australian Senate, which is unlikely to be controlled by one or other of the major political parties (or coalitions), has proved itself capable of investigating the activities of government.

While the American Congress finds it easier to investigate the activities of the Government, it is much harder for it to remove the Head of Government. The removal of a President requires both the Senate and the House of Representatives to vote to remove the President on the grounds only of 'treason, bribery or other high crimes and misdemeanours'.

These offences are more easily alleged than proved — as the attempt to impeach Richard Nixon demonstrated. Mr Nixon finally resigned before the impeachment process had concluded.

The case of Richard Nixon is an interesting one to consider. Nixon resigned before he was impeached. Had he been an Australian Prime Minister his own colleagues in the party room would have sacked him within a few months, if not weeks, of the Watergate conspiracy coming to light. The debilitating 18 months which finally forced Nixon out of office would have been largely avoided in Australia. On the other hand, it is also true that once an Australian Nixon had been sacked by his colleagues, the Parliament would not have followed up all the other conspirators with quite the zealotry that the American Congress did.

An Australian Prime Minister can very readily be removed, but is much more likely to be removed by his or her own supporters in the (relative) privacy of the party room than on the floor of the House of Representatives. An Australian Prime Minister is in many respects more answerable to colleagues in the cabinet and supporters in the party room than he or she is to the House of Representatives. Party discipline will ensure that once the governing party has decided on a course of action all its members, regardless of their private views, will support it. But a Prime Minister can be overruled by cabinet and cabinet can be overruled by the parliamentary party. In the United States, on the other hand, the cabinet has no ability to sway a President who chooses not to heed its advice. An American cabinet is no more than a collection of advisers appointed by the President. Any power an American cabinet member exercises is the power of the President which has been delegated by the President and which can be removed at the President's whim.

So in summary we could conclude as follows:
- The American system of combining the Head of State and Head of Government results in the executive government being much more independent of the Congress than an Australian government is of the Parliament.

- On the other hand, because the American President does not control the House of Representatives (as an Australian Prime Minister must), the American Congress is better able to investigate the activities of government.
- An Australian Prime Minister is always answerable to his or her supporters in the party room and to the cabinet. If the Prime Minister's parliamentary supporters feel the Prime Minister is not likely to lead them to victory they may sack and replace him or her with another, as Labor sacked Bob Hawke and replaced him with Paul Keating in 1991. An American President on the other hand can only be removed by the Congress if it can be demonstrated, after a long and arduous process, that he or she has committed serious crimes.
- An Australian Prime Minister will generally be able to implement a legislative programme, subject only to the attitude of the Senate. The Senate has to be careful, however, that its obstruction does not result in the Government forcing a double dissolution under section 57 of our Constitution. An American President has no reason to believe he or she can implement a programme. The President needs Congress to approve all appropriation legislation, but it has often been the case that there is a Republican President and a Democratic Congress, resulting in a 'gridlock' where important legislation simply cannot be agreed upon.

Few Australians would presume to tell an American 'our system is better than yours'. The Americans have not done too badly with their system of government. And neither have we with ours. While our two countries have a great deal in common, our history and experience are very different. There is neither enough wrong with our system of parliamentary government, nor enough right with their system of presidential government, to justify Australia constituting its new President the Head of Government as well as the Head of State.

It follows from this that I believe, as do my colleagues in the Australian Republican Movement, that an Australian

President should have the same powers and functions as the Governor-General currently exercises. Those powers, as we have seen, are defined by both the terms of the Constitution and the constitutional conventions. The President should be a Head of State but *not* a Head of Government. The real political power should remain with the Prime Minister.

In case it is thought I am too blasé in dismissing the experience of other countries, I would simply note that the only Western democracies with a Head of State who is also the Head of Government are the United States and (to some extent) the Republic of France. So we are in good company, and that should reassure those Australians who need to seek comfort from foreign nations.

CHAPTER SIX

The Election of the President

The President of a republican Commonwealth of Australia should have the same powers and duties as the Governor-General (although more adequately defined). How should we choose that President?

The Governor-General is formally appointed by the Queen. Her Majesty, however, acts on the advice of the Australian Prime Minister, and so the Governor-General can be appointed and dismissed at the whim of the Prime Minister. This ability instantly to advise the Queen to dismiss the Governor-General may have been one of the reasons Sir John Kerr was less than candid with Gough Whitlam prior to the dismissal on 11 November 1975. Kerr may have feared that if he told Whitlam what was in his mind he would find himself out of a job.

The consequence of the office of Governor-General being entirely in the gift of the Prime Minister is that a number of former political colleagues have been rewarded with what must be a very comfortable sinecure. Since the Second World War, there have been four former politicians appointed as Governor-General. Two of them were Liberals (Richard Casey and Paul Hasluck) appointed by Liberal Governments and two of them were Labor men (Bill McKell and Bill Hayden) appointed by Labor Governments.

On every occasion when a former politician is appointed Governor-General there is an outburst of protests against 'political appointments' or 'jobs for the boys'. Nonetheless, it has never been seriously contended that any of these — McKell, Casey, Hasluck or Hayden — has failed to perform his duties with distinction. Indeed, the only Governor-General whose conduct has been the subject of criticism in the post-war era is Sir John Kerr — and he was a former Chief Justice of New South Wales.

It is common to hear Australians expressing support for the idea of a republic, 'As long as we don't have a politician as President'. There is very widespread dislike and suspicion of politicians in Australia. There is little evidence to suggest this antipathy towards politicians is justified, and there is no doubt that by holding our politicians in low regard we make it less likely that talented people will stand for Parliament.

The type of President we have will be very dependent on the method of election or appointment we decide to employ.

Appointment by the Prime Minister

If we were to adopt a truly 'minimalist' approach to establishing Australia as a republic we would leave things as they are now. At present, the Governor-General is appointed by the Queen acting on the advice of the Prime Minister. This means that the Prime Minister can appoint, or dismiss, a Governor-General at a moment's notice. There is no particular constitutional convention to justify this, but the general practice has been that the choice of Governor-General is a decision for the Prime Minister rather than the cabinet or the parliamentary supporters of the Government in their party meeting.

That could be changed, of course. The Labor Party Caucus, for example, could resolve that the Prime Minister will not appoint any person as Governor-General without the approval of Caucus. But as it stands, the occupancy of Yarralumla (and Admiralty House in Sydney for waterfront weekends) is entirely in the gift of the Prime Minister.

Not many Australians would favour our new President being appointed in that fashion. But before we dismiss this method of appointment, we should note that the federal judiciary, including the justices of the High Court of Australia, are all appointed by the Government of the day. In practice, the appointment of federal judges other than those of the High Court is a matter for the Attorney-General, whereas High Court justices are generally chosen by the Prime Minister, although the formal decision is that of cabinet.

The High Court is an immensely powerful body. It is the highest court of appeal in Australia and it is charged with interpreting the Constitution and determining whether federal and state laws conflict with the Constitution. Since much of the wording of the Constitution is fairly general, the justices of the High Court have more than a little latitude in determining what they think the Constitution means. Since the Constitution can only be amended by a referendum supported by a majority of voters across the nation and a majority of voters in four out of six States, a High Court ruling cannot be overturned by Parliament. Yet despite all this power — much more extensive than that wielded by the Governor-General — the High Court justices are appointed by the Government. Unlike the situation in the United States, there is no procedure in Australia whereby the Senate vets the choice of High Court justices. Political cronyism is not unknown, although its results are often unpredictable.

In 1965, Sir Robert Menzies appointed Sir Garfield Barwick Chief Justice of the High Court. Barwick had been Liberal Attorney-General and Minister for External Affairs under Menzies. He was also the most outstanding advocate of his time. It was hard to criticise Barwick's appointment as 'political' since while he was a dyed-in-the-wool Liberal, he was also a very outstanding lawyer. Yet once he became Chief Justice, Barwick was a disappointment to many. His judgments were sometimes lacking in intellectual rigour and his approach to some matters, including taxation cases, was quite out of step with community attitudes. Barwick was not, on reflection, a very good judge.

In 1975, Gough Whitlam appointed Lionel Murphy a Justice of the High Court. Murphy was a Labor Senator and Attorney General. He was not in Barwick's class as an advocate and the professional eminence he had obtained was limited to the area of industrial law. His was clearly a political appointment and it was vehemently criticised, especially by the legal profession. Murphy was impatient with traditional techniques of legal analysis and his judgments often read more like statements of political policy than of dry legal analysis. His last few years on the High Court were dogged with criminal charges (he was finally acquitted) and other allegations of misconduct which were unresolved at his death. Yet because Murphy had a vision which extended beyond the narrow parameters of the traditional lawyer, he was able to influence many lawyers, including some of his fellow judges, into approaching the law in a way that was more in tune with contemporary sentiments. In that sense Murphy's contribution to the High Court has been much more lasting than that of Barwick, and yet his appointment was more contentious and his qualifications to sit on the High Court less obvious.

The vast majority of federal judicial appointments have not been 'political' in any relevant sense, and the standard of the Australian judiciary is correctly regarded as being very high. Is the success of direct governmental appointment of judges an argument for the Government to appoint the President in the same way the Governor-General is appointed?

Figure 6.1: The Election of the President

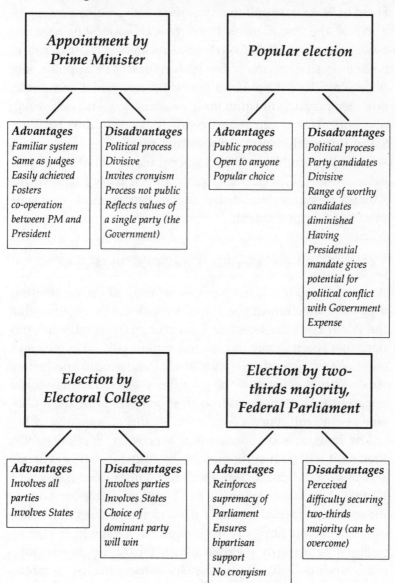

A number of former and serving Governors and Governors-General who spoke to the Republic Advisory

Committee favoured the retention of prime ministerial appointment. They said the present system encouraged a sense of co-operation and trust between the Prime Minister and the Governor-General which might be lost if the new Head of State is appointed by some other process.

While the President will exercise considerably less real power than the High Court, the Presidency is, or ought to be, the personification of the nation itself. The appointment of the President should be a public process which recognises our democratic tradition and ensures that no allegation of political bias can ever be made against our Head of State. While I have little doubt that future Presidents of an Australian republic will be as scrupulous in acting impartially as have Governors-General of the past, I believe the Australian public will not accept a continuation of prime ministerial appointment.

Direct Popular Election of the President

At the other extreme from prime ministerial appointment is a popular election of the President. We could provide that the Australian President will be chosen at a national election. In a recent Morgan Gallup opinion poll, 71 per cent of Australians questioned indicated they would prefer an Australian President to be popularly elected. This would certainly take the selection out of the hands of the politicians — or would it?

The inevitable consequence of a popular election for the President will be that the two major political parties will run their own candidates. There will be a Labor candidate and a Liberal candidate. While it is always possible that other independent candidates may present themselves, the major political parties have a considerable advantage in mounting national campaigns because of their nationwide membership, fundraising capacity and election experience. A popular election will ensure therefore that the President is a politician, endorsed by one or other of the major political parties.

This means that the apparently widespread support for popular election is squarely at odds with an equally widespread desire that the new Head of State not be a politician or a candidate of a political party. During the public hearings of the Republic Advisory Committee I often heard Australians speak in favour of popular election. I invariably said to them, 'I understand and respect your position. But have you considered that the Labor and Liberal parties would undoubtedly run candidates and that one of them would be likely to win? Would you be in favour of popular election if it were almost certainly going to result in a Labor or Liberal candidate winning?' In most cases the response was negative.

One possible means of dealing with this defect of popular election would be to ban political parties from endorsing candidates and even to ban former or serving members of parliament from standing. While I can imagine that such a provision would be appealing in some quarters I would be very concerned about such an extreme restriction on the freedoms of political parties. Similarly, I believe Australians who are prepared to stand for Parliament should be complimented, not stigmatised.

Another consequence of a popular election is that the range of likely candidates for the position will be narrowed. Consider some of the more outstanding Governors-General: Sir Zelman Cowen or Sir Ninian Stephen, for example. It is unlikely that either of those two men would have wanted to go through the rigours of a national election to win the position.

The most troubling aspect of a popularly elected President, from an Australian perspective, is that the President may well regard himself or herself to have a mandate from the people no worse, and perhaps a little better, than that held by the Prime Minister. While our new republican Constitution will almost certainly have a clearer definition of the 'reserve powers' and allow less scope for Presidential discretion, the temptation may well be there for a popularly elected President to overreach the limits of the position.

The President, after all, will largely be confined to ceremonial and formal functions in which he or she will be
expected to represent the entire nation. In moments of constitutional crisis the President will be expected to act as a
scrupulously impartial umpire. How could a President who
had been elected as the candidate of a political party act in
that way?

It should be noted, however, that a number of non-executive Presidents in other countries are elected. The republics
of Ireland, Austria and Iceland are three. Ireland's President,
Mary Robinson, was elected in a contentious campaign and
was the candidate of the Irish Labor Party. Mrs Robinson
was a former member of the Irish Dáil (Parliament). Yet despite this very political background she is widely admired
and applauded and regarded as having done a very good
and inspiring job. The former President of Austria, Mr
Kurt Waldheim, was not so well admired, although his
difficulties relate to his wartime service in the German
army rather than his political background.

Despite the example of Mary Robinson, my view is that a
popular election of the President is not desirable. It would
ensure we had a politician as President. It would narrow the
range of potential candidates for the position. It would
diminish the appearance of impartiality that is so important
for the President. One could add, in conclusion, that it is difficult to see how one could justify the considerable expense
of a national election for a position that does not involve the
exercise of real political power.

Election by an Electoral College

Some countries with non-executive Presidents establish
a special electoral college to choose their Head of State.
Germany's President is elected by a Federal Convention
made up of the members of Germany's equivalent of our
House of Representatives and an equal number of representatives chosen by the *Länder* (or provinces). A similar system
is employed in India and Italy.

It would be quite feasible for a Presidential Electoral College to be established in Australia made up of all members of the Federal Parliament plus an equal number of representatives nominated by the state and territory parliaments. But almost all of the members of federal and state parliaments are members of one or other of the major political parties. Whichever way the electoral college is constituted, one party or other will be in the majority and the result will be that the candidate elected will be seen as being a 'Liberal' or 'Labor' President.

It is also difficult to justify giving state parliaments a direct say in the selection of a President. The people of the States are all represented in the Federal Parliament and the smaller States are, because of the way the Senate is constituted, arguably overrepresented. The States will presumably continue to have their own heads of state (still called Governors) and they will be free to appoint them as they see fit.

We could consider establishing a different type of electoral college. Perhaps all of the members of the Order of Australia (that means people with OAMs, AMs, AOs, ACs and AKs) could form an electoral college and choose the President. But while the Order of Australia seeks to recognise distinction and achievement in Australia, there are no doubt many outstanding Australians without Australian Awards who would regard themselves as having an equal right to participate in the choice of President.

Another possibility might be to constitute the Chief Justices of the High Court, the Federal Court and all the State Supreme Courts as the electoral college. It would certainly make it a non-political choice, but are the judges sufficiently in tune with contemporary Australia to pick the right person?

Election of the President by the Federal Parliament

My preferred position is that the President be elected by a vote of both Houses of the Federal Parliament, sitting together, with the vote requiring the support of a two-thirds majority.

Some supporters of the republic have proposed that the President be appointed by a simple majority vote in a joint sitting of both Houses of Parliament. The problem with a joint sitting is that the party in the majority in the House of Representatives will generally have a majority in a joint sitting because there are only half as many Senators as there are members of the House of Representatives. At present, for example, the Labor Party has 80 out of 147 members of the House of Representatives and 30 out of 76 members of the Senate, giving it a total of 110 votes out of 223 in a joint sitting. If Labor's Senate representation were not so low (by historical standards) it would command a simple majority in a joint sitting but not a two-thirds majority.

Since the Second World War no Australian government has enjoyed sufficient seats in the House and the Senate to carry a joint sitting by a two-thirds majority. Malcolm Fraser obtained the largest House of Representatives majority in Australian history in 1975, but even he fell just short of a two-thirds majority in both Houses sitting together.

There are two objectives in proposing the election of the President by the Parliament. The first is to underline the key principle of our system of democracy: the supremacy of Parliament. It is Parliament which can make and unmake prime ministers, it is Parliament to whom ministers are responsible. The President should be no different. The second objective is to ensure that the President is a person who commands widespread support across the political spectrum and who will not be regarded as the captive of one or other political party.

The way to achieve the second objective is to require that the majority needed to elect the President is two-thirds of the members present and voting in a joint sitting. It is inconceivable that any government would ever control two-thirds of the House and the Senate, and this two-thirds requirement will ensure that the Government and Opposition will have to agree on a candidate.

Some members of parliament have said they are sceptical

about a two-thirds requirement. On a *Four Corners* debate in April 1993, Senators Bill O'Chee (National, Qld) and Bronwyn Bishop (Liberal, NSW) argued forcefully that the parliamentarians would be incapable of agreeing on any candidate. When House of Representatives member Barry Jones (Labor, Victoria) suggested that members of parliament would overcome their party differences and work together constructively to appoint the best candidate, they laughed at him. It is hard to believe Senators O'Chee and Bishop are correct. Many other countries, with much fiercer differences between their parties, manage to select non-executive Presidents in this fashion — Germany and India being two examples. Are German and Indian politicians more conscious of their national responsibilities than Australian politicians? Or are Senators Bishop and O'Chee reflecting their own personal frailties?

In response to this kind of objection, Professor George Winterton has suggested that when an occasion arises to elect a President the Houses of Parliament should be obliged to sit until such time as a result is reached and should not be adjourned 'for a period extending beyond ten days after the first attempted election, until a President has been elected'.[1] Professor Winterton obviously expects the prospect of being stuck in Canberra indefinitely to concentrate the minds of the politicians and force them to reach a decision.

Common sense suggests that the Government and Opposition would not have a great deal of difficulty reaching a decision. If there is a requirement for a two-thirds majority there is no prospect of either major party seeking to reward one of its cronies. If neither party is able to propose one of its 'mates', it is likely that there will be a genuine attempt to find the best person for the job rather than, as is so often the case, the best job for the person.

Who should nominate the President? Presumably the President should be nominated by the Government. Senators O'Chee and Bishop would probably say that a nomination by the Prime Minister would ensure the Opposition would not support the candidate. But it is unlikely that any Opposition which was responsibly led would take such a bloody-minded approach. Similarly, no candidate for the Presidency would allow himself or herself to be nominated without being satisfied there was sufficient bipartisan support to enable the nomination to be approved.

Term of Office

How long should the President's term of office be? Different countries have different terms of office ranging from four years to seven years. The current practice in Australia is that Governors-General can expect to hold their office for five years, although it is open to the Prime Minister to have them dismissed earlier, just as it is possible to extend their term. If the President is likely to be a person reaching the end of his or her career — say someone in their early sixties — a seven-year term may be taking too much of a gamble on their health. It is not desirable to have as President an invalid who is too sick or weak to fulfil his or her duties. On the other hand, if a President does become too frail to do the job, most Australians would be reluctant to see him or her pushed out.

A five-year term seems best. Should the President be able to serve more than one term of office? Most countries allow their non-executive Presidents to serve as many terms as they are chosen to serve; a few others, such as Germany and Austria, allow only one further term.

The arguments in favour of limiting the President to one term are: first, it gives more people a turn (probably not a very good reason) and second, it ensures that a President does not have any reason to curry favour with the Parliament during his or her term of office. Neither argument is very convincing in the context of an Australian Presidency. The President should be able to serve as many terms as he or she is elected to serve.

Qualifications for Office

I remember one (uncharacteristically) sunny day in Oxford, I was sitting in the quadrangle of my college reading a book. (I was probably dozing, but reading sounds more scholarly.) The Principal of Brasenose College was hurrying through the quad with a worried look on his face and I greeted him and inquired as to his apparent concern. He told me that he had been asked by a large stockbroking firm, whose senior partners were Brasenose men, if he had any young men who were about to graduate and who were qualified for stockbroking. Brasenose College had an excellent record in mathematics and I said I felt he could find any number of mathematicians who would be wizards in the financial markets.

'No, no,' replied the Principal, 'the brokers need a special sort of man. They need Old Etonians who are very tall, and I am afraid most of our Old Etonians are too short.'

I told him I could understand why the snobbish stock-broking community favoured men who had been to England's most elite private school, but what was the relevance of height?

'Well, if they are not tall, nobody can see them, or their Old Etonian ties, on the floor of the exchange.'

This is a digression, but it does illustrate the difficulty of laying down qualifications for any job, let alone that of the Head of State. Many countries with non-executive Presidents require a candidate for the office to be of a certain age, older than the age at which a person is qualified to vote. Even the United States requires its executive President to be at least 35 years of age. In Germany a minimum age of 40 is required, in Austria, Iceland, India and Ireland it is 35 and in Italy it is 50.

We have no minimum age requirements (beyond adulthood) for any public office in Australia, and it is hard to see any need to make an exception for the Presidency. The only qualifications for the Presidency should be that the President is an adult Australian citizen.

Removal of the President

How do we get rid of an unsatisfactory President? The President could disgrace himself, and the nation, by turning up drunk to the Melbourne Cup. The President could start accepting bribes in return for procuring awards in the Order of Australia. He or she could become deranged, cursing everybody in sight and using the most violent language. Or perhaps some terrible, scandalous skeleton could emerge from his or her past.

As we have seen, at present, getting rid of a Governor-General is just a matter of the Prime Minister sending a fax to Buckingham Palace. If we have gone to all the trouble of electing a President by a two-thirds vote of both Houses of Parliament we shouldn't allow the Prime Minister to turf that President out with a phone call.

Two issues arise for consideration. First, should the same two-thirds majority apply to the removal of the President as it does to his or her appointment? Second, before a President is removed, should there be some proven misconduct or physical or mental incapacity?

Section 72 of the Constitution deals with the appointment and removal of federal judges, including the justices of the High Court. It provides that they will be appointed by the Governor-General and it goes on to say that they may be removed 'on an address from both Houses of Parliament in the same session, praying for such removal on the ground of proven misbehaviour or incapacity'.

There has only been one occasion upon which a federal judge has been accused of misconduct. Justice Lionel Murphy of the High Court spent the last three years of his life besieged with allegations of misconduct. Criminal charges were laid against him in 1985 and he was ultimately acquitted. After his acquittal, more allegations of misconduct surfaced and the Senate established a judicial committee to inquire into whether Murphy had conducted himself in such a way as to amount to misbehaviour justifying his removal. Murphy died before the inquiry was finished. The question of what kind of conduct justifies removal of a judge was never decided.

Most constitutions around the world provide that their Head of State (be it of the executive or non-executive variety) can be removed by a parliamentary vote. But they generally also require that either some misbehaviour or misconduct be proved or that the Head of State's incapacity be established.

There is no clear definition of either 'misbehaviour' or 'incapacity' in our current law, and if the removal of a President were to be based on establishing either, it would be necessary to define both terms so they related to the particular functions of the President. Private vices may be quite acceptable in a judge, so long as the judge's work on the bench is satisfactory. So if a High Court justice is having a love affair with the spouse of the Prime Minister, that may not disqualify him or her from holding office. But a President is the Head of State and what may be a private matter in the lives of other people is a public matter in the life of the President. As Napoleon observed: 'Kingship is a role. The sovereign is always on stage.'

The President should be removable by the same process by which he or she was appointed. It should not be necessary, or appropriate, to establish the President's misconduct or incapacity before he or she is removed. Establishing a two-thirds majority in a joint sitting as the prerequisite for removal eliminates any prospect of the President being sacked simply because he or she has offended the Government of the day. It is difficult to imagine the Government and Opposition banding together to remove the President unless the President had acted in a manner that justified his or her removal.

In many circumstances it may be quite embarrassing to be obliged to establish misconduct or incapacity. If, for example, the President developed an unacceptable addiction to alcohol and regularly attended state occasions in a drunken condition, should the Parliament be obliged to listen to days of medical testimony as to whether this alcoholism rendered the President incapable of fulfilling his or her task? Should the Parliament have to listen to the President's pleas that drunkenly mauling the spouse of the British High Commissioner was not an example of misconduct?

It is likely that strong views will be expressed that a President should not be removed other than on the ground of misconduct. Why should a President be different from a High Court justice, it will be asked? If, however, a President has reached a point at which both major political parties in the Parliament want to remove him, then whatever the rights or wrongs of the matter, the President has clearly lost the confidence of almost all the members of parliament; and if our political system has one great, overriding principle, it is that Parliament is the supreme political body, subject only to the Constitution. In practical terms, including a requirement that misbehaviour or incapacity be proved may not make much difference. It is doubtful if Parliament would ever sack a President unless his or her unfitness for office was most apparent.

If, on the other hand, it were decided that the appointment and removal of a President should be determined by a simple (50 per cent plus one) majority, then removal should be conditional upon proven misbehaviour or incapacity to protect the President against being removed by one political party which has managed to gain control of both the House of Representatives and the Senate.

CHAPTER SEVEN

States, the Commonwealth and Public Opinion

The States

Discussion about a republican Australia has naturally focused on the position of the Commonwealth. But Australia is a Federation of six States and the Queen occupies the position of Head of State of each of them. In each State the executive power of the State is carried out in the name of the Governor, as the Queen's representative. The legislative power of the State is exercised by the State Parliament, consisting of the Queen (represented by the Governor) and the two Houses of the State Parliament (other than in Queensland, where the Legislative Council has been abolished).

There are two clear alternatives open to republicans when considering the position of the States. Either the Commonwealth Constitution can be amended to eliminate the role of the Queen in each State, or the decision can be left to each

State. The latter course could have the consequence that we would have a republican Commonwealth of Australia and one or more monarchist States.

Assuming the Queen was prepared to remain, for example, Queen of Tasmania, there is no constitutional reason why the Tasmanians should not retain the monarchy. However, it is not at all clear that the Queen would want to remain as Head of State of a particular State of Australia when she was no longer Head of State of the whole nation, especially since her position as Head of State of that particular State would remain a contentious matter for years to come. Ardent monarchists may well regard such a role as demeaning to Her Majesty.

If her attitude to the award of Imperial honours was any indication, the Queen is more likely to take the view that if the Australian people wish to have an Australian as the Head of State of their nation, then it would be inappropriate for her to remain as Head of State of particular States within the Federation. Labor Governments have traditionally not recommended the granting of Imperial honours. Imperial honours are those established in the United Kingdom — such as the Orders of the British Empire (OBE, MBE, CBE and KBE) or the Order of St Michael and St George (CMG, KCMG etc.). The most desirable of these were knighthoods of various rankings, and conservative governments (following the very best of British traditions) had traditionally used them as a means of rewarding their loyal supporters.

When Nick Greiner became the Liberal Premier of New South Wales in 1988 he announced that he would not reintroduce the award of Imperial honours and would content himself with recommending worthy citizens for awards under the Order of Australia, which had been established as an entirely Australian honours system by Gough Whitlam. Some state branches of the Liberal Party, including the West Australian one, indicated they would reintroduce Imperial honours if they won government. To date the recently elected Liberal Premier of Western Australia, Richard Court, has shown no sign of trying to revive Imperial honours. It appears that the Queen took the view that the on-again, off-again affair with Imperial honours had become too ridiculous and she let it be known that she would not agree to the award of any more Imperial honours in Australia regardless of the attitude of the governments in power there.

If Her Majesty took a different view on this issue, and agreed to remain, for example, Queen of Western Australia, it would create some interesting matters of precedence. If she were, as the Queen of Western Australia, to encounter the President of Australia she would be obliged to give precedence to the Head of State of Australia, since she would only be Head of State of one of its constituent States. Alternatively she could, upon encountering the Australian President, quickly turn back into the Queen of the United Kingdom of Great Britain and Northern Ireland — in which case she would meet the Australian President as the Head of State of another nation.

The parliaments of New South Wales, South Australia and Tasmania are free to abolish the role of the Queen in their respective States. Subject to obtaining an absolute majority in its Legislative Council, so is Victoria. The Queensland and West Australian constitutions would require the change to be approved by a referendum. It is therefore quite legally feasible for the States to adopt a different approach.

Would differences between the States be desirable? It is worth noting that Malaysia is a federation of 13 States, nine of which have their own particular royal family from whose ranks is drawn a Sultan of each State. The King of Malaysia is a position which rotates between the nine royal families. But in Malaysia each of the royal families has connections with its respective State. In Australia, while it is legally feasible, an arrangement by which the Queen was no longer Head of State at the national level, but retained that function in some States, would be ridiculous.

It has been suggested in some monarchist quarters that it is not possible to remove the Queen as Head of State of Australia without a majority of the voters in all six States supporting the change. The Republic Advisory Committee considered this issue very carefully and obtained the advice of the Acting Solicitor-General, which it published. It is quite clear in my view that a normal constitutional amendment would be sufficient to abolish the monarchy at the federal level and, if it were felt desirable, at the state level also.

Another issue which will undoubtedly emerge is whether the States should continue to maintain their own local heads of state, the State Governors. The cost of the Governors is not inconsiderable, as Figure 7.1 shows.

The budgeted cost of maintaining the Governor-General and his residences and staff is $9.5 million. The difference in cost between the Commonwealth's vice-regal personage and those in the States is due to the Governor-General having two official residences (Yarralumla in Canberra and Admiralty House in Sydney) rather than just one; the Governor-General also travels a great deal around Australia. Finally, the cost of the State Governors is understated in the official figures, which do not reflect the entirety of the expense of maintaining the official Government Houses and gardens.

All up, Australia spends about $20 million a year on its Governor-General and six Governors. The retention of the State Governors is entirely a matter for the States concerned. The expense is not inconsiderable and while the money saved by abolishing the office of Governor could be put to better use, the truth is that it probably wouldn't be.

A number of options present themselves for the States in a republican Australia.

Maintain the Governor, but More Humbly

An attractive option may be for the States to maintain their Governors in a republican Australia, but drastically to reduce the cost. If the State Governor was to fulfil only constitutional duties and was to cease playing host at Government House to royal visitors, garden parties and other entertainments, the office of Governor could be operated with only two or three staff. The Governor, like the Premier and the Chief Justice, could live in his or her own home at

Figure 7.1: The Funding of State Governors

	NSW	Vic	QLD	WA	SA	Tas	Total
Governor's salary (tax free in States)	$83 000	$84 720	$89 000	$95 000	$65 300	$112 000	$529 020
1992–93 budgeted operational costs†	$1 947 000	$1 820 040	$2 607 000	$1 102 000	$1 134 700	$1 040 000	$9 650 740
Total	$2 030 000	$1 904 760	$2 696 000	$1 197 000	$1 200 000	$1 152 000	$10 179 760

† Costs not including Governor's salary.

Source: Official Secretaries to the various State Governors; Qld and WA Budget papers 1991–92 to 1992–93

private expense. It would not be a grand office, but it would be an honourable one and appropriate for a retired judge.

A variant on this approach may be to combine the office of Governor with, say, the office of Chief Justice. In terms of strict constitutional theory it is not correct for the same person to act as head of the judicial branch and as head of the executive branch of government. Nonetheless, in most States the Lieutenant-Governor (who fills in when the Governor is away) is usually the Chief Justice. No harm seems to have come from this practice, even if anomalous, and it could be a means of maintaining the office of Governor but at a very reduced cost.

Retain the Governors as they Stand

The most likely course of action would be for the States to retain the office of Governor in its present form, save that the State Governor would not be the representative of the Queen. The States would have to decide how their new republican Governor was to be appointed. They could choose to have the Governor appointed by the Government of the day, in the same way judges are appointed. Or they could copy the system most likely to be used at the federal level: appointment by a vote of both Houses of Parliament.

Abolish the Office of Governor Entirely

A radical, and unlikely, course of action would be for the States to abolish the office of Governor. If the States were to have no traditional Head of State it would be necessary carefully to rewrite the state constitutions to cover the kinds of 'nightmare' constitutional problems that a Governor or Governor-General has been traditionally expected to arbitrate. Should a Premier who has been defeated on the floor of the Legislative Assembly be able to call an election or should the Opposition Leader be given an opportunity to form a Government? There are precedents in both Austria and Germany for a non-executive President at the national level without an equivalent at the state or provincial level. The Australian Capital Territory operates its Parliament without a local Head of State and has done so without any apparent problems.

Call Upon the President As and When Required

Another option, which may be justified by cost, would be to constitute the President of the Commonwealth as the Head of State of each of the States. In acting as, say, the Governor of Tasmania, the President would rely only on the advice of the Premier of that State. Given the bipartisan method proposed for appointing the President, this could be acceptable. In the rare event of there being a need for the exercise of the reserve powers or discretions of the Head of State, the President would be able to fill in.

In practical terms this option would be the same as not having a Governor at all, since the President would not have the time to fulfil his or her own national ceremonial duties as well as those previously performed by the Governors. But it would ensure that the occasional, but critically important, constitutional functions of a Head of State at the state level would still be able to be fulfilled.

These choices are basically driven by considerations of cost. Is it worth $2 million a year to the taxpayers of New South Wales, for example, to maintain the State Governor in the accustomed style? Before answering that question it would be necessary to examine how much it would cost to maintain Government House with an alternative use. The various Government Houses could never be sold, they would have to be maintained as some form of museum or public building — all of which would require public funding. Closer examination may reveal that not much money would be saved by either abolishing the Governor's office or operating it on a more low-key basis.

The principal issue for the States as Australia moves towards a republic is whether the States should become republics by operation of the same constitutional amendments that render the Commonwealth a republic, or whether they should be able to make their own independent decisions to become republics. Before insisting loudly on their right to maintain their own monarchical institutions, however, they would be well advised discreetly to inquire whether Her Majesty would contemplate remaining Queen of a State in a republican Federation. If she takes the view that the monarchy should be dealt with on a national basis, as she has with Imperial honours, then even those States whose leaders prefer a monarchy may well consider the matter to be best dealt with by a constitutional amendment that covers both state and federal governments.

The better course, in my view at least, is for the nation to move to republican status together. The Australian republic is an expression of national identity, or it is nothing. Earlier this year both the Queensland Premier, Mr Goss, and the New South Wales Opposition Leader, Mr Carr, have proposed that their respective state parliaments should legislate now to remove some references to the Crown. Mr Goss backed off his proposal fairly quickly when he realised he would need a referendum to implement it. Mr Carr's proposal got as far as a debate in the Legislative Assembly (where it was defeated); it would have changed the name of 'Crown Lands' to 'State Lands' and 'Crown Prosecutor' to 'State Prosecutor' and so on.

Mr Peter Collins[1] spoke eloquently against Mr Carr's Bill on 1 April. Mr Collins said he shared the republican views of his leader, Mr Fahey, but chided the Opposition for trying to use the issue as a means of scoring cheap political points.

I have been looking forward to the commencement of this debate. I only regret the way that some members of Parliament have attempted to hijack this debate to date. That must stop. We must share the debate; we must share this issue. What we will be sharing is the future identity of Australians, the future structure of this nation, and the way it will be perceived around the world. The matters we are talking about are of profound and lasting significance and should not be belittled by the usual cut and thrust — the jabs of political barbs — across this Chamber ... This is too important an issue for any one party to wholly appropriate. It must be owned by all parties.

Mr Collins was entirely correct in his criticism of the Opposition. There is nothing to be gained by state politicians trying to jump the gun on the republican debate. There is a national discussion going on at the moment and the decision in favour of a republic should be a national one.

The Commonwealth of Nations

The Commonwealth of Nations is a voluntary association of 50 independent nations, all of them being former colonies or dependencies of the United Kingdom. Of those 50 countries, 28 are republics, six are monarchies with their own local monarch and the remaining 16 (including the United Kingdom) recognise the Queen as the Head of State. Most of the Commonwealth countries recognising the Queen as Head of State are small island nations in the Caribbean. The Queen's realms within the Commonwealth are as set out in Figure 7.2.

Figure 7.2: Nations recognising the Queen as Head of State

Nation	Population	Area (sq km)
United Kingdom	57 000 000	244 100
Canada	27 100 000	9 215 430
Australia	17 682 000	7 682 300
Papua New Guinea	3 800 000	3 390 000
New Zealand	3 400 000	267 844
Jamaica	2 550 000	10 991
Solomon Islands	319 000	27 556
Barbados	260 000	430
The Bahamas	254 000	13 939
Belize	191 000	22 965
St Lucia	153 000	616
St Vincent and Grenadines	108 000	389
Grenada	98 000	344
Antigua and Barbuda	78 000	441
St Christopher and Nevis	44 000	262
Tuvalu	9 000	26

An Australian republic would be perfectly entitled to remain a member of the Commonwealth. The first republican member of the Commonwealth was India. The British Parliament passed the *India Independence Act* in 1947 and constituted both India and Pakistan as independent dominions. The King remained the Head of State of both of the new nations and was represented by a Governor-General in the normal way. The ruling party in India, the Congress Party, had resolved that India should become a republic, and this was affirmed by a constituent assembly which drafted the new Constitution. The British Prime Minister, Clement Attlee, was initially opposed to the idea of India remaining in the Commonwealth as a republic. However, at a Prime Ministers' Conference in London in 1949 it was agreed that republican India could remain. The conference made the following declaration of principle:

> The Governments of the United Kingdom, Canada, Australia, New Zealand, South Africa, India, Pakistan and Ceylon, whose countries are united as Members of the British Commonwealth of Nations and owe a common allegiance to the Crown, which is also the symbol of their free association, have considered the impending constitutional changes in India.
>
> The Government of India have informed the other Governments of the Commonwealth of the intention of the Indian people that under a new constitution which is about to be adopted India shall become a sovereign independent Republic. The Government of India have, however, declared and affirmed India's desire to continue her full membership of the Commonwealth of Nations and her acceptance of the King as the symbol of free association of its independent member nations and as such the Head of the Commonwealth.
>
> The Governments of the other countries of the Commonwealth, the basis of whose membership of the

Commonwealth is not hereby changed, accept and recognise India's continuing membership in accordance with the terms of this declaration.

Accordingly the United Kingdom, Canada, Australia, New Zealand, South Africa, India, Pakistan and Ceylon hereby declare that they remain united as free and equal members of the Commonwealth of Nations, freely cooperating in the pursuit of peace, liberty and progress.[2]

Pakistan became a republic in 1955, followed by Ceylon (later Sri Lanka) in 1956. The trend in Commonwealth countries has been overwhelmingly towards republicanism, and continues. As recently as last year, Mauritius became a republic and remained in the Commonwealth.

As an international association, the Commonwealth's character has drastically changed over the last 50 years as almost all of the old British Empire has become independent. Out of 50 countries only six — the United Kingdom, Canada, Australia, New Zealand, Malta and Cyprus — have a predominantly European population. The sheer size of the Commonwealth, with 50 members representing one-fifth of the world's population and 29 per cent of the members of the United Nations, means that the old intimacy of the early Prime Ministers' Conferences is a thing of the past. There is no longer any commonality of race, religion or even language. The majority of its members, and the vast majority of its overall population, are from Asia and Africa, and it is no surprise therefore that the principal diplomatic activity of the Commonwealth has been the combating of racism, be it apartheid in South Africa or the white supremacist regime of Ian Smith in Rhodesia.

There has been considerable criticism of the Commonwealth in the United Kingdom. British governments, especially those led by Mrs Thatcher, refused to impose economic sanctions on South Africa despite sustained pressure from the rest of the Commonwealth (including Australia) and the United Nations. In many respects Britain is now the odd one out in the Commonwealth and many

Conservative politicians in Britain regard the Commonwealth as something of an embarrassment. They point out
that while Britain, Canada and Australia between them
pay for over 50 per cent of the costs of administering the
Commonwealth secretariat, the Commonwealth has become
no more than a vehicle for promoting Third World com-
plaints against developed countries including Britain,
Canada and Australia.

The only diplomatic achievements of the Commonwealth
in the post-war period have been in southern Africa. The
Commonwealth nations were instrumental in securing the
demise of Ian Smith's regime in Rhodesia (now Zimbabwe)
and procuring its replacement, following an interim Government led by Bishop Muzorewa, by that of Robert
Mugabe. Australia's Malcolm Fraser played an important
and prominent part in that process.

Apart from securing the transfer of power from Mr Smith
to Mr Mugabe, the significance of the Commonwealth in
international affairs has dwindled enormously in the post-
war years. The regional, economic, cultural and ethnic
diversity of its members means that there is no longer any
prospect of the nations of the Commonwealth banding
together against a common foe in the way the old 'white'
Commonwealth did in the Second World War. The Commonwealth nations simply do not have enough in common
to enable them to constitute a strong influence in the world.
Many of the leaders of the newly independent former
colonies had been educated in Britain and shared a common
cultural and educational background as a result. Nowadays
the elite of the various Commonwealth countries are more
likely to have been educated in their own countries, or in
the United States, than in Britain.

Britain's principal international commitment has been,
since January 1972, to the European Community. A few
months previously, Prime Minister Edward Heath, justifying the decision to join Europe in the House of Commons,
assured members that the Commonwealth offered Britain
no prospects for dynamic growth: the future lay in Europe.
And so it has proved.

Once Australia becomes a republic, our nation will continue to recognise the Queen as Head of the Commonwealth, as do the other republics that are members of the Commonwealth. The Queen will always be a welcome guest in Australia, both in her capacity as the Head of State of the United Kingdom and as Head of the Commonwealth.

Public Opinion

There are 'lies, damned lies and statistics',[3] and of statistics the worst are opinion polls. The accuracy of an opinion poll depends on many factors. The two most important are the nature of the question and the nature of the sample. Polling companies have been asking Australians about a republic for many years, but only one polling company has asked an informative question.

Newspoll, for example, published in the *Australian*, asks in its republican poll:

Thinking about whether you want Australia to become a republic, are you personally in favour or against Australia becoming a republic? If in favour is that strongly in favour or partly in favour? If against is that strongly against or partly against?

The oldest polling company in Australia, Morgan Gallup, has been asking Australians about a republic since 1953. Its question is:

In your opinion, should Australia remain a monarchy — or become a republic with an elected president?

The Saulwick poll, published in the *Sydney Morning Herald* and the *Age* has this question:

There has been some talk over recent years about whether Australia should become a republic. Which of the following statements comes closest to your views?
I would prefer Australia to remain in the

Commonwealth with the Queen as Head of State.

I would prefer Australia to remain in the Commonwealth but as a republic.

I would prefer Australia to become a republic outside the Commonwealth.

Of these three polls the most misleading is the Morgan Gallup poll question. It shares the defect of both Saulwick and Newspoll in not explaining what is meant by the term 'republic', and offering the choice of a 'republic with an elected president' inevitably leads the person being questioned into believing that the republic proposed is an American-style system with a popular election.

The only opinion poll whose question is genuinely informative is that asked by Quadrant Research Services. It is:

There has been a good deal of talk lately about Australia becoming a republic. By the year 2001 which one of these alternatives are you likely to prefer for Australia?

Continue with the present system of federal parliamentary government with the Queen as Head of State.

Continue with the present system of federal parliamentary government but with an Australian as Head of State chosen by both Houses of Parliament.

Change to a system like the United States system.

Don't know.

Despite the misleading or inadequate nature of most of the questions used by the pollsters, the trend towards acceptance of a republic is very clear. The percentages shown by the Quadrant poll to be in favour of a republic have risen steadily from April 1992 (57 per cent), October 1992 (61 per cent) to January 1993 (65 per cent).

The trend in the Saulwick poll is also clear (see Figure 7.3). The proportion of respondents wanting to stay in the Commonwealth with the Queen as Head of State has fallen, with a few ups and downs in between, from a high of 45 per cent in June 1991 to 34 per cent in August 1993. The support

for staying in the Commonwealth as a republic has grown
steadily, from 30 per cent in June 1991 to 43 per cent in
August 1993. Support for a republic outside the Commonwealth has fluctuated between 22 per cent and 15 per cent
over the period, with the August 1993 level of support being
19 per cent. The Saulwick poll thus shows overall support
for a republican option growing from 52 per cent in June
1991 to 62 per cent in August 1993.

Figure 7.3: Public opinion — Saulwick polls
June 1991 to August 1993

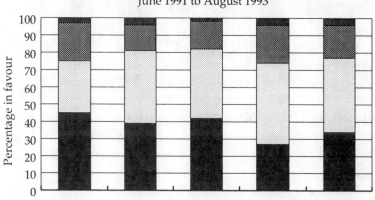

With the exception of the most recent poll taken in September 1993, which is discussed in Chapter 9, *The Politics of
the Republic*, the Newspoll trend is also clear, although the
nature of the question militates against a republican choice
and in favour of either a 'Don't know' or a monarchy choice.
Until the September figure, the poll showed that support for
a republic had grown steadily between October 1987 and
July 1993 from 21 per cent to 46 per cent, while support for a
monarchy dropped from 64 per cent to 36 per cent over the
same period (see Figure 7.4).

The Morgan Gallup poll has been asking its (in my view
misleading) question since June 1953 and even there the
trend is similarly clear: support for the monarchy has
dropped from 77 per cent in 1953 to 36 per cent in 1993;

Figure 7.4: Public opinion — Newspoll polls
October 1987 to September 1993

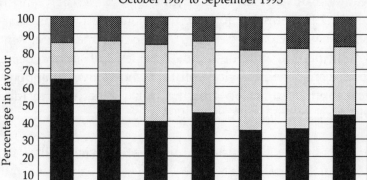

support for the republic has grown from 15 per cent to 52 per cent over the same period. The 'undecided' level has fluctuated between eight and 15 per cent over that time (see Figure 7.5).

The largest single leap in republican support shown on the Morgan Gallup poll has been since the foundation of the Australian Republican Movement in July 1991. It is a matter for considerable regret that Morgan Gallup continues to

Figure 7.5: Public opinion — Morgan Gallup polls
June 1953 to April 1993

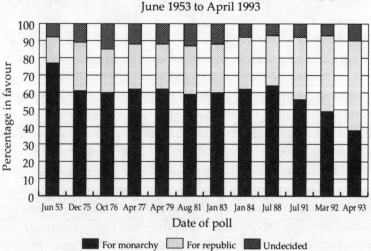

employ such a misleading question. It is perfectly plain that an Australian republic is most unlikely to be one with an executive President along American lines. Yet the question clearly gives that impression. Mr Morgan even acknowledges this, noting in his press release accompanying the March 1992 poll results that one of the comments from supporters of the monarchy was 'we don't need a President like America'.

Finally, AGB/McNair has been polling with the question 'Should Australia become a republic?' since 1979. The results of this poll (see Figure 7.6) are consistent with the others: support for a republic has increased from 31 per cent in 1979 to 48 per cent in October 1993; support for the monarchy has declined from 61 per cent to 42 per cent over the same period.

Figure 7.6: Public opinion — AGB/McNair polls
1979 to October 1993

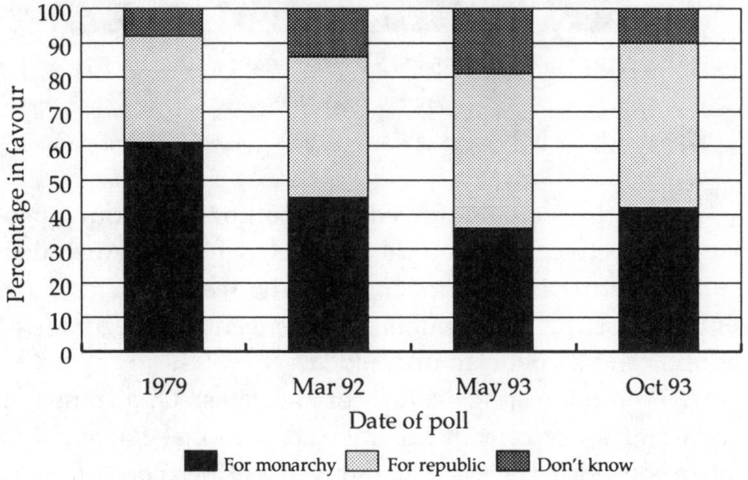

Two interesting features apparent in all the polls is the way support for the monarchy is much stronger among those aged 55 years and over. Older age groups will always favour certain issues more than younger ones — increased pensions or improved medical and hospital care are obvious examples. Those Australians aged 55 years and over had their school education in the 1930s and 1940s (or earlier). In those years, as we have seen, Australia saw itself as being part of the British Empire, Australians saw themselves as being just as British as their 'kith and kin' in London or Edinburgh. Those early feelings of identity are slow to fade. The January 1993 Quadrant poll (Figure 7.7) illustrates the differences between the age groups.

Figure 7.7: Public opinion — Quadrant poll
January 1993

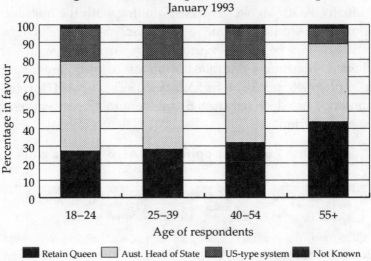

These figures are reinforced by a poll of 3000 young people aged between 14 and 24 conducted for the Australian Youth Institute in September 1993. The results were 51 per cent supporting the republic, 21 per cent opposed to the republic and 27 per cent undecided.

Another interesting feature of the latest Quadrant poll was that 51 per cent of Liberal and National Party voters polled supported a republic, whereas 79 per cent of Labor voters supported the republic. I have been informed by the Liberal Party that their own polling during the election campaign showed 45 per cent of their voters supported the republic.

While these trends are encouraging, they are no more than that. Supporters of the republican cause need to be mindful of how few proposed amendments to the Constitution have been successful, and why.

Amending the Constitution

Australia's mechanism for amending the Constitution recognises the democratic and federal nature of the Australian nation. Under section 128 of the Constitution, a constitutional amendment must be proposed by at least one House of the Federal Parliament. It is then put to a referendum. In order for the proposal to succeed and amend the Constitution it must be approved by a majority of voters throughout Australia, and by a majority of voters in a majority of the States (i.e. four out of six States).

Since Federation, 42 constitutional amendments have been proposed. Only eight have been successful. The referendum results are set out in Figure 7.8 below, with successful referendums shown in bold and referendums which achieved a national majority but failed to carry four States shown in italics.

Of the 34 rejected proposals, only five attracted a majority of the total number of voters, but failed to attract a majority in four or more States.

Of those five proposals which won a majority of votes but failed to get a majority of States, only one, the 1977 Simultaneous Elections proposal, received more than 54 per cent of the votes (it received 62.2 per cent).

One lesson can be drawn fairly quickly. Would-be constitutional reformers need to be satisfied that there is overwhelming public support for a constitutional change before they contemplate putting it to the people.

They also need to ensure that all political parties support the proposal. In 1988 the Hawke Labor Government proposed four amendments to the Constitution in a referendum held on 3 September. The first amendment was to establish a four-year fixed term for the House of Representatives and the Senate. The second was to ensure that all electorates both for federal and state Houses of Parliament were as nearly as practicable equal. The third was to recognise the role of local government in the Constitution and the fourth was to affirm the right of freedom of religion, to ensure that all serious criminal charges were tried before a jury and to

Figure 7.8: Amendments proposed to Australian Constitution

Year	Subject	Government submitting	States where voters in favour of proposal	Percentage of voters in favour of proposal
1906	**Senate Elections**	***Protectionist**	**6**	**82.65**
1910	Finance	*Fusion	3 (Qld, WA, Tas.)	49.04
	State debts	***Fusion**	**5 (all except NSW)**	**54.95**
1911	Legislative Powers	Labor	1 (WA)	39.42
	Monopolies	Labor	1 (WA)	39.89
1913	Trade and Commerce	*Labor	3 (Qld, SA, WA)	49.38
	Corporations	*Labor	3 (Qld, SA, WA)	49.33
	Industrial Matters	*Labor	3 (Qld, SA, WA)	49.33
	Railway Disputes	*Labor	3 (Qld, SA, WA)	49.13
	Trusts	*Labor	3 (Qld, SA, WA)	49.78
	Monopolies	*Labor	3 (Qld, SA, WA)	49.33
1919	Legislative Powers	*Nationalist	3 (Vic., Qld, WA)	49.65
	Monopolies	*Nationalist	3 (Vic., Qld, WA)	48.64
1926	Legislative Powers	Nat–C.P.	2 (NSW, Qld)	43.50
	Essential Services	Nat–C.P.	2 (NSW, Qld)	42.79
1928	**State Debts**	***Nat–C.P.**	**6**	**74.30**
1936	*Aviation*	U.A.P.	2 (*Vic., Qld*)	53.56
	Marketing	U.A.P.	0	36.26
1944	Post-war Powers	Labor	2 (SA, WA)	45.99
1946	**Social Services**	***Labor**	**6**	**54.39**
	Marketing	*Labor*	3 (*NSW, Vic., WA*)	50.57
	Industrial Employment	*Labor*	3 (*NSW, Vic., WA*)	50.30

Year	Topic	Party	States	%
1948	Rents, Prices	Labor	0	40.66
1951	Communists	Liberal/C.P.	3 (Qld, WA, Tas.)	49.44
1967	Nexus	Liberal/C.P.	1 (NSW)	40.25
	Aboriginals	**Liberal/C.P.**	**6**	**90.77**
1973	Prices	Labor	0	43.81
	Incomes	Labor	0	34.42
1974	Simultaneous Elections	*Labor	1 (NSW)	48.32
	Amendment	*Labor	1 (NSW)	48.02
	Democratic Elections	*Labor	1 (NSW)	47.23
	Local Government	*Labor	1 (NSW)	46.87
1977	*Simultaneous Elections*	*Liberal/N.C.P.*	*3 (NSW, Vic., SA)*	62.20
	Casual Vacancies	**Liberal/N.C.P.**	**6**	**73.30**
	Territorial Votes	**Liberal/N.C.P.**	**6**	**77.70**
	Retirement of Judges	**Liberal/N.C.P.**	**6**	**80.10**
1984	*Simultaneous Elections*	*Labor	*2 (NSW, Vic.)*	50.60
	Interchange of Powers	*Labor	0	47.10
1988	Four-Year Term	Labor	0	32.92
	Fair Elections	Labor	0	37.60
	Local Government	Labor	0	33.62
	Rights and Freedoms	Labor	0	30.79

*Referendum held at the same time as a federal election.

ensure that state governments could not acquire property from any person except on just terms.

These proposed amendments had all been recommended by the Constitutional Commission established by the Hawke Government in 1985. The Liberals and Nationals opposed all four amendments. None of the proposals secured a majority in any State. Indeed, only the 'fair elections' proposal secured better than 40 per cent in two States. The support nationwide ranged from 30.79 per cent for the amendment relating to freedom of religion, trial by jury etc. to 37.6 per cent for the fair elections proposal. The result was regarded as a catastrophe for the cause of constitutional reform.

It is surprising that the Government bothered to propose constitutional amendments which had not previously obtained the support of the Liberal and National parties.

What lessons can be learnt for the cause of the republic? In my view the lessons are these:

- The republican cause needs the support of all major political parties to succeed. The Prime Minister has acknowledged this on many occasions, and some of his more enthusiastic supporters should follow his lead rather than trying to make the republic a purely 'Labor' achievement. If the republic is to be a 'Labor achievement' then there will no republic, and no achievement. The republic must have the support of all major political parties and its attainment will be an achievement of all of the parties, and, most importantly, all of the people.
- The Prime Minister has invited the Opposition to be involved in the process of determining the amendments. The Opposition parties should accept that invitation.
- There needs to be a continuing public discussion between now and the referendum to ensure that all Australians understand the issues and, in particular, understand the effect of the changes proposed.
- No referendum should be called unless there is clear evidence that a very large majority supports the change throughout Australia.

The republican referendum will be very different from

any other constitutional amendment proposal. Most proposed amendments have been fairly technical in content and the level of public awareness and interest has been very low indeed. The only referendum in my lifetime which had anything like the same level of awareness was the 1967 proposal to enfranchise the Aboriginal population. That was carried by 90.77 per cent of the votes and all six States.

This high level of awareness will make it difficult for either the Liberals or Nationals to oppose the referendum simply for the sake of frustrating the Government. The political party that is responsible for preventing Australia becoming a republic will, in my view, commit political suicide.

CHAPTER EIGHT

Amending the Constitution

Amending the Constitution to make Australia a republic is not especially difficult. Some constitutional lawyers are prone to wring their hands and make it sound much harder than it is. Rather than talk about the problems, let us address them by considering the particular amendments we need. Remember that most lawyers like to make simple things sound complicated. After all, if they were not complicated, you would not need a lawyer, would you?

A complete copy of the Constitution as it stands today, together with proposed amendments for a redrafted republican version, appears at the end of the book as Appendix One. But we can see how easy constitutional amendment is by doing the job ourselves. So let's start at section 1 and work through to the end.

1. The legislative power of the Commonwealth shall be vested in a Federal Parliament, which

shall consist of the ~~Queen,~~ *President*, a Senate
and a House of Representatives, and which is
hereinafter called 'The Parliament' or 'The Parliament of the Commonwealth'.

Section 1 is easy. We delete 'Queen' and insert 'President'.
On to section 2.

2. ~~A Governor-General appointed by the Queen
shall be Her Majesty's representative in the
Commonwealth, and shall have and may exercise in the Commonwealth during the Queen's
pleasure, but subject to this Constitution, such
powers and functions of the Queen as Her
Majesty may be pleased to assign to him~~.

This section should be deleted entirely, and should be
replaced with a new section 2 which tells us who the President is, and how he or she should be elected. We have
already proposed that the President should not be popularly
elected, but should be elected by a joint sitting of both
Houses of Parliament. If the majority required in the joint
sitting were a simple majority (i.e. one vote more than 50
per cent) it would mean that the Government of the day,
which by definition has a majority in the House of Representatives, would often be able to carry a majority in the
joint sitting as the House of Representatives has nearly
twice as many members as the Senate. No Government has
ever controlled enough votes in the House and the Senate to
carry two-thirds of a joint sitting, so this formula would
mean the President will need the support of both major
political groups. A new section 2 could look like this:

(a) *The Head of State of the Commonwealth shall
be the President of the Commonwealth who shall
exercise his or her powers in accordance with this
Constitution.*
(b) *The first President of the Commonwealth shall
be the person occupying the position of Governor-*

General at the date of the enactment of this clause. As soon as practicable thereafter, and in any event not later than 90 days thereafter, the Prime Minister shall, after consulting the leaders of the other parties represented in the Parliament, propose the name of a person to fill the position of President. Upon the House of Representatives and the Senate voting together in a joint sitting to approve, by a two-thirds majority, the appointment of such person, he or she shall be deemed appointed President of the Commonwealth and shall hold that office until the expiry of five years from the date of his or her appointment or his or her death, resignation or removal in accordance with this section.

(c) During any vacancy in the office of the President of the Commonwealth or during the absence from Australia of the President of the Commonwealth, the duties and functions of the President shall be undertaken by the most senior State Governor, or in the event of his or her disability or inability to act, the next most senior State Governor. The seniority of a State Governor is determined by the length of his or her service as State Governor. In the event of more than three States abolishing the office of Governor, the Parliament shall be empowered to enact legislation for the purpose of providing for the appointment of a person to fill the office of President in the event of a vacancy, provided that no such person shall fill the office of President for more than 120 days.

(d) The President must be a citizen of the Commonwealth of Australia entitled to vote for the election of members of the House of Representatives.

(e) Upon the passage, by a two-thirds majority, of a resolution to remove the President by a joint sitting

of the House of Representatives and the Senate, the President shall cease to hold the office of President and a casual vacancy in the Presidency shall be created.

(f) The House of Representatives and the Senate shall appoint a President in accordance with this clause within 90 days of the position of President becoming vacant for whatever reason. When the Houses meet to elect a President, the Parliament shall not be prorogued, nor shall the joint sitting be adjourned for a period extending beyond five days after the first attempted election until a President has been elected.

(g) The President shall enter upon the office by making and subscribing publicly the following declaration: 'I, A.B., do solemnly and sincerely promise and declare that I will maintain the Constitution and uphold the laws of the Commonwealth and that I will fulfil my duties faithfully and conscientiously in accordance with the Constitution and the law, and that I will dedicate my abilities to the service and welfare of the people of Australia.'

(h) The President may resign his or her office by writing addressed to the President of the Senate, or the Speaker if there is no President of the Senate or if the President of the Senate is absent from the Commonwealth. Such resignation shall take effect at the time specified therein.

Particular points to note in the new section 2 include the requirement in section 2.(b) that the Prime Minister consult with the leaders of the other political parties in the Parliament before nominating the President. This does not mean that the Prime Minister is bound to nominate somebody the other parties suggest, but since a two-thirds majority will require support from all the major parties, it does ensure that the views of all parties will be canvassed before the nomination. Another important point to note in section 2.(f) is that once the joint sitting starts to consider the election of the President it cannot adjourn for more than five days until the election is complete, thereby putting considerable pressure on fractious politicians to make up their minds.

Section 3 of the Constitution deals with the Governor-General's salary. The only important principle here is that the President's salary should not be capable of being altered during his or her term of office. So a new section 3 should read:

> 3. *The salary of the President shall be provided for by Parliament and shall not be altered during the President's term of office.*

We have now amended the Constitution to say how the office of President will be filled. What should the President's powers be? At present, our Constitution gives the impression that the Governor-General is all-powerful. In fact, we know that constitutional convention ensures that the Governor-General always acts in accordance with the advice of his or her ministers, except in the exercise of the reserve powers. So we have a choice here. We could either spell that out and state that the President has to act in accordance with the advice of ministers except in specified circumstances, or we could leave the Constitution as it is and trust to the operation of the constitutional conventions as we have in the past.

Presidential Powers

The Republic Advisory Committee considered four distinct approaches to the powers of the President. The first was simply to include a clause which expressly stated that the constitutional conventions applying to the office of Governor-General will continue to apply to the President. Such a clause would read as follows:

> The President shall exercise his or her powers and perform his or her functions in accordance with the constitutional conventions which related to the exercise of the powers and performance of the functions of the Governor-General,

but nothing in this section shall have the effect
of converting constitutional conventions into
rules of law or of preventing the further development of these conventions.

This clause, of course, invites the question as to what the
constitutional conventions actually consist of. As we have
seen in Chapter 6 that is a very debatable question. Having
said that, we have managed reasonably well without
spelling out the powers of the Governor-General in the past
and a clause along these lines would continue the status quo
without any change at all. It could be described as the ultra-
minimalist solution. It has also been used in a number of
other countries which replaced the British monarch with a
locally chosen President.[1] Since the mid-1960s, however, the
usual practice has been to define the powers rather than rely
on constitutional conventions.

My own view is that the powers of the President should
be comprehensively set out in the Constitution. There are
two reasons for this. First, just as good fences make good
neighbours, so do clear ground rules make for stable and
predictable government. It is important in this most important area of our democratic life that all the players — the
President, the Prime Minister, the two Houses of Parliament
and the High Court — know precisely what their responsibilities and obligations are. The second reason is that it is
quite wrong in a democracy such as ours to have fundamental elements in our democratic system left to so-called
unwritten rules or conventions. As we have seen, our Constitution is a quite misleading document, giving the impression that the Governor-General is an all-powerful ruler who
appoints and dismisses ministers at his pleasure. Australians should be able to pick up their Constitution and
find in it an accurate description of how their democracy
works. Therefore, I support a full codification of the powers
of the President.

The Republic Advisory Committee considered two other
options short of codification. First, it considered empower-
ing some form of Constitutional Commission to formulate
an authoritative statement of the constitutional conventions.

This authoritative statement would not have the force of law but would be able 'to illuminate some of the darker corners of the reserve powers'. While this approach would be an improvement on the status quo there are at least two significant areas of concern. First, it is very doubtful whether a body like a Constitutional Commission would be able to reach a sufficient level of bipartisan agreement to formulate a statement of the conventions which all political parties were prepared to accept as binding. Since the sacking of Whitlam in 1975 there have been several attempts by such bodies to describe the agreed conventions and while there has been some success in the less controversial areas, there has been no success in respect of the contentious questions such as the power to sack a Prime Minister and the appropriate approach to a Senate blockage of Supply. The second area of concern is that no matter how eminent or bipartisan a statement of constitutional conventions may be, it is by no means clear that those conventions would be followed by a President or a Prime Minister when faced with a constitutional crisis. After sacking Whitlam in 1975, Sir John Kerr responded to critics who claimed he had breached convention by saying:

> The Constitution must prevail over any convention because, in determining the question how far the conventions of responsible government have been grafted on to the federal compact, the Constitution itself must in the end control the situation.[2]

There are really only three areas where there is scope for a Governor-General (or a President) to act otherwise than in accordance with the wishes of his or her ministers. They relate to the decision to appoint and to dismiss a Prime Minister, the decision to dissolve the House of Representatives and call a general election, and the decision to dissolve both Houses of Parliament (a double dissolution) and cause an election for all of the House of Representatives and all of the Senate.

Double Dissolution

Dealing with these areas of possible discretion in reverse order, section 57 of the Constitution is intended to provide a mechanism for tie-breaking in the event the House of Representatives and the Senate cannot agree. It provides that if the House of Representatives passes a law and if the Senate rejects it or fails to pass it in a form acceptable to the House of Representatives and if the process is repeated a second time after three months, then the Governor-General may dissolve both Houses of Parliament simultaneously and all seats in the Senate and the House of Representatives would be up for election in the same election. Normally, only half the Senators come up for re-election every three years as their term of office is six years.

If, after the double dissolution, the House of Representatives and Senate still do not agree, there will then be a joint sitting of the two Houses to decide the matter. Given that there are nearly twice as many members of the House of Representatives as there are Senators it is likely that the party with the majority in the House of Representatives would prevail.

There have been five double dissolutions in our history (in 1914, 1951, 1974, 1975 and 1983). While there are early examples of Governors-General declining to agree to a dissolution, the modern view advanced by both Liberal and Labor Governments is that once the Governor-General is satisfied the preconditions of section 57 do in fact exist, he or she should act in accordance with the advice of the Government.

Dissolution of the House of Representatives

The next area of discretion relates to the dissolution of the House of Representatives. Section 28 of the Constitution says the term of the House of Representatives shall be three years 'but may be sooner dissolved by the Governor-General'. In the first decade of Federation, Governors-General declined to dissolve the House of Representatives on the advice of the Prime Minister on three occasions. Since then, prime pinisterial recommendations have always been acceded to.

It is clear that the electorate does not like overly frequent elections and that a Prime Minister who calls an excessively early election is likely to be criticised. If there is not to be a fixed term for the House of Representatives, then there seems no reason why the President would wish to disregard a Prime Minister's advice except in the special circumstances where a majority of the House of Representatives has voted to displace one Prime Minister and has indicated that another person has its confidence instead. This situation can occur where members of the Government cross the floor and vote with the Opposition, or where independent members decide to support the Opposition Leader rather than the Prime Minister.

Appointment and Dismissal of Prime Minister

The third, and most controversial, area is that relating to the appointment and dismissal of a Prime Minister. The convention is that the Governor-General appoints as Prime Minister that person who can command the support of a majority in the House of Representatives. That principle should be spelt out in the Constitution. The controversy arises in circumstances where a Prime Minister is dismissed. The most obvious circumstance in which a Prime Minister should be dismissed is where he or she has lost the confidence of the majority of the House of Representatives and refuses to resign. If, for example, Bob Hawke had refused to resign after the Labor Caucus had voted to elect Paul Keating, the first meeting of the House of Representatives would have resolved that Mr Hawke no longer had the confidence of the House and that Mr Keating did. If Mr Hawke had not then resigned, the Governor-General would have been entitled to dismiss him and appoint Mr Keating in his place.

But what does a Governor-General do if the Prime Minister is breaking the law? In 1932, the Governor of New South Wales, Sir Philip Game, dismissed Premier Jack Lang and appointed the Leader of the Opposition, Mr Stevens,

Premier on condition that an election was immediately called. The reason for this dismissal was that Sir Philip considered Mr Lang's Government to be acting in breach of certain Commonwealth regulations.

The Lang dismissal was a misuse of the Governor's power. A Governor-General (or a President) who believes his or her ministers are breaking the law should be entitled to ask the Attorney-General for a legal opinion on that matter. If the Governor-General or President is unconvinced by this, he or she should be able to obtain a declaration from the High Court. If the Government continued to act in breach of the law, as declared by the High Court, then the Governor-General or President should be entitled to dismiss the Prime Minister and appoint a new Prime Minister who, not having control of the House of Representatives, would be immediately obliged to call a general election.

The final reason for dismissing a Prime Minister is that the Senate has refused to pass an Appropriation (or Supply) Bill. The Commonwealth Government cannot spend public moneys unless its appropriation from the Treasury has been approved by Parliament.

The events of 1975 should not be unduly simplified, but similarly the emotion of the time should not be allowed to complicate something that is really quite straightforward. A Government cannot govern without money. If the Senate refuses to give the Government that money, then the Government must go. If people disagree with the Senate having that right, then they should agitate for a change to the Constitution so that the Senate (like the New South Wales Legislative Council) can no longer block Supply Bills. So long as the Senate has that power, it can bring the business of government to a halt.

If a Prime Minister were denied money by the Senate and if he or she tried to govern without it, nobody would argue that the Governor-General would have to dismiss the Prime Minister and cause an election to be called. A Prime Minister who spends money which has not been lawfully appropriated by the Parliament is breaching section 83 of the

Constitution. The criticism of Sir John Kerr's actions in 1975 is not that he sacked Prime Minister Whitlam, but that he did so sooner than he needed to and without any warning. Indeed, some Labor ministers insist that Sir John Kerr went out of his way to mislead Whitlam into believing that he would not be dismissed.

So how do we resolve this problem of the Senate not passing a Supply Bill? First, we could abolish the Senate's right to block Supply. That would be opposed by the Liberals and Nationals and would not be passed at a referendum. So that is out.

Second, we could write down some rules. We could say that if the Senate refused to pass a Supply Bill which the House of Representatives insisted upon it passing and if it persevered in this course for, say, three months, then there would be a double dissolution. In that way, we would remove any need for the President to exercise his or her discretion. Everyone would know, including the Senators, that if they blocked Supply there would be a double dissolution, followed by an election in which their conduct would no doubt be a very central issue!

The third approach is to leave things as they are. It is unlikely that a President in this situation would be afraid of telling a Prime Minister bluntly that if Supply was not obtained within a nominated period he would have to call an election or be sacked. The President would have nothing to fear from the Prime Minister. There is always the risk that a President would act dishonestly — but that risk is inherent in all our public offices. The criticism of Sir John Kerr was so intense that I doubt whether any future Governor-General or President would allow his or her conduct ever to be the subject of such controversy.

The fourth approach is remove the right of the President to sack a Prime Minister who has the confidence of the House of Representatives other than on the ground of illegality. This would mean that if the Senate blocked Supply, the Prime Minister could stay in office until such time as he or she had spent all the money that had been lawfully appropriated. This would not remove or qualify the Senate's right to block Supply, nor would it affect the President's right to sack the Prime Minister if he or she tried to spend unappropriated moneys. It would, however, ensure that all the players in the parliamentary drama knew where they stood and it would prevent the President making a pre-emptive strike against the Prime Minister in the way Kerr did in 1975.

Given that the first and second options are likely to be strenuously opposed by the Labor and Liberal parties respectively, the best approach is to be found between the third and fourth options. For the sake of clarity we will opt for the fourth.

It is as much a matter of taste as anything else where to put the new provisions in the Constitution, and views may differ about the appropriate spot. We will, however, remove the old section 4 and insert a new set of sections which will deal with the question of the powers of the President. In order to keep the rest of the numbering the same we will just call these new sections 4A, 4B and so on. That will make the revised Constitution at the back of the book easier to follow, although it would be expected that a more elegant approach to drafting would be taken once the changes were generally agreed upon. These sections are essentially the same as those proposed by the Republic Advisory Committee in its 'full codification' option.

4A Executive power of the Commonwealth

(i.) *The executive power of the Commonwealth is vested in the President and is exercisable either directly or through Ministers of State (including the Prime Minister) or persons acting with their authority.*

(ii.) *The executive power of the Commonwealth extends to the execution and maintenance of the Constitution, and of the laws of the Commonwealth.*

(iii.)*The President shall exercise his or her powers and functions in accordance with the advice tendered to him or her by the Federal Executive Council, the Prime Minister or such other Ministers of State as are authorised to do so by the Prime Minister.*

(iv.) *Subsection (iii.) does not apply in relation to the exercise of the powers or functions of the President under sections 4B, 4C(v.), 4D, 4E and 4G.*

4B Appointment of the Prime Minister

(i.) *The President shall appoint a person, to be known as the Prime Minister, to be the Head of the Government of the Commonwealth.*

(ii.) *Subject to subsection 4C(iv.), whenever it is necessary for the President to appoint a Prime Minister, the President shall appoint that person who commands the support of the House of Representatives expressed through a resolution of the House, and in the absence of such a resolution, the person who, in his or her judgment, is most likely to command the support of that House.*

(iii.) *The Prime Minister shall not hold office for a longer period than 90 days unless he or she is or becomes a member of the House of Representatives.*

(iv.) *The Prime Minister shall be a member of the Federal Executive Council and shall be one of the Ministers of State for the Commonwealth.*

(v.) *The Prime Minister shall hold office, subject to this Constitution, until he or she dies or resigns or the President terminates his or her appointment.*

(vi.) *The exercise of a power of the President under paragraph (ii.) shall not be examined in any court.*

4C Other Ministers

(i.) *Ministers of State shall be appointed by the President acting in accordance with the advice of the Prime Minister.*

(ii.) *One of the Ministers of State may be nominated Deputy Prime Minister.*

(iii.)Subject to this section, the President shall only remove a Minister from office in accordance with the advice of the Prime Minister.

(iv.) Upon the death of the Prime Minister, the President shall appoint the Deputy Prime Minister or, if there is no Deputy Prime Minister, the Minister most senior in rank, to be the Prime Minister.

(v.) In this section, 'Minister' does not include the Prime Minister.

Comment

This clause restates convention; it is intended to operate in addition to an updated version of section 64. Subclause (iv.) reflects the past practice of appointing the Deputy Prime Minister as Prime Minister if the Prime Minister dies in office. After that appointment, the parliamentary party will of course elect a new leader and if necessary the 'interim' Prime Minister will as a consequence resign.[3]

4D Dismissal of the Prime Minister: no-confidence resolutions[4]

(i.) If the House of Representatives, by an absolute majority of its members, passes a resolution of confidence in a named person as Prime Minister (other than a person already holding office as Prime Minister), and the Prime Minister does not forthwith resign from office, the President shall remove him or her from office.

Comment

Subclause (i.) simply restates convention.

(ii.) If the House of Representatives passes, other than by an absolute majority of its members, a resolution of confidence in a named person as Prime Minister (other than a person already holding office as Prime Minister), and the Prime Minister does not within three days resign from office or secure a reversal of that resolution, the President shall remove him or her from office.

Comment

Subsection (ii.) allows the Prime Minister three days' grace after a vote of no-confidence to try to reverse the vote. This is appropriate because the resolution referred to may have been procured by the Opposition taking advantage of the temporary absence of Government members.

(iii.)*If the House of Representatives passes a resolution of no-confidence in the Prime Minister or the Government by an absolute majority of its members and does not name another person in whom it does have confidence, and the Prime Minister does not, within three days of the passing of that resolution, either resign from office, secure a reversal of that resolution or advise the President to dissolve the Parliament, the President shall remove him or her from the office of Prime Minister.*

Comment

Subsection (iii.) deals with a 'simple' no-confidence motion (that is, one in which confidence is not expressed in an alternative Prime Minister). The House has, by an absolute majority, decided it does not want the Prime Minister but has not nominated an alternative. In those circumstances an immediate resignation may not be appropriate, so this subclause allows the Prime Minister three days in which to reverse the resolution, resign or, as would be most likely, call an election. (If the House of Representatives wishes to avoid dissolution, it must decide in whom it has confidence, so that subclause (i.) or (ii.) applies.)

(iv.) *If the House of Representatives passes a resolution of no confidence in the Prime Minister or the Government other than by an absolute majority of its members and does not name another person in whom it does have confidence, and the Prime Minister does not, within seven days of the passing of that resolution, either resign from office, secure a reversal of that resolution or advise the President to dissolve the Parliament, the President shall remove him or her from the office of Prime Minister.*

Comment

Subsection (iv.) deals with a 'destructive' no-confidence resolution other than by an absolute majority — for instance because some Government members are absent. The seven-day period has the same purpose as the shorter period in subclause (ii.).

4E Dismissal of the Prime Minister: constitutional contravention

(i.) If the President believes that the Government of the Commonwealth is contravening a fundamental provision of this Constitution or is not complying with an order of a court, the President may request the Prime Minister to demonstrate that no contravention is occurring or that the Government is complying with the order.

(ii.) If, after giving the Prime Minister that opportunity, the President still believes that such a contravention or non-compliance is occurring, the President may apply to the High Court for relief.

(iii.) If, on application by the President, the High Court is satisfied that the Government of the Commonwealth is contravening a provision of this Constitution or not complying with the order of a court, the High Court may grant such relief as it sees fit including a declaration to that effect. The High Court shall not decline to hear such application on the ground that it raises non-justiciable issues.

(iv.) If on an application by the President, the High Court declares that the Government of the Commonwealth is contravening this Constitution or not complying with the order of a court and the Prime Minister fails

to take all reasonable steps to end the contravention or to comply with the order, the President may dissolve the House of Representatives.

(v.) If the President dissolves the House of Representatives under this section, he or she may also terminate the Prime Minister's commission and appoint as Prime Minister such other person as the President believes will take all reasonable steps to end the contravention and who will maintain the administration of the Commonwealth pending the outcome of the general election following the dissolution referred to in subsection (iv.) above.

(vi.) The exercise of the powers of the President under this section shall not be examined by any court.

Comment

This clause recasts the existing reserve power to dismiss a Government which is persistently engaging in illegal conduct. Instead of the President having to make up his or her own mind on the legal status of the Government's conduct, the President is obliged to seek the advice of the High Court which, in our Constitution, is the appropriate body to rule on questions of law.

4F Refusal of dissolution

The President shall not dissolve the House of Representatives —

(i.) on the advice of a Prime Minister in whom, or in whose Government, the House of Representatives has passed a resolution of no-confidence, if the House has, by an absolute majority of its members, also expressed confidence in another named person as Prime Minister;

Comment

Subsection (i.) is simply designed to ensure that no election can be advised between the passage of the resolution referred to and the commissioning of the Prime Minister. It complements subclause 4D(i.).

> (ii.) *on the advice of a Prime Minister in whom, or in whose Government, the House of Representatives has passed a resolution of no-confidence, if the House has, other than by an absolute majority of its members, also expressed confidence in another named person as Prime Minister unless the House has reversed the resolution;*

Comment

Subsection (ii.) prevents a Prime Minister in whom Parliament has passed a vote of no-confidence calling an election where Parliament has also expressed confidence in another person, unless he or she can convince the House to reverse the resolution. It complements subclause 4D(ii.).

> (iii.) *while a motion of no-confidence in the Prime Minister or the Government is pending; or*
>
> (iv.) *before the House of Representatives has met after a general election and considered whether it has confidence in the Prime Minister or the Government, unless the House of Representatives has met and is unable to elect a Speaker.*

Comment

Subsection (iv.) again conforms to the underlying principle of this clause: that before a dissolution is advised the House should have the opportunity of agreeing on a new Prime Minister.

For the purpose of paragraph (iii.), a 'motion of no-confidence' is one which expresses confidence in another named person as Prime Minister and is to come before the House of Representatives within eight days.

The next sections that need substantive amendment are those relating to the grant, or refusal, of the Governor-General's consent to legislation. Archaic provisions (such as sections 59 and 60) relating to the ability of the Queen to disallow Australian laws or reserve her consent to them should be deleted in their entirety as several Constitutional Commissions have recommended. Section 58 will remain as amended below (changes in italics):

58.*(i.) Subject to sub-section (ii.),* when a proposed law passed by both Houses of Parliament is presented to the ~~Governor-General~~ *President* for ~~the Queen's~~ assent, he *or she* shall ~~declare, according to his discretion, but subject to this Constitution, that he assents in the Queen's name, or that he withholds assent, or that he reserves the laws for the Queen's pleasure.~~ *assent to it if so advised by the Federal Executive Council.*

58.*(ii.)* The ~~Governor-General~~ *President in Council* may return to the House in which it originated any proposed law so presented to him *or her*, and may transmit therewith any amendment which ~~he~~ *the President in Council* may recommend, and the Houses may deal with the recommendation.

The next important part of the Constitution we need to consider amending is that relating to the executive government. Since we have already dealt with the respective roles of the President and the Prime Minister in an expanded section 4 we do not need to change much in section 61.

61. The executive power of the Commonwealth is vested in the ~~Queen~~ *President* and is exerciseable ~~by the Governor-General as the Queen's representative~~ *on the advice of the Federal Executive Council,* and extends to the execution and maintenance of this Constitution and of the laws of the Commonwealth.

We have already made it clear now that the President acts on the advice of the Federal Executive Council which is, by convention, made up of the members of the ministry appointed on the advice of the Prime Minister. We will recognise that change by amending section 62. The old section 62 reads as follows and we will amend it as follows:

62. There shall be a Federal Executive Council to advise the ~~Governor-General~~ *President* in the government of the Commonwealth, and the members of the Council shall be chosen and

summoned by the ~~Governor-General~~ *President in accordance with the advice of the Prime Minister* and sworn as Executive Councillors, and shall hold office ~~during his pleasure~~ *until such time as the President is advised by the Prime Minister to terminate such office.*

As a result of the changes we have made (and the consequential changes which are set out in Appendix One) we have simply and effectively substituted a President, elected by Parliament, for the Queen and Governor-General. All of our constitutional arrangements remain in place. The only change which we have made to the powers of the President is to establish a procedure for dealing with the situation where the Senate blocks a Supply Bill.

The only remaining substantive issue for us to consider in the Constitution is the role of the States. As we have seen earlier in Chapter 7, there are two clear alternatives. First, we can say nothing about the States and allow the respective States to decide whether they want to continue with the Queen as Head of State of their particular State, or second, we can decide to amend the Constitution so as to ensure that the Queen cannot be the Head of State of any Australian State. Assuming we took the latter course, the section of the Constitution to amend is section 110 (additions in italics).

110.*(i.)* The provisions of this Constitution relating to the Governor of a State extend and apply to the Governor for the time being of the State, or other chief executive officer or administrator of the Government of the State.

110.*(ii.) Subject to this Constitution, including this section, the manner in which a State Governor is appointed and removed, and the tenure, powers, functions and all other matters relating to the office of Governor shall be such as are prescribed by the law of the State.*

110.*(iii.) The Governor of a State shall be the Head of State of that State and no State Governor shall represent or be appointed by any person who is the Head of*

*State of another country or is an officer in the Gov-
ernment of another country.*

*110.(iv.) The Commonwealth Parliament shall, sub-
ject to this Constitution, have the power to make laws
which enact and implement the provisions of this
Section.*

We have now amended the Constitution. In Appendix
One there is a complete version of the Constitution showing
all the amendments proposed. All the substantive ones have
been discussed above. The others are either consequential
(such as removing 'Queen' and inserting 'President') or they
involve the deletion of archaic or spent provisions that are
no longer applicable.

It is very important to note that the amendments proposed are neither the only way the Constitution can be
amended to introduce a republic nor necessarily the way
that is most likely to be adopted. As the process of establishing an Australian republic continues, many talented Australians will be able to suggest variations on these
amendments which may more effectively set out the powers
and duties of the President. The purpose of these amendments, and this chapter, is simply to demonstrate that the
task is not some mysterious process that ordinary people
cannot understand. It is simply a matter of using plain
English to express straightforward political ideas.

Finally, there are two important, but largely symbolic
parts of the Constitution which should be dealt with. As we
have seen, the Constitution itself is a schedule to a British
Act of Parliament called the *Commonwealth of Australia Constitution Act*. As it stands the preamble to the *Constitution
Act* is almost entirely inappropriate. Various suggestions
have been made to change it. It is quite common for the pre-
ambles to constitutions to contain declarations about the
democratic principles which guide the nation. The United
States Constitution provides in its preamble, for example:

We, the People of the United States, in Order to form a
more perfect Union, establish Justice, insure domestic
Tranquillity, provide for the common defense, promote

the general Welfare, and secure the Blessings of Liberty to ourselves and our Posterity, do ordain and establish this Constitution for the United States of America.

There is a great temptation to write ringing phrases about human rights, equality, the rights of the Aboriginal people, devotion to peace and other noble causes into the preamble. Before doing that, however, we need to bear in mind the advice received by the Republic Advisory Committee from the Acting Solicitor-General. He pointed to a recent High Court case in which several judges relied upon certain words in the present preamble as the basis for holding that the Federal Parliament could not enact laws that distinguish between persons in different areas on grounds that are not relevant and sufficient in the opinion of the court. In other words, general inspirational language is very likely to be given a specific application by the High Court, unless the preamble clearly states that it is not intended to be relied on by any court.

It is probably safer, then, not to make reference to controversial issues such as Aboriginal prior occupation of Australia and leave matters of that kind to be dealt with in substantive legislation of the Parliament or in specific provisions of the Constitution itself.

I favour a relatively modest rewrite of the preamble which owes a great deal to Donald Horne and Henry Finlay, both of whom made submissions on this point to the Republic Advisory Committee. So we will elect to make the following change:

WHEREAS the people of New South Wales, Victoria, South Australia, Queensland, ~~and~~ Tasmania *and Western Australia*, humbly relying on the blessing of Almighty God, ~~have~~ agreed to unite in one indissoluble Federal Commonwealth under the Crown of the United Kingdom of Great Britain and Ireland, and under the Constitution hereby established:

~~And whereas it is expedient to provide for the admission~~

into the Commonwealth of other Australasian Colonies and possessions of the Queen:

And whereas that Federal Commonwealth, the Commonwealth of Australia, evolved into an independent nation under the Crown of Australia:

We, the people of Australia, united in an indissoluble Commonwealth of States, acknowledging the equality of all under the law regardless of colour, race, sex or creed, declaring ourselves to be free, sovereign and independent, agree to be bound by these principles of equality and by the provisions of this Constitution.

The final matter which needs to be addressed is the oath. I would favour amending the oath in a manner consistent with the new citizenship oath.

OATH

I, A.B., do swear that I will be faithful and bear true allegiance to Her Majesty Queen Victoria, Her Heirs and Successors according to law. *pledge my loyalty to Australia and its people whose democratic beliefs I share whose rights and liberties I respect and whose Constitution and laws I will uphold and obey.* SO HELP ME GOD!

AFFIRMATION

I, A.B., do solemnly and sincerely affirm and declare that I will be faithful and bear true allegiance to Her Majesty Queen Victoria, Her Heirs and Successors according to law. *pledge my loyalty to Australia and its people whose democratic beliefs I share whose rights and liberties I respect and whose Constitution and laws I will uphold and obey.*

(NOTE. The name of the King or Queen of the United Kingdom of Great Britain and Ireland for the time being is to be substituted from time to time.)

CHAPTER NINE

The Politics of the Republic

The Australian Republican Movement (ARM) made its first public appearance on 7 July 1991. Its committee, chaired by writer Thomas Keneally, included former New South Wales Premier Neville Wran, playwright David Williamson, Labor MLC and long-time republican Franca Arena, journalists Geraldine Doogue and Mark Day, architect Harry Seidler, poet Faith Bandler, writer Donald Horne, designer Jenny Kee, industrialist Franco Belgiorno-Nettis, cricketer Ian Chappell, ABC chief executive David Hill and me. Most of the ARM's original committee had publicly supported a republic for many years.

It was not the first time Australians had called for a republic. A few weeks before the ARM launch, the Australian Labor Party's federal conference had passed a resolution calling for a republic by 2001, but the ALP had passed a similar motion in 1981 and nothing had been done.

When we established the ARM in late 1990 we had hoped to launch the movement early in 1991. But an election in New South Wales intervened and the launch was delayed until July. From the outset the republican issue was dismissed by most federal Liberal politicians, who spoke about it as a diversion from the more pressing economic issues.

Our strategy was very deliberately aimed at keeping party politicians out of the debate. Our two committee members who were prominent members of the ALP, Franca Arena and Neville Wran, deliberately kept a low profile. Few Labor Party politicians in 1991 — with the possible exception of South Australian Senator Chris Schacht — had anything to say about the issue. The Prime Minister, Bob Hawke, repeated his observation that a republic was inevitable, and when asked to nominate a date suggested 2041, which was far away enough to put even the most determined monarchist at ease.

The ARM recognised that if the republican issue became a matter for full-blown debate between the two political parties it was likely that the Liberal Party would paint itself into the monarchist corner. The Liberal Party, after all, included support for the constitutional monarchy in Australia among the political principles in its platform. Its rank-and-file membership was, overall, older and more conservative than those people who voted for it, let alone the population at large. If the issue became a party political one it was most likely that the Liberals would oppose the republic.

In order to amend the Constitution we needed a majority of Australian voters both nationally and in four out of six States to support the change. Historically Australians have been very reluctant to approve changes to their Constitution. Forty-two constitutional amendments have been put to voters in referendums. Of those only eight have been approved by the requisite majorities. Of the 34 rejected proposals, only five were supported by a majority of voters throughout Australia.

Conventional political wisdom dictated that for a referendum to have any chance of success we needed to secure the support of all major political parties. That would only come about when the opinion polls were showing a substantial majority of the order of 60 per cent or more in favour of a republic. At that point, we reasoned, even the most die-hard monarchists in the Liberal Party would support us. But in order to get to that point we needed to maintain a people's debate for some years: a debate during which public opinion could be informed and, would, we hoped, shift towards a republic.

But by July 1991 no major opinion poll had suggested support for the republic was over 50 per cent. There was enormous ignorance about what a republic would involve and our opponents were not slow to allege that a republican Australia would spell an end to parliamentary democracy and the rule of law. The Victorian President of the Returned Services League, Mr Bruce Ruxton, even suggested our first President could be Idi Amin, the former dictator of Uganda.

In order to ensure the debate remained narrowly focused on the issue of the nationality of the Head of State, the ARM opted for the narrowest possible form of republic. We proposed simply that the Queen and the Governor-General be replaced by a President, the President be elected by a vote of both Houses of Parliament, the President have the same duties and functions as the Governor-General and Australia remain a member of the Commonwealth of Nations. A number of our supporters were anxious to include other issues in the ARM's platform. We persuaded them, however, that every additional change to the Constitution which we proposed was certain to create more opposition.

The ARM's platform had to be as simple and short as possible, so that our opponents would be left without anything to defend except the monarchy itself. We believed that in 1991 a coherent case could no longer be made for retaining the British monarchy in Australia.

While Labor Party politicians stayed out of the debate, a number of Liberal politicians became very actively involved. John Howard and Senator Bronwyn Bishop were regular opponents of Tom Keneally and me in numerous debates on television and radio and in public meetings. They succeeded in creating an impression in the public mind that while the ALP was in favour of a republic, but not enthusiastically so, the Liberal Party was aggressively against it.

Shortly after the ARM launch, the *Midday* programme on the Nine Network hosted a debate between some republicans and monarchists. Normie Rowe, a singer and Vietnam veteran, was for the Queen; among the republicans was the veteran Sydney radio announcer, Ron Casey. Casey offended Rowe, who leapt to his feet and pushed Casey back into his seat. Rowe was no doubt aware that Casey was old enough to be his father, but he did not know that he had begun his career as a boxing writer. Casey landed a perfect left hook on Rowe's chin. It was the first and only blood spilled for the republic.

It was also a most regrettable distraction and we feared that it would serve to justify those who claimed the debate would be violently divisive of Australian society. On 30 July, Mr Ruxton demanded that the New South Wales Attorney-General prosecute the committee of the ARM for treason. The Attorney-General, Mr Peter Collins, declined the invitation to make himself as big a fool as Mr Ruxton.

The rest of 1991 passed quietly enough. The debate continued in the media, the ARM committee members gave speeches, wrote articles and were interviewed on radio and television. The Labor Party was absorbed with the power struggle between Bob Hawke and Paul Keating, who became Prime Minister on 20 December that year.

Prior to his becoming Prime Minister Keating had said nothing publicly about the desirability of a republic. His first foray into the field of national symbols was about the flag. On 31 January 1992 he supported the idea of Australia having a new flag. Speaking on radio he said: 'I suppose people around the world are entitled to say, "We look at your flag — you've got the flag of another country in the corner. Are you a colony or are you a nation?"'.[1] The Liberals and Nationals were not impressed. Before long each of the

Opposition members in the House of Representatives had placed a little Australian flag on the desk in front of his seat. Many of Keating's supporters in the ALP were puzzled by this outburst. It made no sense to launch an attack on the Australian flag 12 months before an election.

The Queen arrived in Australia on 18 February for a seven-day visit to Sydney, Dubbo, Canberra and Adelaide. It was another example of Australians' inability to celebrate any significant occasion without a member of the British royal family in attendance. This time it was the 150th anniversary of the Sydney City Council. While in Sydney, the Queen conferred the Order of Merit (a British award) on opera singer Dame Joan Sutherland. 'La Stupenda' was scathing about the republican movement, demanding that we all be locked up on Fort Denison. Her loyalty to the Queen, however, does not extend so far as to incline her to live in one of Her Majesty's many dominions. Dame Joan prefers the fresh air, and low taxes, of that very stable republic, Switzerland.

When the Queen arrived the press remarked that the welcoming crowd at the airport was smaller and older than normal. Was this due to a growing republican sentiment? Or was it simply that the grandmother of 1992 was not quite as fascinating as the glamorous princess of 1954? In an age of celebrities, how can the Queen compete with Madonna, or even our own Kylie? Perhaps we were just bored.

In any event, the ARM had decided to lie low during the royal visit. As Harold Scruby had shrewdly observed, Australia had few monarchists but a great many Elizabethans. There was no point being seen to be anti-Queen. Our cause was pro-Australian, not anti-British or even anti-royalty. So we waited for the visit to finish before resuming our seditious activities.

Republicanism was far from the Prime Minister's mind also. The Queen visited Parliament in Canberra on 24 February and Mr Keating gave a short speech of welcome. It was upbeat and thoughtful, but hardly revolutionary.

> I know that on this visit it is your primary purpose to
> participate in Sydney's sesquicentennial; but today it is
> my primary purpose to congratulate you on the 40th
> anniversary of your accession to the throne.
>
> Your Majesty we have all changed in that time. The
> men who sat in the Australian Parliament on your first
> visit — they were practically all men in those days — had
> memories of Empire. Not a few of them saw the world
> through Imperial eyes. Many of them had been born in
> Queen Victoria's day and remembered the several
> monarchs in between.
> ...
>
> This is an altogether different generation, reflecting the
> profound change in our two countries and the
> relationship between them ... Just as Great Britain some
> time ago sought to make her future secure in the
> European Community, so Australia now vigorously seeks
> partnerships with countries in our own region. Our
> outlook is necessarily independent.

Keating's speech was frank, but unremarkable. It is hard to
believe it could have caused any offence to the Queen. After
all, she is the Queen of Australia and monarchists never tire
of assuring us Australia is an independent nation and that
the monarchy is an Australian institution. But Keating's reference to independence shocked some members of the
Liberal Party. Opposition Leader John Hewson described
Keating's speech as 'embarrassing' and giving a tilt to republicanism. Tim Fischer, the Leader of the National Party,
described the speech as 'shocking and inadequate'. The
Shadow Minister for Trade, Alexander Downer, headed his
press release 'Keating Brings Bovver Boy Tactics to National
Occasion' and described the speech as '... poorly conceived,
weakly delivered and downright ungracious'. The Reverend
Fred Nile suggested it was not long before the declaration of
the 'Atheist Socialist Republic'.

The Prime Minister was surprised by the reaction. His
speech had made no reference to republicanism. It was a
thoughtful *tour d'horizon* of an elevating kind suited to such

occasions. He had made reference to Australia's independence, in the presence of Australia's Head of State, and the Opposition went berserk. Perhaps this was a soft spot that called for more prodding.

Mr Keating would have been excused for thinking no-one understood him. Hot on the heels of the Liberals' reaction to his speech, the London press flayed him for *touching the Queen*. A casual reader would have imagined that the Prime Minister had, in Barry Humphries' words, 'stuck his hand up her frock and gone the grope'. 'HANDS ORF, COBBER' said the London *Daily Star* in a typical headline. In fact, at a large reception at the Parliament, the Prime Minister had gently guided the Queen towards some old friends.

The Australian press was delighted. The *Financial Review*, the *Age* and the *Herald Sun* editorialised in support of the Prime Minister and joined the call for a republic. The Prime Minister was encouraged.

On any estimation the tour could not be described as a public relations success. The *Age*[2] neatly summed it up:

> The crowds, although warm, were predominantly elderly
> women. Their numbers have been dwindling since the
> first royal tour of 1954 ... The lasting image of this visit
> was the division of the crowds. The older generation sang
> only 'God Save the Queen'. The schoolchildren knew
> only the words to 'Advance Australia Fair'.

On 27 February, the House of Representatives heard the Labor member for Kalgoorlie, Mr Graeme Campbell, criticising the republican movement which he regarded as being a front for supporters of 'multiculturalism' who wanted to wipe the slate of Australia's history clean and start again. This example of monarchism in the ALP ranks did not deter the Prime Minister. Responding to a pre-arranged question from one of his colleagues he rose to deliver a broadside against the Opposition.

> In the past week we have had one of those rare
> philosophic outbursts from the Opposition ... They

started off with the Leader of the Opposition ... talking
about 'I never learned respect at school'. You see, I should
never have said in front of Her Majesty the Queen of
Australia that Australia was now trading with the
Asia–Pacific area. I should never have said that we have
independence from Britain and Europe, as Britain joined
the Common Market and as Australia trades now 70 to 80
per cent of its imports and exports with the Asia–Pacific
area. I should never have made that remark about
independence to the Queen of this continent. I should
have had more respect. How dare I even reflect modestly
on the old links with Britain, on the British bootstraps
stuff?

...

   I said today at the Press Club that one of my
colleagues, the Minister for Administrative Services,
Senator Bolkus, has always been at the Cabinet about the
future development of the old Parliament House and
whether it ought to be a constitutional museum or
museum of Australian cultural history. We thought we
could basically make the changes and put some of the
cultural icons of the 1950s down there. The Morphy
Richards toaster, the Qualcast mower, a pair of heavily
protected slippers, the Astor TV, the AWA radiogram.
And, of course, the honourable member for Wentworth
[Dr Hewson] and the honourable member for Bennelong
[Dr Howard] could go there as well. When the kids come
and look at them they will say 'Gee, mum is that what it
was like then?' And the two Johns can say 'No, kids this
is the future'. Back down the time tunnel to the future —
there they are. I was told that I did not learn respect at
school. I learned one thing: I learned about self-respect
and self-regard for Australia — not about some cultural
cringe to a country which decided not to defend the
Malayan peninsula, not to worry about Singapore and
not to give us our troops back to keep ourselves free from
Japanese domination. This was the country you people
wedded yourself to, and even as it walked out on you
and joined the Common Market you were still looking for

your MBEs and your knighthoods, and all the rest of the
regalia that comes with it. You would take Australia right
back down the time tunnel to the cultural cringe where
you have always come from … These are the same old
fogies who doffed their lids and tugged their forelock to
the British establishment … We will not have a bar of it.
You can go back to the fifties, to your nostalgia, your
Menzies, the Caseys and the whole lot. They were not
aggressively Australian, they were not aggressively
proud of our culture, and we will have no bar of you or
your sterile ideology.

Keating's speech was as dramatic as it was unexpected. His
violent attack on Britain's alleged lack of support of Australia in the Second World War created an enormous storm
both in Australia and Britain. His colourful rhetoric reinvig-
orated the Labor Party which was exhausted and disillu-
sioned by both the recession and the recent leadership
struggle which Keating had won. Despite its dominance of
Australian politics for over a decade, the Labor Party likes
to see itself as a party of underdogs, standing up to the
establishment. This self-image is, of course, almost entirely a
self-indulgent fantasy. Any definition of the Australian
'establishment' which did not include the leaders of the
labour movement would be quite inadequate. The days
when Australia was run by Anglophile products of the
Protestant private schools are well and truly past. Nonetheless, in the mythology of the Labor Party, history and sentiment often count for more than current affairs and while
Keating's remarks may not have done much for Anglo-Aus-
tralian relations, he had done a great deal for the morale of
his own supporters.

Some of the more cautious Labor MPs were taken aback. I
spoke to one of Keating's closer allies shortly after the
speech. 'Geez mate,'[3] he said, 'I don't know what went
wrong. Some bloody fool in his office gave him the speech
notes for the IRA fundraiser on Saturday, and it was too late
before we realised the mistake.'

The ALP may have been ecstatic, the British establishment

affronted and the Opposition outraged, but the Australian Republican Movement was far from pleased. This was exactly the sort of speech we did not want to hear. It was calculated to make the republic an election issue, which we wanted to avoid. It was needlessly and inaccurately offensive to the British and even more so to the Liberal Party. As we have seen in Chapter 4, the Labor Party had been a most enthusiastic supporter of the British Empire during the 1940s and 1950s and Labor icons like Curtin and Evatt had tugged the forelock with the best of them.

There was an easy response to Keating on his misinterpretation of history. But, sadly, no-one on the Opposition benches appeared to know it. The cream of the professional and business classes of Australia apparently had little interest in the history of either their own country or their own party.

Keating's speech was over the top, and most Australians recognised it for what it was. But Australians like fighters, and they like leaders who are aggressively nationalistic. Just as Paul Hogan made himself a fortune by creating an Australian bushman who went to New York and made fools of the Americans, so Keating was setting himself up, for the first time in his political career, as an Australian champion. Hitherto Keating had presented as a sophisticated man of the world, preaching international free trade in an elegant Italian suit. The more the British press dubbed him 'The Lizard of Oz', the more British politicians chided Keating on television, the more Australians liked him.

Two days later, the *Sydney Morning Herald* and the *Age* published another Saulwick poll, this time showing 57 per cent in favour of the republic. For the first time a poll had shown a substantial majority in favour of the change.

This was the point at which the Liberals could, and should, have defused the debate. It was preposterous of Keating to characterise Hewson as a 1950s, British-to-the-bootstraps Menzies clone. It was equally preposterous to suggest that the conservative parties had been alone in tugging the forelock. But the only Liberal to engage in this aspect of the debate in any substantive way was Malcolm Fraser, the former Prime Minister. Fraser endorsed Keating's remarks about Australia's independent role in the Asian region and acknowledged there was more than a little truth in his criticism of Britain's failure to defend Malaya properly in the Second World War. But Fraser also rightly defended previous Liberal governments, pointing out that Menzies and his foreign minister, Richard Casey, had promoted trade and diplomatic contacts with the Asian region during the 1950s.

The republic issue was a difficult one for the Liberals to deal with. It was clear enough, both on the published poll results and their own research, that support for a republic was growing rapidly, especially in the age groups under 55 years. A shrewd response would have been, first, to demonstrate that all political parties, including Labor, had been effusively pro-British in the 1950s and before; second, to say 'We in the Liberal Party believe our constitutional monarchy has served us well. We note there is a public debate on this issue and think it is a good thing as it will promote public understanding of our Constitution. We believe it is better that party politicians stay out of the debate for the time being. You can rest assured that if a strong consensus for change emerges, the Liberal Party will not stand in the way of the Australian people'.

This approach would have denied the Labor Party the appearance of being the pro-republican party and, so they would argue, the only party with a nationalistic vision. Individual Liberals would have been free to take one side of the debate or the other, if they chose. Instead the Liberals allowed themselves to appear as defenders of the monarchy and the British connection generally. A Tandberg cartoon summed it up neatly showing Hewson and other colleagues being told by a gleeful John Howard: 'If a federal election were held in Britain we'd win in a landslide.'

It is no easy matter, so close to the events and writing from the midst of them, accurately to assess the impact of the Prime Minister's advocacy of a republic through 1992.

His public espousal of the cause gave it a credibility and profile that it had not had before. Any cause for change which has the Prime Minister's endorsement has to be taken very seriously. On the other hand, because the Prime Minister is a leader of a political party and hence a political partisan — and is, by definition, the most important public figure in the nation — the cause of the republic became excessively identified with him. It did not matter how large was the republican bandwagon, how long it had been running or how many others were on it, from the moment the Prime Minister stepped on board he tended to overshadow everybody else.

On the other hand, Keating would argue that matters of national identity are entirely appropriate subjects for the leader of the nation to address. He saw it as his responsibility to embrace the issue and make it his own. His critics suggested that Keating saw the republic as an irresistible diversion from the apparently intractable problems of the economy. The economy was depressed and his own role in the policy mistakes of the past made it hard for him to sound credible in promising to improve it. In the 1980s Keating had impressed the Australian electorate with his confidence as an economic manager. His vision splendid had been a bold programme of economic reform, abandoning Labor Party orthodoxy at every turn. By 1992 that vision was tarnished, to say the least. He needed a new vision; more importantly, perhaps, he needed one which would inspire his own supporters who had become dispirited and bored with years of economic rationalism.

As 1992 progressed the republican cause became increasingly identified with Keating. It became 'Keating's republic' or the Prime Minister's republican push. He was criticised for politicising the issue. And he was politicising the issue. He was staking out the Labor Party's claim over what many saw as an inevitable constitutional development. The republican cause was a certain winner for the Labor Party. It was clear on all the polls that support for the republic exceeded support for the Labor Party by a substantial margin. It could not hurt the ALP to be associated with it. Never mind the damage it was doing to the republican cause overall. Moreover, if you took the view that the change was inevitable, there were enormous advantages for the ALP in being associated with the move. The longer the Liberals took to climb on the bandwagon the more anachronistic they would look. Already word was filtering back from the Labor Party branches that the republic was encouraging new memberships, especially from young people. One young ALP parliamentary aspirant who had been struggling to stack the branches in his electorate for years told me, 'Until this republic thing came along, I could only get my relatives and really close friends to join up. Now it's easy. Everyone I know of my age wants to get involved'. It was clear that while ALP support for the republic was a short-term or possibly medium-term liability for the republican movement, it was very good politics in the long term for the ALP.

It is probably too late now to correct the public impression that Keating was solely responsible for 'politicising' the republican cause. However, the truth is that until February 1992 Keating had said nothing about the issue. The republican debate had been proceeding vigorously for more than six months and the only prominent federal politicians engaged in it were Liberals — in particular John Howard and Bronwyn Bishop. Indeed the first television debate I engaged in on this issue was with Senator Bishop, closely followed by another with John Howard.

The republican issue continued to bubble along during 1992. The letters pages were full of it, a schools essay competition was sponsored by the *Australian* and ARM directors continued their busy round of speeches. Our ambivalence about the value of the Prime Minister's support was heightened when he returned to an earlier theme, changing the flag. Some members of the cabinet, including Senator Nick Bolkus, the Minister for Administrative Services, were urging that a change to the flag be made immediately so that Australian athletes could compete in the Barcelona Olympics under a new national banner.

A change to the flag did not require a referendum, or even a national plebiscite. It could be effected simply by legislative action. Keating repeated his criticism of the flag again and again, and on one occasion did so during a visit to Indonesia. This provoked an uproar and it quickly became apparent that while support for the monarchy was diminishing, support for the flag was strong and, if anything, growing stronger.

While there was a large overlap between those groups who supported a republic and those who wanted to change the flag, there is an important distinction between the two objectives. No matter how well intentioned the incumbent, the monarchy can never become representative of Australia. The Constitution specifically decrees that our Head of State is to be whoever occupies the British throne and for as long as that remains unaltered we will have a Head of State whose principal role in life is being Queen (or King) of Britain.

The flag, on the other hand, is a more ambiguous symbol. It is an exclusively Australian flag, in the sense that we do not share it with another country (as we do our Queen). Having said that, the most honoured position on that flag is occupied by the flag of the United Kingdom, the Union Jack. That place of honour is no accident. The first of the conditions for the design competition which produced the flag stated: 'The design should be based on the British ensign as were the flags of the other Dominions and Colonies: The red ensign of the Homeland with the sign of the country added to its folds in these far off lands signals to the beholder that it is an Imperial union ensign of the British Empire.' The present Australian flag was selected in 1903. It was no more than either a red or blue British ensign (as used on British ships and government establishments). At that time Australia was unquestionably a British colony, self-governing in many domestic matters, but legally, constitutionally and politically a *subordinate* part of the British Empire. The new flag required the approval of the British Government before it could be adopted and that new flag was designed to make this statement: 'This is the flag of Australia, a subordinate part of the British Empire.' Subordination was recognised through the requirement that the Australian flag (red or blue) be flown in a *subordinate* position to the Union Jack which was the senior flag, as that of the Empire.

At that time very few Australians would have quarrelled with these sentiments. Australians were proudly British. The Australian red or blue ensign would never have been appropriate for adoption by Australia had it been an independent nation. The flag was then avowedly a mark of subservience to the British Empire of which we were part.

The Australian blue ensign was rarely used other than by Government until after the Second World War. The Australian blue ensign only achieved the status of a national flag in 1953, and its official description is as 'the British blue ensign defaced by the Southern Cross and Federation Star'.

But despite its undoubted colonial origins, there is little doubt that to many Australians the blue ensign does, in fact, represent Australia. The Union Jack (flying undefaced as the flag of the United Kingdom) is not the constant presence in Australia that it used to be and it is argued that many Australians see the Australian blue ensign as one coherent Australian symbol, rather than a composite of symbols the most prominent of which is unmistakably British.

Flags are designed to distinguish one nation from another. They are not only intended to symbolise a nation to its own citizens, but to the citizens of other nations as well. In this respect, even if the Australian blue ensign does represent Australia to some Australians, it cannot unambiguously represent Australia to people abroad.

Taking account of the views of foreigners on this issue has been characterised by some people as forelock-tugging. In making this characterisation they are displaying their ignorance and chauvinism. The truth is that the Union Jack (together with the flags of the USA, Canada and Japan) is one of the best-known national flags in the world. As a national symbol our flag (which is not nearly so well-known) is confusing precisely because it displays the well-known Union Jack in the position of honour. This confusion is particularly intense because of the similarity of our flag with that of New Zealand and some other Commonwealth countries (most of which are either colonies or very recently independent). If we believe it is important to have a flag which is distinctively Australian, then we should favour a change.

But it should also be acknowledged that the flag debate will be stillborn until such time as an alternative design for a flag is proposed which can command widespread support. Because the options for an Australian republic are well understood, the republican campaign is in this respect further advanced.

On 14 May, I addressed a fundraising luncheon for the Melbourne branch of the ARM and used the occasion to criticise the Prime Minister's attempt to reinvent Australian history. I pointed out that the Labor Party had been a devoted supporter of the British connection and far from wanting to come to terms with Asia had been the only party which included the maintenance of a white Australia in its platform.[4]

The fourth of June 1992 saw the launch of a monarchist group called 'Leadership Beyond Politics — Australians for Constitutional Monarchy'. Its charter is considered in detail in Chapter 10. The emergence of this monarchist group came as a great relief to the ARM. For the first time it offered the possibility of debating the issue with a citizens' group on the other side, rather than with Liberal politicians. It also meant that the public exposure of the case for the monarchy would result, so we believed, in people perceiving its weaknesses.

The silliness of the monarchist case was neatly demonstrated at a public debate held during Melbourne Writers' Week in September 1992. The monarchist team was made up of Lloyd Waddy, Dame Phyllis Frost and Richard Cobden. For the republic were Dr Jocelynne Scutt, a Melbourne feminist and barrister, Dr John Hirst and me. Lloyd Waddy is a better comedian than a political scientist and the high-

light of his speech was accusing me of planning to take over
Australia. 'Mr Turnbull is a McCarthyist,' he declaimed. I
responded, in my best Joe McCarthy accent: 'And if there is
only one monarchist in the State Department ... that is one
monarchist too many.'

Dame Phyllis read out large chunks of the monarchists'
charter and then, perceiving the audience was not with her,
observed as she sat down:

> I've got as much chance persuading you lot to respect
> Her Majesty as I would persuading a bunch of Jews to
> invest in a business promoting artificial insemination in
> pigs.

There was a stunned silence. But more was yet to come. Mr
Richard Cobden rose as the third defender of the Crown. He
said that he liked the royal family because it was good to
have people dressing up in sequins and tiaras — indeed, he
said, he liked wearing sequins and tiaras, and long gowns
too. He said the marital difficulties of the royal family did
not worry him at all, and he particularly liked Prince
Edward because, he assured the audience, he understood he
was a bachelor for all the right reasons.

As he sat down, I could only reflect that if I were the
Queen I would rather Australia became a republic than
have to put up with champions like that.

There is an interesting postscript to Richard Cobden's
involvement with Australians for a Constitutional Monarchy. Though Mr Cobden was a 'Foundation Councillor' and
signed the charter of the organisation, Mr Cobden resigned
from the monarchist organisation on 15 April 1993. In a letter to the *Sydney Morning Herald* published on 13 May 1993
he said in part:

> A year of articulating the arguments, both in public and
> in private, for the retention of the British monarch as
> Australia's head of State, only convinced me more and
> more of how weak those arguments are ... What kind of

symbol is a privileged, remote and insulated foreign woman, who despite the speed and ease of travel today ... has managed only a handful of visits over 40 years to a country she allegedly treasures? It is a symbol of indifference. What kind of symbol is a person who makes no attempt to change her job description, which places women last in the queue to take over, and bans Roman Catholics completely? It is a symbol of prejudice, discrimination and profound conservatism.

I couldn't have said it better myself.

The growing sentiment in favour of a republic in Australia was the least of the Queen's problems in 1992, a year she was to describe as her *'annus horribilis'*. A biography of Princess Diana was published by Andrew Morton in which he alleged that the Wales's marriage had become a miserable pretence, that Diana had attempted to kill herself on a number of occasions and that Prince Charles had maintained, throughout his marriage, a sexual liaison with Mrs Camilla Parker-Bowles, who was married to a close friend of the royal family.

As if that were not enough, Sarah Ferguson, the Duchess of York and wife of Prince Andrew was photographed barebreasted and cuddling her lover in what was meant to be a secluded hideaway in the south of France. Worse still, the prying photographer recorded her admirer, one Johnny Bryant, sucking her toes. All of this 'indecent' behaviour was taking place in full view of her two daughters.

A fire damaged Windsor Castle and the British Government committed itself to paying for the repairs. The barrage of public criticism which followed these incidents resulted in the Queen succumbing to pressure and agreeing to pay tax. There was even talk of Britain becoming a republic before Australia.

The Australian Republican Movement was tactful about the royal scandals, if that is the right term for them. The ARM's argument was simply that the Queen was not Australian, and we confined ourselves to expressing sympathy for the distressing marital disharmony in London. Nonetheless, there can be no doubt that it all worked to the advantage of the republican cause. While the Queen still generated enormous affection and respect, it was difficult to believe that Prince Charles could ever be accepted as King. The more conservative members of the community who were inclined to support the monarchy were shocked at his apparently unashamed adultery with the wife of another man. Women — who as a whole tended to be more supportive of the monarchy than men — were repelled by his apparent coldness towards Diana. And while many sympathised with the Princess's plight, it was increasingly difficult to envisage her as Queen of England, let alone of Australia.

Keating continued to fuel the republican fire by announcing in Sydney on 26 June that he proposed to amend the oath of allegiance in the *Citizenship Act* by deleting all reference to the Queen. The oath required new Australian citizens to swear 'true allegiance to Her Majesty Queen Elizabeth the Second, Queen of Australia, Her Heirs and Successors according to law.' The Prime Minister said he would replace the present oath with one in which new Australian citizens would make a commitment to Australia, its democratic way of life and its Constitution.

The Opposition denounced the proposal as 'part of Mr Keating's Irish agenda to turn Australia into a republic'.[5] Once again the Liberals allowed themselves to be seen as supporting an archaic attachment to an increasingly unpopular royal family, while the Labor Party was advocating more explicit commitment to Australia. The Liberals were confirming the libel that Keating had uttered back in February. Faced with the choice between an oath of citizenship that emphasised allegiance to the Queen and an oath that emphasised commitment to Australia, the Liberals went for the Queen. They were becoming the un-Australian Party. Even the *Sydney Morning Herald* supported Keating, as did every other important newspaper in the country.

It took some time before the oath was officially changed. The Bill was shunted off to a Senate Committee before being carried in the Senate on 29 September 1993. It was a tight vote: 33 votes to 32. The Democrats and Greens supported the Government against the Coalition and Senator Brian Harradine from Tasmania. The Coalition had opposed the removal of an oath which requires new Australian citizens to swear allegiance to 'Her Majesty Queen Elizabeth the Second Her Heirs and Successors' and its replacement with an oath which pledges that:

> From this time forward [under God], I pledge my loyalty to Australia and its people, whose democratic beliefs I share, whose rights and liberties I respect, and whose laws I will uphold and obey.

A new preamble to the new law refers to Australia's cultural diversity, democratic beliefs, the reciprocal rights and obligations of citizenship and the common bond of citizenship.

The libel that all republicans were embittered Irish Catholics continued to develop as an effective slur on the republican cause. It was somewhat unfortunate that a number of the republic's supporters tended to indulge a little too much in Irish sentimentality.

I have always found it rather bizarre that Australians who are separated from Ireland by many generations continue to revel in their Irishness in a way that Australians from other parts of the British Isles do not. Proponents of the republic should not bundle it up with half-remembered wounds inflicted on the Irish Catholics, or for that matter any other ethnic group, of past generations. It doesn't help. The republic is an Australian aspiration not an Irish one.

The bad news from London continued to undermine the monarchist cause. A number of illegal tape recordings of conversations emerged. In one the Princess of Wales (allegedly) conducted a very intimate conversation with a male friend. The conversation reinforced the impression that her marriage was a disaster and suggested she might be as indifferent to her marital vows as her husband. The next tape was (allegedly) that of Prince Charles and his mistress,

Camilla Parker-Bowles. It was an intimate conversation of the most revealing kind. Those who were able to get over the outrage that such intimate conversations were being eaves-dropped upon at all, could only reflect that Prince Charles had absorbed very little of the English romantic tradition during his extensive, and expensive, education.

Shortly before the release of the Charles and Camilla tele-phone tape, Quadrant Research conducted another poll. This showed another increase in support for the republic, at a new high of 65 per cent. Even more interestingly, it showed that 51 per cent of Liberal and National Party voters also favoured a republic. A large majority (82 per cent) of Australians polled wanted Australia to remain a member of the Commonwealth. Paddy McGuinness, writing in the *Australian*, said this was a rebuff to the Australian Republi-can Movement — overlooking the fact that the ARM's plat-form actually advocated Australia remaining in the Commonwealth as a republic.

Both Government and Opposition had been in election mode for the previous year, and when the election date of 13 March was announced in February, it only served to quicken the political tempo. The ARM, consistent with its desire to prevent the republic becoming a party political issue, again decided to lie low during the campaign. Together with other members of the ARM, I urged the leadership of the Liberal Party to maintain an open mind on the issue. At that time the federal leadership both at the parliamentary and organi-sational level had no difficulty on that score. Their own pri-vate polling was showing a majority in favour of a republic and even showed 45 per cent of their own supporters being in favour.

On 24 February 1993 Paul Keating gave the Labor Party's policy speech at Bankstown Town Hall. He spoke briefly about the republic:

It is perhaps in part because Australians are growing in confidence that more and more of them are questioning whether it is appropriate for Australia to have as its head of state the monarch of another country.

Many Australians — some surveys suggest a majority — believe that we will be better able to succeed in the world with the unique and unambiguous identity which an Australian head of state, chosen by the Australian people, could provide.

While it is far from the most pressing matter facing the nation, it is nevertheless important that we do not let this decade leading to the centenary of the Federation pass without advancing the debate.

To do this we will set up a broadly based committee of eminent Australians, including representatives of the States, to develop a discussion paper which considers the options for a Federal Republic of Australia.

Any options developed by the committee would not seek to change our way of Government, only to have an Australian, chosen by Australians, as Australia's head of state.

I would like to extend an invitation to the Opposition to participate in the workings of this committee.

It would be the intention that as a result of this committee's deliberations and the public discussion that would follow, the Australian people would be in a position to decide by referendum later in the decade whether Australia should become a republic by the year 2001.

John Hewson was no longer prepared to defend the monarchy, the polls had put an end to that. He simply dismissed the republican element in Keating's speech as 'a facile distraction', observing there was 'not one job in it'. Tim Fischer commented that if at the end of the debate there was a majority in favour of a republic he would go along with it.

The following week saw another conservative convert. Gerard Henderson is Executive Director of the Sydney Institute, a conservative think-tank. Writing in the *Sydney Morning Herald* he justified his support for a republic by pointing to the appalling prospect of a King Charles III of Australia. He referred to a speech made by Prince Charles in

December 1992 to a learned academy in France. The heir to the throne of Australia (*inter alia*) went out of his way to praise French protectionism and French farmers. France, Charles proclaimed, 'sets the rest of us an inspiring example of civilised values ... underpinned ... by giving due importance to the kind of rural traditions without which it would be impossible to enjoy the way of life that recognises the importance of elements in our lives which enrich and ennoble us, but which are not "cost effective" in strictly economic terms'.

> The future King of England (and Australia) was lending his support to the protectionist policies of the French government. And, by implication, he was identifying with militant French farmers who maintain that the highly protectionist European Common Agricultural Policy is not protectionist enough.[6]

Henderson was quite right, of course. The European Community's protectionist approach to agriculture was one of the factors bankrupting rural Australia. And here was the heir to the Australian throne encouraging the selfish policies of inefficient French farmers at the expense of the efficient Australian farming community.

As the campaign came to an end, Hewson promised his own review of the Constitution and options for a republic. And then the unbelievable happened. Labor was re-elected with an increased majority.

CHAPTER TEN

The Monarchists

On 4 June 1992 a group of well-known Australians launched the charter of a group called 'Leadership Beyond Politics — Australians for Constitutional Monarchy'. The Foundation Council of the new monarchists' group included Sir John Atwill, a former President of the Liberal Party, Mr Neville Bonner AO, an Aborigine and former Liberal Senator, Mr Richard Cobden, a solicitor and President of the Sydney Gay and Lesbian Mardi Gras, Sir Harry Gibbs, formerly Chief Justice of Australia, Justice Michael Kirby, President of the New South Wales Court of Appeal, Dame Leonie Kramer, the Chancellor of Sydney University, Alderman Doug Sutherland, formerly Lord Mayor of Sydney, and Mr Lloyd Waddy QC, a Sydney barrister.

The monarchists kicked off with a meeting in Sydney attended by about 400 people. As might be expected from the monarchist support base we see reflected in the polls, they were mostly in the older age groups. They sang *Advance Australia Fair*, which, I was told, sounded half-hearted. This may have been because they had not yet learned the words. Then, with considerably more gusto, they sang *God Save the Queen*. They published a charter, the principal author of which was Michael Kirby. Justice Kirby is one of Australia's best-known, and most widely published, lawyers. So his views should command our close attention. Under the heading 'Why We Support the Australian System of Government', the monarchists set out their case. We shall examine it carefully. I have not set it out in full, because much of it is very repetitive, but I have taken care not to overlook any of their arguments.

1 **Constitutional History** — The Crown is part of Australia's history. It is a reminder of the long struggle for constitutional reform and freedom to which we in Australia are heirs. It is no less Australian because its story began in England. Inescapably, the Queen of Australia provides in her person an authentic reminder to all Australians of the history of our freedoms; of the great struggles over the centuries to secure them; and of the transient nature of contemporary political debates and the importance of always perceiving current events from the perspective of a constitutional history which stretches back for more than a millennium.

2 **Free, Tolerant and Temperate** — The freest, most tolerant, stable and temperate societies in the world today tend to be constitutional monarchies. The Netherlands, Denmark, Norway and Sweden are good examples. Spain was rescued from Fascism, division and strife by the unity provided by a constitutional monarchy. Of the 24 advanced democratic economies in the OECD half are constitutional monarchies ... Republics on the other hand are much more common. With few notable exceptions they have tended to be prone to populist politics and military pretensions. In the name of the 'People' republican governments all too frequently do great wrongs.

3 **Limiting Populist Politics** — A glance around the world today demonstrates the peril of populist politics. It is often of the nature of those who are engaged in political life to fall victim to delusions of grandeur, coming to a view of their own indispensability. Where ministers, judges and officials are appointed in the name of the Crown, they are reminded by that designation of the fact that they are servants of the whole people, delegated for a time only with the responsibility of power.

4 **Opponents' Shallow Arguments** — The fact that Australia shares its monarch with Canada, New Zealand, Papua New Guinea and many other countries of the Commonwealth of Nations is a proper source of pride in an age of divisive nationalism …The notion that Australia should change a system of government that works perfectly well for it because unspecified Asian societies are said to be 'confused' is a paltry argument. It underestimates the sophistication of our Asian neighbours and patronises them. Many Asian countries are monarchies; Japan, Thailand and Malaysia would regard it as ludicrous that we should feel it necessary to change our Australian system of government to save explaining monarchy to them!

5 **A Personal Living Symbol** — From time to time in the nation's affairs it is necessary to rise above divisive political debates; to represent the things we hold in common as Australians. Countries which do not enjoy the system of constitutional monarchy are forced to create such symbols from other things. In some such countries, citizens put their hands on their heart when the national song is sung. They venerate a Bill of Rights, a Declaration of Independence or some other document. They revere the flag. But for us in Australia, the existence of a living symbol in the form of the Queen, above politics, provides a more tangible representation of national unity, than songs, paper and bunting can possibly provide.

6 **Modern and International Monarchy** — The monarchy today in Australia is both modern and international. Many of the arguments voiced for a republic in Australia

resound with the calls of outmoded, divisive, nineteenth-century republicanism rather than a commitment to the needs of Australia today. After Hiroshima, in a world so profoundly changed, where the Queen visits regularly by intercontinental jet and in a country which has embraced the diversity of multiculturalism, the demand for provincial nationalism is singularly unconvincing. We in Australia should be building and reinforcing, not recklessly destroying, international institutions which we share with other lands. The calls to republican nationalism are the antithesis of diverse, tolerant, multicultural Australia.

7 **Leadership Beyond Politics** — Sometimes the Queen and her representatives, and members of her family, can give leadership on issues in ways which politicians and officials often find difficult or impossible. For example, President Reagan could not mention the acronym AIDS during the first four years of his presidency of his American republic for fear of perceived political consequences. Hundreds of thousands of his citizens became infected whilst he was silent. In Britain and Australia it was different. The Princess of Wales took an early lead in reaching out to people living with HIV and AIDS. In Australia the Queen's representative took the initiative to found the AIDS Trust.

8 **A Monarchy of Service** — For the whole period of Australian Federation, despite the most profound changes in our country's history and in the world, we have been specially fortunate with our monarchs ... They have set standards of service, dedication to duty, personal simplicity, integrity and honesty ... In a world of constant change, the Crown provides an element of continuity and stability.

9 **'If It Isn't Broken, Don't Fix It'** — It is trite to say, but it needs to be said, that the form of government embodied in our Constitution has served the Commonwealth and people of Australia well for nearly a century... Under it liberty has flourished and democracy has prevailed for

the best part of the century. These facts are and should be a matter of pride within Australia and a matter of encouragement to less fortunate, less democratic lands.

The Crown is certainly part of our history. But it is hardly a reminder of a struggle for freedom, especially since that struggle, both in the United Kingdom and Australia, was waged by ordinary citizens and their parliamentary representatives against the Crown. The assertion that the Crown is an Australian institution is, of course, the 'big lie' of the whole monarchist case, although it is often repeated. Shortly after being made executive director of Australians for Constitutional Monarchy Tony Abbott, speaking to a Senate Committee, said: 'Support for the Queen, the flag and the Constitution (is) part of being Australian.'[1] As we have seen, the Crown is an entirely British institution and has always been seen as such by Australians, including its most devoted admirer, Sir Robert Menzies.

The monarchy is not Australian simply because the monarchy is established by laws of the United Kingdom, beyond the ability of our Parliament to alter. The monarch must be a member of the Church of England. If Prince Charles, in his restless search for meaning, embraced the Roman Catholic Church or became a Muslim he would not be able to succeed to the throne. And yet a man as otherwise rational and intelligent as Michael Kirby will contend that this thoroughly sectarian institution is a reminder to Australians of our 'long struggle for constitutional reform and freedom'.

One of the many struggles for freedom waged by people in Australia, and the United Kingdom, was the struggle for religious tolerance. It is not so long ago that nobody but Protestants were allowed to be members of parliament, study at a university or sit on the bench as judges. The British monarchy, far from being a reminder of freedom is a reminder of prejudice, bigotry and the second-class status which a Protestant elite inflicted on those people who practised a different religion.

The disgracefully un-Australian aspect of this is that our own Constitution guarantees religious freedom. Section 116 provides:

> The Commonwealth shall not make any law for establishing any religion, or for imposing any religious observance, or for prohibiting the free exercise of any religion, and no religious test shall be required for any office or public trust under the Commonwealth.

If the monarchy is, as Michael Kirby asserts, an Australian institution, then why is it not subject to Australian laws? The answer is, of course, that the monarchy is not Australian any more than it is an 'office or public trust under the Commonwealth'. The Constitution makes it quite clear that the Commonwealth was established 'under the Crown of the United Kingdom of Great Britain and Ireland'. In other words, the succession to the Crown of the United Kingdom is a matter for its Parliament, and not ours. Our monarchy is *ex officio* and we have as our Head of State whoever is the Head of State of the United Kingdom. If Britain became a republic, the British President would become the Australian Head of State — and until we had amended our Constitution there would be nothing Australians could do about it.

It is preposterous to suggest that the political stability of Australia has anything to do with the British monarchy. The monarchists apparently have too little respect for their fellow Australians to imagine that political stability is due to the good sense of Australians. But let us suppose, just for a minute, that the monarchists are right, and that the Queen is a wondrous force for political stability. If that were so, then we should stop being so selfish. We should become a republic and allow that wondrous stability-giving royal family to concentrate on its other realms. The Queen's principal realm is the United Kingdom of Great Britain and Northern Ireland. There is a civil war in Northern Ireland and as a direct consequence of that, the IRA is letting off bombs in

Great Britain. If she could get out of her occasional royal visits to Australia those few extra days of giving stability to Belfast could make all the difference. What about Canada? The French half of Canada wants to secede and the English-speaking half cannot agree on what to do with the balance. Or what about Grenada? Her Majesty's sublime presence was not sufficient to prevent the US marines from invading and overthrowing the Government in 1979. And of course there is Papua New Guinea. Her Majesty's stabilising presence is desperately needed in Bougainville. And finally Fiji: if the Queen had not been so busy stabilising Australia during the Bicentenary she could have had a tea party in Suva and stopped the coup.

It is easy to poke fun at the puerile reasoning so typical of the monarchists' arguments. It is subject to the same logical fallacy as the proposition: The Australian Don Bradman was a great batsman, therefore all great batsmen are Australians. The longest-standing monarchy in the world is that of Japan. The stability and harmony induced by the reign of the Japanese monarchies did not prevent that country going to war in 1941. The Chinese Emperors were overthrown by revolutionaries who established a republic. Is it seriously contended China was better governed under a monarchy? Our political system owes a lot to Britain, and to other countries. But the achievements and failures of Australia can only be sheeted home to Australians.

Every nation in the world is different, and every nation's particular system of government has characteristics unique to itself. There is no doubt that many modern constitutional monarchies are able to serve as non-political, living symbols of the nation and its people in a way that party politicians cannot. But there is something about the monarchies of the Netherlands, Denmark, Norway and Spain that is different from the monarchy in Australia. The Queen of the Netherlands is Dutch, the Queen of Denmark is a Dane, the King of Norway is Norwegian, the King of Spain is Spanish — and unlike 'our' monarch all of these Kings and Queens actually live in their own countries.

Monarchies have inherent problems of their own. Because the office of King, or Queen, is inherited there can be no guarantee that a particular monarch will be competent to fill the role. As Thomas Paine observed 200 years ago: 'An hereditary governor is as inconsistent as an hereditary author.' The modern constitutional monarchies will survive so long as the monarchs are capable of fulfilling their largely decorative and ceremonial roles with dignity.

The monarchists argue that many crimes have been committed in the name of the 'People', but just as many have been committed in the name of Kings and Queens. One of the least attractive aspects of a constitutional monarchy is that because government is administered in the name of the Crown, a quite unjustified lustre is added to what are straightforward political deeds.

It does seem puzzling that in order to remind ministers, judges and officials that they are appointed to act as servants of the whole people, we tell them they are appointed in the name of the Crown. Common sense would suggest that if you want to remind Australian public office holders that they are there to serve the people of this country, you would tell them precisely that. As it stands members of the Australian Parliament swear an oath that they 'will be faithful and bear true allegiance to Her Majesty Queen Elizabeth, Her Heirs and Successors according to law'.

We republicans may lack the subtlety of the monarchists, but it does seem right that if you say what you mean people are much more likely to understand you. Late in 1993 the Prime Minister announced that the oath of allegiance required of new Australian citizens would be changed from:

I swear by Almighty God that I will be faithful and bear true allegiance to Her Majesty Elizabeth the Second, Queen of Australia, Her Heirs and Successors according to law, and that I will faithfully observe the laws of Australia and fulfil my duties as an Australian citizen.

to:

From this time forward (under God), I pledge my loyalty
to Australia and its people, whose democratic beliefs I
share, whose rights and liberties I respect and whose
laws I will uphold and obey.

The new oath was finally passed into law by the Senate on
29 September 1993.

The oath required of members of parliament is set out in
the Constitution and cannot be changed other than by a constitutional amendment. When our Constitution is amended
to make Australia a republic we should replace the current
oath with one similar to that taken by new Australian
citizens.

One strong theme in the monarchists' arguments is a dis-
trust of 'divisive nationalism' or elsewhere in their charter,
'provincial nationalism'. While they will become so red-
faced as to endanger their health denying it, the truth is that
deep down, many of the supporters of the monarchy here
believe Australia is second-rate. They acknowledge that the
French, the Germans, the Malaysians, the Indonesians, the
Japanese, the Americans (and almost every other nation in
the world) is entitled to insist on having a Head of State
who is one its own citizens. They do not regard the Japanese
or the French as suffering from 'provincial' or 'divisive'
nationalism, because they regard Japan and France as being
nations in a way they cannot regard Australia as being one.

If the Queen were a genuinely international symbol, their
argument would have more validity. But the Queen is not
living in her own international enclave. She is not the mistress of her own destiny, above the laws of nations like some
sort of secular Pope. The Queen (and the monarchy) is a
British institution, governed by British laws. She lives in
Britain, she is supported by the taxpayers of Britain. When
she travels abroad she represents Britain, not Australia or
Papua New Guinea or Tuvalu.

The monarchists often argue that republicans are trying to
change Australia's Constitution to make it more acceptable
in Asia. This argument about Asia is a not-so-subtle piece of

racism. The real message they seek to convey is: Why should we change our system of government to suit all these coloured neighbours to our north? The answer is that we should not change our Constitution for that reason, and to the best of my knowledge nobody is suggesting we should. It is as difficult to explain the Australian monarchy to Japanese as it is to explain it to Germans or Brazilians or even Americans. Everyone, including the Japanese, Thais and Malaysians, understands the institution of monarchy. But the Emperor of Japan is Japanese, the King of Thailand a Thai and the King of Malaysia a Malay. The problem with our system is that our monarch is not Australian.

Nonetheless, the monarchists continue to contend that republicans believe we should 'reject this country's British cultural inheritance'[2] in order to become closer to Asia. Others have suggested we want Australia to become Asian.

It is very misleading even to use the term 'Asia' and 'Asian'. The differences (in every respect) between Bengalis and Koreans, or between Japanese and Indonesians, is so considerable that generalising about Asia and the Asians is almost completely fatuous. 'Asian' is almost a meaningless concept, except when used as a geographical adjective — and even there the area covered is so vast that it serves only to draw a (contentious) distinction between Asia and other continents.

The monarchists have attempted to distort an argument I made as far back as a National Press Club Speech I delivered on 18 March 1992:

> ... many Asians are sceptical about our commitment. Are we part of Asia, or are we (spiritually at least) moored in the mid-Atlantic between New York and London? I do not believe we should tailor our affairs to gratify our neighbours, but a real nation is perceived as such by other nations.

Barely two weeks after the launch of the Australian Republican Movement in July 1991 an editorial headed 'Kingdom of the Blind' appeared in *Asiaweek*.[3]

The cold war discouraged tinkering with national institutions — however much they might be riddled with anachronisms. But no one is afraid of the Russians any more, and people everywhere are giving the musty old status quo a good shaking. Few countries are immune from the temper of renewal ... And now, reappraisal of the establishment has begun to agitate Australians.

Elizabeth the Second, by the Grace of God, Queen of Australia sounds downright silly in Jakarta and Manila. Not that South-east Asians would ever say so; they no more desire to stick their noses in Australia's internal affairs than they welcome Canberra's occasional interference in their own. *But distant royal connections are vaguely disturbing to neighbours with whom Australians have been anxious to strengthen their position.* Although overtures of friendship have so far won less than unrestrained enthusiasm, most Asians recognise that in this case geography ought to take precedence over history and culture. Australia's eagerness to be accepted is akin to Turkey's ambition to be considered part of Europe. *A sign of commitment would help its cause. Asians are therefore observing with interest moves in Australia to declare the country a republic.*

...

Having a foreign lady as head of state detracts from nationhood ... It is a matter of urgency for Australia to fashion a place for itself in the new world order. *As Britain disappears into Europe, the link to Buckingham Palace looks sillier and sillier.* But a republic would be more than an overdue constitutional correction. Australia must recognise that its future lies with the Asian Community of Nations. Most Asians agree that Australia has a rightful place there, but membership is not automatic. It is Australia's natural destiny to be a rich, important and powerful nation of the 21st century, a thickly populated, pluralist society of industrious immigrants. Only Australians can decide whether they really want that. If they do, it might be a good idea to send a signal by cutting the royal apron strings. [Emphasis added]

Exactly this point has been echoed in the statements of the Foreign Minister, Gareth Evans. Nick Greiner, in an interview with the *Sydney Morning Herald* on 19 June 1993, said he had recently been on a trip to six Asian nations and was amazed that local people stressed the significance of Australia's becoming a republic. 'It didn't occur to me that this would be a matter of interest in Malaysia, but it is. There is a strong view that it symbolises to the world the nature of our priorities.'

The Hong Kong based investment banker Michael Dobbs-Higginson in his new book, *Asia Pacific: Its Role in the New World Disorder* writes of the republican objective:

> If achieved, this restructuring of Australia's identity should give it a greater sense of self-confidence. And it should facilitate considerably the improvement of its relations with its Asian neighbours. It could also make it easier for Asia to consider Australia as a free and independent member of the Asia Pacific region.

Australian Financial Review foreign editor, Stephen Mills, recently wrote that if Dr Hewson was looking for reasons to support a republic he should examine the 'bizarre anomalies that the monarchy inflicts on Australia's trade diplomacy'. In an article titled 'Queen Confuses Trade Diplomacy' he wrote:

> ... a senior Australian diplomat based in Europe was surprised recently to be told that the Queen — Australia's Head of State — was about to pay a visit to the country in which he serves.

This piece of information was conveyed to him not by Canberra but by his counterpart from the British Embassy.

> When the 'Queen of Australia' arrived, she opened a British Trade Fair and promoted on behalf of the British exhibitors. She spoke about the British economy and

espoused British trade policy. Her visit was arranged by the British Embassy.

...

> But when ... the Governor-General travels abroad, he frequently has less access and less influence precisely because he is not seen as the 'real' Head of State.

...

> In terms of protocol, a Governor-General is only a vice-regal, not a regal, figure. He is not on a par with, say, the president of a republic. As such, his level of influence is inevitably diminished.

> As one diplomatic source put it, the Governor-General 'might only get an official lunch instead of a full State dinner'.

...

> Australia should have a Head of State who is an authentic and effective advocate for Australian commercial interests abroad.

A practical example of the above occurred in the mid-1980s when Sir Ninian Stephen was forced to cancel a visit to Indonesia because Indonesia's President Suharto refused to participate in the welcoming party. He quite rightly identified the Queen and not the Governor-General as the Head of State of Australia.

Governor-General Bill Hayden visited France in 1993 to commemorate the 75th anniversary of battles on the Western Front in which thousands of Australians died defending French territory. Writing in the *Bulletin*, Laurie Oakes observed:

> His program shows that the highest French official with whom he came in contact was the veterans affairs minister and when he left he was farewelled only by a ministerial staffer. No one regarded as a genuine head of state would be treated so dismissively.[4]

During the course of the Republic Advisory Committee

inquiry I received hundreds of letters relating to various aspects of the republican debate. Two of the most interesting were from the Asian–Australian Resource Centre (AARC) and the Australian Malaysian–Singapore Association. Both letters were unsolicited. The first of these said:

> Australia is an evolving nation with people seeking and forging a new identity. While the past history of Australia has to be acknowledged, the moulds from the past do not totally fit or suit an Australia which is vibrantly multicultural and different from the past. Evolution means past configurations have to mesh in, coalesce with, more contemporary, appropriate ones. Becoming a republic is one aspect of this evolutionary process.

The second, from the Australian Malaysian–Singapore Association, said:

> We see the Republic issue as a matter of crucial and urgent importance. We also see it as being inextricably tied to Australia's quest for closer links with Asia. We believe it will determine how Australia is perceived in this region and the rest of the world.
> ...
> The present constitution may have served Australia well, but that is not because it was framed by men of genius but because of the qualities of the Australian people. It may have been adequate in a previous era when the world was a very different place. It is no longer adequate to Australia's future.

The final word on this whole issue of relations with our region and trade in general goes to someone who should know a little about trade: the Chairman of Austrade, Bill Ferris. In a speech titled 'The Republican Advantage: A Marketing Opportunity for Australia's Exports', he had this to say:

In these tough economic times, many people argue that the Republican debate is irrelevant, and perhaps even a dangerous distraction from the main game of boosting Australia's economic performance.

But I take a different view ... A move by Australia to a Republic status would, in my view, present a windfall marketing opportunity to Australian exporters. Getting the international market's attention is always a challenge, but especially if your image has become outmoded and possibly harmful to the promotion of your products and services.

...

And this is where the Republic comes in. Being a republican is neither about being arrogant, nor about being thankless and embarrassed about our past. It assumes a certain pride and self-confidence derived from an understanding of one's history combined with a clear sense of an independent way ahead.

The Republic comes in as a rare (indeed one-time) opportunity to focus the world's attention on a fresh and invigorated Australian image. I tie these two things together because it is not possible to properly present an image abroad if it is not first built on and derived from a self-image. Taking hold of our national identity at home will help us promote it overseas more confidently.

The Republic will be an opportunity on a grand scale for us to remind ourselves, and to showcase to the world, that Australia is not a second-rate, derivative, one-dimensional society ... The process towards a Republic offers us a marketing opportunity like no other to achieve an important advance in this re-definition of self and representation of Australia in our major markets abroad.

...

Becoming a Republic is partly a symbolic exercise, but the power of this symbol is immense. It will provide a perfect opportunity to update and re-frame our mental image of ourselves — and to promote that new image to the world. The process is not a distraction from the real issues; handled sensibly, it will provide a very real boost to national exports.

Australia's identity should be Australian. Our culture is an English-language one. Our institutions are more influenced by British models than by those of other countries, although we should not overlook the contribution of other nations (especially the United States). A change of the Head of State does not make us 'Asian' any more than it constitutes 'a rejection of our British cultural inheritance'. There are considerably more teachers, and students, of British literature in the United States than there are in the United Kingdom, and in many areas of British cultural studies (particularly literature) the leading writers are predominantly American. There is more to our culture than the royal family.

Indeed, our English-language culture is of enormous advantage to us in this region. Our first language, English, is the second language of almost every country in the Asia–Pacific region (other than those where it is the first). In that respect it is often easier for us to communicate with Japanese and Malaysians than it is for them to communicate with each other.

The best way for us to deal with all of our neighbours, in Asia or elsewhere, is to be true to ourselves; to be Australian and to be proud of that. As long as we have the British Queen as our Head of State, other nations everywhere, not just in Asia, will regard us as somewhat less than independent.

In Asia, our diplomats are ashamed of the monarchy. I have seen more than one Australian embassy where the portrait of the Queen is not hung. Whenever I notice the absence of the Queen's portrait I ask why it is not there, and the answer is always the same. Hanging the Queen's portrait in an Australian embassy only invites, at worst, confusion — and at best, embarrassing questions as to why the Queen of England is occupying pride of place on an Australian wall.

This confusion is hardly surprising. If we were to visit South Korea, for example, and if we were to notice that the coins were all impressed with the profile of the Emperor of Japan, and if we saw the Emperor's picture in public offices and if the Government was conducted 'in the name of the Emperor...', would we not suspect that in some way or other Korea was still subordinate to, or dependent on, Japan? If the Koreans hastened to add that the Emperor's title for use in Korea was 'Emperor of Korea', would that change our minds? Or would we note that the Emperor lived in Tokyo, represented Japan when he travelled abroad and was paid for by the Japanese taxpayer?

The monarchists continually assert that the monarchy represents the things Australians hold in common. One is reminded of Humpty Dumpty's remark to Alice in Lewis Carroll's *Through the Looking Glass*:

When I use a word, it means just what I choose it to mean — neither more nor less.

How can a public office, that of the Head of State, which can only be occupied by the Protestant descendants of a particular British family, constitute an institution which represents those things Australians hold in common? It would be more correct to say that the monarchy represents things which are not held by any Australians.

The monarchists are scornful of nations, like the United States, who 'venerate a piece of paper' such as their Declaration of Independence or their Bill of Rights. Those pieces of paper are the record of Americans' struggle for independence from the British Crown. They establish in a legally binding document the rights and liberties of every American citizen. It almost beggars the imagination that a group of rational, educated Australians would prefer to bow and curtsy to a foreign monarch rather than pay respect to the institutions and anthems of their own country. It is hard to avoid reaching the conclusion that they are somehow or other ashamed of those institutions that are distinctly and unequivocally Australian, and would prefer to continue to venerate an institution from another country.

The monarchy is not, as we have seen, an international institution, but a British one which a number of other countries are also allowed to make use of as their Head of State. It is extraordinary that the monarchists would defend the Crown on the basis that it is a multicultural institution. One of the arguments against retention of the British monarchy in Australia is that it represents only one of the cultural traditions which have melded together to form our Australian culture. People have come to Australia from many lands and many cultures. The things we all have in common are those things that are Australian. A grandchild of English migrants may have some sense of cultural connection with the British monarchy, but will a grandchild of Italian or Chinese migrants?

It is rarely appropriate to vilify the arguments of your opponents, but it is not possible other than to despise that part of the monarchist charter which claims that monarchies are more responsive to the tragedy of AIDS than are republics. It is hardly surprising that the 75-year-old Ronald Reagan, whose own political beliefs were intensely conservative, was slower to come to terms with the AIDS epidemic than the 30-year-old Princess of Wales. The difference in their respective attitudes may say a lot about the conservatism of the Republican Party in the United States, the differences between the generations or even the differences between the United States and Great Britain. But to suggest that it is relevant to the monarchy-versus-republic debate is ludicrous. It is also quite contemptible. AIDS is an intensely emotional and tragic issue. To try to enlist the emotion generated by that epidemic on the side of the monarchy is a cynical exploitation of human suffering to support a political argument.

The fact is — and Michael Kirby knows this as well as anyone — that in Australia both politicians and Governors-General and Governors were active in taking steps to control the AIDS epidemic. The AIDS Trust which Michael Kirby says was founded 'on the initiative of the Queen's

representative' was heavily supported by government fund-
ing and the Governor-General accepted the position of
Patron on behalf of the Australian Government. An Australian President would have done exactly the same thing.

The monarchists contend that the Crown is a symbol of
continuity. But continuity of what? The continuity provided
by the Crown is that of the appearance of political subordination to Great Britain. It is a symbol without substance,
because Australia is no longer politically subordinate to
Britain — but it nonetheless misleads and confuses because
instead of providing Australians with a national symbol
that is unequivocally Australian, it offers one which is, for
all the world to see, thoroughly British.

The last, and most dependable, argument of the monarchists is to say 'If it ain't broke, don't fix it'. This is really
cave-man conservatism, for after all there would have been
no human progress if our ancestors had not striven to
improve. One might more appropriately ask, 'If it's of no
use, why have it?' The fact is, however, that the institution
of monarchy in Australia is now well and truly 'broken'.
How can the monarchy function as a symbol of unity and
nationhood when more than half of the population wish to
have it replaced by a republic?

The poverty of the arguments of the monarchists is one of
the reasons public support for a republic has grown as
quickly as it has. The problem the monarchists have is that it
is no longer acceptable to state the truth about the monarchy: that it is a British institution which, insofar as it represents anything in Australia, represents Britain and the
British Commonwealth. It does not now, any more than it
ever has in the past, represent the Australian nation.

In June 1993 Australians for Constitutional Monarchy
released a pamphlet, somewhat ironically titled *Monarchy or
Republic?: Read the Facts and Then Decide,* which deliberately
set out to mislead Australians about the Constitution. It
preyed on ignorance and sought to promote and enhance
ordinary Australians' ignorance. For example, it states that
'Australia has been an independent nation since 1901'.
In fact, as we have seen, Australia neither sought, nor

obtained, independence at the time of Federation.

The monarchists must have been aware of this. After I pointed this out to Mr Abbott on national TV, a second version of the pamphlet was printed which said:

> Australia has been completely independent at least since the passage of the *Statute of Westminster* in 1942 ...

Another classic error in the original pamphlet stated that the Governor-General makes no laws, and does not direct government policy, *but has the authority to approve or reject all laws, on behalf of the people of Australia* (my emphasis). As Mr Abbott and his colleagues should know, neither the Governor-General nor the Queen has any discretion in granting royal assent to legislation if so advised by the Government of the day. The monarchists were attributing to the Crown an independent discretion that it has not claimed for itself for at least 150 years! Not surprisingly, the highlighted passage does not appear in the second version of the pamphlet.

It is remarkable how the monarchist cause has attracted to itself, like a political magnet, some of the ugliest and most prejudiced elements in our society. During the public consultation phase of the Republic Advisory Committee, I was asked by a man at the Sydney meeting why the republican push was dominated by Irish Catholics. He then proceeded to name Keneally, Kelly, Keating and Fahey. I, in jest, mentioned to him that he had forgotten O'Kostakidis, O'Turnbull, O'Winterton and O'Greiner. He responded by saying he could explain Mr Greiner being a republican: his wife was a Catholic!

On another occasion we visited Canberra for a public meeting at the National Conference Centre. It was a well-attended meeting of more than 200 people. As was the normal course of events, we had a number of prepared speakers who had some expertise in the areas that the committee was investigating. One of those was Professor John Molony, former Professor of Australian History from the Australian National University. Professor Molony had recently returned from three years in Ireland at the University of Dublin, where he had taught both Australian and Italian history. It was a scholarly address that mentioned in passing how a large number of Irish and Italian people had posed the question, 'Why was Australia not a Republic?'

We then heard from other speakers and took questions from the floor. The first speaker identified himself as Tony Miller, Chairman of the Canberra branch of Australians for Constitutional Monarchy. Early on in his remarks he stated:

> ... it's an observation that we've been listening to the Turnbulls and the Molonys and the Galligans and one might be forgiven for thinking that we've walked in on the southern Australian chapter of the Irish Republican Army.

Not surprisingly this resulted in some disquiet within the audience. But instead of moderating his remarks, Mr Miller got worse.

> Professor John Molony who is just returned from Ireland seemed to be rather surprised that the Irish and Italians were asking us why we weren't a republic. Now it strikes me as somewhat odd that the two countries whose history and political heritage are so far removed from democracy should be questioning the democratic institutions of Australia. Let's not forget that it was the Italians that gave us the fascists and Mr Mussolini and it's the Irish who've given us blowing up women and children as a means of solving a political debate in their country.

There was considerable uproar in the meeting including the cry from some people that this was 'racial vilification'. At the conclusion of Mr Miller's comments, I responded in these terms:

> Let me simply make this observation. I believe that Australians see themselves as Australians, not delving into each other's pasts to determine ethnic or racial

backgrounds. I thought we'd grown out of all of that. I find this sort of ridiculous Orange Lodge circa 1821 bigotry against Roman Catholics quite despicable. If it's of any interest to Mr Miller, whose understanding of ethnicity is perhaps not as great as his deep understanding of constitutional law, Turnbull is not even an Irish name. Indeed, not that I'd think there's anything turns on it, my forebears built the first Presbyterian church in this country. I might add also, that the first proponent of a republic in Australia was none other than John Dunmore Lang, the first Presbyterian clergyman in Australia, who gave one of his first communions in the church that my forebear John Turnbull built. So, I think that we would all be well advised to avoid caricaturing either side of this debate in terms of ethnic, racial or religious grounds. It is a despicable business to characterise our fellow Australians in little religious or ethnic boxes. I happen to think that the most important thing about the republican cause is that it offers to represent the one thing that every Australian has in common and that is not his religion, not his ethnicity, not his political party, but the fact that we are Australians and this is the one country, the one place to which we owe our first and foremost commitment as citizens of this great, secular egalitarian nation.

Shortly after I spoke, another person attending the meeting, Mr Michael Corscadden, rose and with a strong Belfast Irish accent explained:

Twenty years ago, I came to this country and this town to build a new life, and to get away from sectarianism, bitterness, hate. I thought I'd succeeded until tonight and this gentleman [pointing to Mr Miller], and I use the word advisedly, sitting staring at me at the front just gave me a feeling of déjà vu. I thought I was back in Belfast 20 years ago. You're a slur, you insulted me, you insulted most of the people of this country, who immigrated here for a better life. You do yourself no service. You do your cause a great disservice.

The meeting concluded and I hoped that would be the end of it. But unfortunately I was wrong.

A couple of days later I received a letter from Mr Corscadden in which he detailed the events referred to above and then told me:

This afternoon I answered my home telephone to a male voice which, in a quiet, controlled and intense fashion proceeded to tell me that 'we have ways of dealing with IRA trash like you. We string them up...'

On 26 July Mr Corscadden appeared on the Matt Abraham programme on Canberra Radio 2CN. As Mr Corscadden explained, subsequent to his letter to me he received a number of other similar telephone threats and then, 'The following day a rock came flying through my living room window'.

Following the media exposure on this issue, I spoke with Tony Abbott, the Executive Director of Australians for Constitutional Monarchy, who told me that Mr Miller was no longer the chairman of their ACT chapter. He then issued a press statement saying only their national chairman and directors were entitled to speak on their behalf. Nonetheless, on 3 September, less than six weeks after the public meeting, Mr Miller was speaking on Canberra radio again as the representative of Australians for Constitutional Monarchy in Canberra.

This 'ethnic explanation' was used by Robert Manne, the editor of the conservative monthly *Quadrant*, wrote in its March editorial this year:

Three groups in Australia care passionately for the republic.
    The first, of course, are the self-conscious Irish. Their folk memory is suffused with stories of harsh British rule in Ireland — of Cromwell and the famine and the Easter

Rising of 1916 — and of the sectarian struggles and the Protestant ascendancy in Australia. Irish Australians are instinctively both anti-British and anti-monarchy … In part at least, republicanism is their revenge.

The Irish Australian elite is not alone. The republican cause is of passionate interest to two other groups, the ethnic intelligentsia and the left. The ethnic intelligentsia have a variety of particular reasons, drawn from political struggles in their ancestral homelands, for cheering on republicanism. The kind of historical memories which made the Irish anti-British, make many Australian Greeks anti-monarchy and many Arabs anti-colonial.

As Gerard Henderson neatly put it:[5]

Never mind that such leading republicans as Malcolm Turnbull, Jenny Kee and David Williamson do not fit into any one of Manne's little (academic) boxes.

I responded to Manne's remarks after his editorial was reprinted in the *Age*.[6]

Apart from Tom Keneally and Geraldine Doogue I am not aware of any director of the Australian Republican Movement who is of obviously Irish descent, but then unlike Mr Manne I do not make a practice of characterising people by reference to their ancestry or religion. Those, like Mr Manne, who insist on doing so say a great deal about their own lack of national consciousness.

As one of the leading proponents of an Australian republic, I am puzzled which of Mr Manne's three categories of republicans I fall into. I am neither of Irish extraction nor a Roman Catholic. I would not qualify as a member of the ethnic intelligentsia on at least two grounds, and if Mr Manne regards me as a member of 'the left' I would hate to meet anyone he regards as being of 'the right'.

Mr Manne seems unable to appreciate that most Australians regard themselves as being Australian, not Irish, Scottish, Italian, Chinese, etc. and their enthusiasm for a republic is an expression of Australian national pride, and nothing more. They believe their Australian identity is more important than their ethnic background, their religion or their political philosophy.

The cause of the republic is the cause of the Australian nation. It is a means of affirming that Australia is not just an expression of geography, an enormous caravan park full of transients looking back to their real homes far away.

The republic will unite Australians, affirming the one thing all Australians have in common, their love of this land and its people above all others.

When the monarchists are not lambasting republicans because their forebears were Greek, or their religion is Catholic, they claim that a republican President would be a 'virtual dictator' as Sir Harry Gibbs said, ignoring the fact that there is a greater chance under the current constitutional arrangements for collusion between the Prime Minister and Governor-General than there would be under a republic.

But perhaps the most remarkable contribution (apart from whatever he contributed to the charter of Australians for Constitutional Monarchy, discussed earlier in this chapter) came from Justice Michael Kirby when he appeared on a BBC programme hosted by Bob Hawke. Justice Kirby made some remarkable suggestions about what he would do if he were a republican.

If I were a republican I would be seeking to make radical changes. Abolishing the States, securing two levels of government, national and local, an elected President with completely different powers from the Governor-General. They are radical and true republican notions.

...

The debate will divide the Australian people very severely as it hots up. It would divide people if they are denigrated because they are of an older generation who don't happen to climb on a bandwagon ... if the anglo-celts, the old Australia, are in some way to be divided from new Australians who have some greater legitimacy.

I am thankful that Michael Kirby is not a republican. I have no idea where he got the idea that two tiers of government were somehow crucial to a republican platform. And his point about the older generation is also rather offensive. No group or section of the community should be left out, or feel unable to contribute to this debate. However, to imply that if older people don't like something we shouldn't change it is preposterous. And perhaps Michael Kirby should consider that the older generation should take some notice of young people, the people that will inherit this great country and that the views of 'new Australians' have as much legitimacy (but no more) as Michael's 'old Australia'.

As we have seen, the monarchists' most effective tactic is to raise the fear of unforeseen change. The republic will abandon our parliamentary system, threaten the rule of law, endanger the liberties of the citizen ... and induce horrible fungi in geraniums everywhere.

When I hear scaremongering about the terrors of life without the Queen, I am reminded of the verse of that great Australian poet, Victor Daley, about Queen Victoria's Diamond Jubilee procession in 1897. It is entitled 'A Treat for the London Poor'. The last verse reads:

Sixty years their gracious Queen has reigned a-holding
   up the sky,
And a-bringing round the seasons, hot and cold, and wet
   and dry;
And in all that time she's never done a deed deserving
   gaol —
So let joy-bells ring out madly and Delirium prevail!
O, her Poor will blessings pour
On their Queen whom they adore,
When she blinks with puffy eyes at them they'll hunger
   never more.

CHAPTER ELEVEN

Exploring the Options

For a few months after the March 1993 federal election it looked as though the ARM's most cherished objective was about to be achieved: bipartisan support for the republic. On 27 March 1993 the Liberal Premier of New South Wales, John Fahey, told a Liberal Party conference that it was inevitable Australia would become a republic by the year 2001. He urged Liberals to get involved in the debate.

A month later in a message to a republican function at the Marconi Club in Sydney the NSW Premier went further, saying:

> While we will be forever grateful for the wonderful institutions of law and democracy which we inherited from Britain, we must also accept that we are an evolving and uniquely Australian society.
> This is not just because of our rich multiculturalism.

Australians of British and Irish origins have also developed a new cultural independence, and are developing a constructive relationship with Aboriginal Australians.

We are what we are, not what we were.

It is inevitable that such comprehensive change will be recognised in new structures and institutions.

Above all, the debate about a republic should not become politicised or belong to one side of politics. This is the quickest way to divide, rather than build, a nation.

Mr Fahey's public conversion to the republican cause closely followed a newspaper article by Nick Greiner, the former Liberal Premier, in which Mr Greiner also endorsed the republican goal. Mr Fahey's views were endorsed by the Liberal Premier of Tasmania, Mr Ray Groom, the Country–Liberal Chief Minister of the Northern Territory, Mr Marshall Perron, and the Liberal Opposition Leader in South Australia, Mr Dean Brown. Only the Liberal Premiers of Western Australia and Victoria declined to get on the republican bandwagon.

A few days before, a Saulwick poll published in the *Sydney Morning Herald* disclosed that 70 per cent of voters questioned in New South Wales supported the idea of Australia becoming a republic. A republican Australia seemed not merely inevitable, but imminent. On 30 March the Legislative Assembly in New South Wales approved, on the voices, a motion endorsing the inevitability of the republic and supporting community consultation on the form and structure of an Australian republic.

Suddenly it seemed that many of the traditional supporters of the monarchy had vanished. Only Wal Murray, the then National Party Leader in New South Wales, and his federal counterpart, Tim Fischer, remained loyal to Her Majesty. 'Australia at the moment has got a lot of problems and the diversionary tactic of talking about referendums is rather stupid given the fact Australia has a large number of problems.'[1]

The outburst of conservative support for the republic followed Paul Keating's unexpected election victory. It appeared to most observers that a Labor defeat was certain, given that Labor had been in office for a decade and that the one million Australians who were unemployed represented the highest level of unemployment since the Great Depression in the 1930s. There was no doubt the people were angry and wanted to punish the Government.

The Liberal Party, led by former economics professor Dr John Hewson, confounded the pundits. Its election platform included the radical restructuring of government finances, including a new 15 per cent Goods and Services Tax as well as a shift away from publicly funded universal health coverage. The Liberals' policies were a product of the tough-minded economic rationalists who had taken over the Liberal Party during its years in Opposition.

The Australian electorate did not want Mr Keating, but they wanted Dr Hewson's GST and other reforms even less. The Liberals lost the unlosable election. They had committed the ultimate crime of any Opposition. They had made themselves unelectable. Their reaction to the election was one of shattered disbelief. Hewson announced the GST would be dropped from the Liberals' platform, then changed his mind and said it wouldn't be, and then had it changed for him by a parliamentary party who wanted to make a clean break from the policies that had cost him office. Hewson was retained as leader, but most commentators explained his re-election on the basis that there was no alternative available.

The republic had not been an issue in the election. Keating had mentioned it in his policy speech, and the applause was deafening, but Hewson did not rise to the debate. The Liberals' response during the election was consistently dismissive. The Labor Party was talking about the republic as a diversion, to avoid talking about unemployment. In truth the Labor Party was not saying much about the republic at all. It had no need of diversions. Hewson had already provided Labor with the ultimate diversion in the GST.

In fact the Liberal and Labor Party election policies on the republic were much closer than most people recognise. While Labor had promised to establish a committee to consider the options for a republic, the Liberals had proposed to give much the same brief to the Constitutional Centenary Foundation.

The period from late April to early May 1993 was probably the high point — so far — of republican support. The polls were very favourable, the Prime Minister was enthusiastically pushing the proposal and many Liberals were falling over themselves to declare as either republicans or inevitablists. This upsurge in support had occurred in just 21 months since the formation of the ARM in July 1991. Given that the increase in support had been so dramatic it is perhaps not surprising that we could not maintain that forward momentum. The Saulwick poll of September 1993 showed support for a republic had fallen four points: from 66 per cent to 62 per cent in favour. Then, in the last week of September, a Newspoll survey showed republicans trailing monarchists by 44 to 39. It was the first poll we had lost in 18 months. Although an AGB/McNair poll which appeared in the *Bulletin* 10 days afterwards showed republicans leading the monarchists by six points, the fact remains that the republican momentum had slowed. The important question, of course, was why.

Undoubtedly the media's description of the republican movement as 'Keating's Republic' is a two-edged sword for republicans. When Keating is riding high with the public, as he was after the surprise election win in March 1993, the polls appeared to reflect the pro-Keating enthusiasm. As his support waned with the difficulties over the tax cuts, the budget, *Mabo* and industrial relations, the support for the republic has suffered.

The monarchist group, Australians for Constitutional Monarchy, also lifted their game after the election. They appointed Tony Abbott as their executive director and for the first time had at their disposal a very articulate full-time advocate. Abbott was valuable to the monarchists not so much for what he said, but for who he was. At 36 years of age, he is much younger than their other spokesmen. He is a Roman Catholic and indeed a former seminarian. He is a graduate in law and a Rhodes Scholar. Since returning from Oxford 10 years ago he has worked as a journalist and a political adviser until early this year with John Hewson, whom he now professes to despise. He has worked for Bronwyn Bishop and is angling for a safe Liberal seat in the House of Representatives. Given the monarchist leanings of most rank-and-file Liberals, Abbott's acceptance of his present position is probably a shrewd way of garnering the support he needs to topple a sitting member.

His principal theme has been to promote a scare campaign. The republic, he has claimed, will put at risk all of our principles of democracy. A republican President could become a dictator. The republic is no more than a Labor Party plot to take over Australia and abolish the States, the Senate and all of our liberties. His credibility has started to suffer in recent times, however, because of his unwillingness to engage in any substantive discussion of the issues. He knows that he cannot win the intellectual debate and so has refused to engage in it. Shortly after the Republic Advisory Committee's report was published I was invited to engage in a debate with Abbott, moderated by Paul Kelly, editor of the *Australian*. Abbott agreed with me that conservatives like himself regard the most important function of the Head of State as defending the Constitution against abuse by the Government of the day. I pointed out that under the option I personally favoured, the new Head of State would not be instantly dismissed by the Prime Minister as is the Governor-General and that under the Committee's codification of the reserve powers the new Head of State would have the ability to refer suspected breaches of the Constitution by the Government to the High Court. I asked Abbott whether he conceded that such a Head of State would be better able to fulfil the very role conservatives regarded as most important. Abbott declined to answer the question.[2]

Bob Hawke was particularly unhelpful to the republican cause. He served as the presenter of a BBC programme on

Australian republicanism and spent most of his time both on and off camera endeavouring to embarrass the Prime Minister. The programme was selectively edited so as to damage the republican cause and in what must be one of the most extraordinary political untruths of all time Hawke stated that the monarchists were winning the intellectual debate. They may have been winning the debate, but certainly not on intellectual grounds.

Governor-General Bill Hayden observed in his interview with Hawke that if a republican President were elected to the office and if the reserve powers were left in their present undefined state there was considerable potential for conflict between the President and the Prime Minister. Hawke edited the interview so that Hayden appeared to be saying that conflict between the two office holders was an inevitable consequence of a change. Hayden was so annoyed by Hawke's conduct that he released the entire text of his interview to the press. Nonetheless, the damage done by the television programme was not fully repaired.

But more than all of these factors, the popularity of the republic was a victim of the leadership struggle within the Liberal Party. In my view it would be fair to characterise Hewson's personal position on the republic as broadly sympathetic. He is not particularly interested in the Constitution or its history and he certainly does not regard it as a burning issue. Like most politicians he is profoundly suspicious of his opponents and especially so of Mr Keating. Nonetheless in April 1993 the re-elected Hewson said:

> I have no doubt, given the shift of community attitudes, that the hardline monarchist position is out of touch with the realities of Australia today. The only way in the end you're going to make genuine changes is if you fully inform the electorate of the proposals.[3]

Hewson's April position was in fact very close to that of the Prime Minister, who had on 28 April established the Republic Advisory Committee. The Committee's terms of reference required it to produce an options paper describing the 'minimum constitutional changes necessary to achieve a viable federal republic of Australia while maintaining the effect of our current conventions and principles of government'.

Keating's aim in commissioning the report was to do precisely what John Hewson had said was so important, namely 'fully inform the electorate of the proposals'. The Report of the Committee was intended to provide a solid base of information about the fairly narrow range of options for replacing the British monarch with an Australian citizen as our Head of State.

Hewson's clear intention at this stage was to manoeuvre the Liberal Party to a position where it had an open mind on the republic and could not be painted as either a monarchist or republican party. Yet Darryl Williams, his shadow Attorney-General, had asked me in a private meeting on 22 April 1993, 'How do we get this issue off the political agenda?' Nothing was further from Hewson's mind at that time than manning the barricades in defence of the Queen.

However, Hewson's credibility and authority as leader of the parliamentary Liberal Party was very tenuous. He had lost the unlosable election and he had retained the leadership of his party only because the alternative was John Howard, another loser. The sentiment within the federal parliamentary Liberal Party was strongly anti-republican, largely on the basis that anything Keating supported should be opposed. John Howard and Bronwyn Bishop, each of whom saw themselves as potential leaders, thumped the monarchist drum.

The first sign that Hewson was retreating into the arms of the monarchists was in May, when he declined Keating's invitation to appoint a representative to the Republic Advisory Committee. Then in June, speaking at the Queensland Liberal Party Convention, he said:

The starting point for those who argue the need for constitutional changes to establish an Australian republic must be clear evidence that existing arrangements are flawed, inappropriate or simply do not work. At this stage advocates of a republic offer an essentially emotional rationale that tries to equate patriotism with republicanism.[4]

The shift in approach was very significant. Prior to June Hewson had accepted there was a strong case for change. It was, and remains, an essentially emotional or symbolic issue and the case for change had been put time and time again. The important priority had been to put flesh on the republican bone and to spell out precisely how the change would be effected. That, in the first instance, was the task of the Republic Advisory Committee.

Dr Hewson's apparent change of heart was also due to his belated recognition that the rank and file of the Liberal Party was still overwhelmingly in favour of the status quo. In some States, especially Victoria, support for the monarchy in the branches probably exceeds 75 per cent. This should come as no surprise. The Liberal Party's rank-and-file membership is older than average, has fewer Australians from non-English speaking backgrounds than the community at large and is generally more conservative. These rank-and-file members were becoming tired of Mr Hewson leading them down radical avenues of economic change that they did not support or understand, and the republic was the last straw.

Had Hewson been an unchallenged leader, as he would have been had he won the election, he could have taken the party in any direction he chose. But he was crippled after the election loss. More importantly, those Liberals who fancied themselves as potential leaders — Howard, Bishop, Reith and Costello, to name just four — all started to thump the monarchist drum with increased fervour. They saw the republican issue as one which would enable them to gather more support from the party's rank and file. They also saw it as an issue which would reinvigorate the demoralised Liberal Party members in the way Keating had seen the other side of the argument reinvigorate the Labor Party branches.

By July, the official position of the federal Liberal Party had hardened even more. On 9 July the party's federal executive claimed it would enter into the debate constructively, but then went on to say:

> ... we are totally opposed to the hidden agenda that
> Labor has in supporting the move to a republic, including
> its long-term plans to undermine the power of the States,
> to abolish the Senate, change the flag and eliminate the
> reserve power of the Governor-General.[5]

This allegation of a Labor Party 'hidden agenda' was, even by political standards, an extraordinary piece of political hysteria. While it is true that the Labor Party does support, in a largely theoretical sense, the abolition of the Senate, it was no part of the republican agenda. The Prime Minister had nailed his colours firmly to the minimalist mast. The terms of reference of the Republic Advisory Committee precluded its canvassing any of the matters allegedly part of the hidden agenda. And in any event, how could an agenda for constitutional change be hidden? The process of constitutional amendment is so laborious that any proposed changes will emerge long before the referendum.

The *Sydney Morning Herald* had this to say about the federal executive's approach:

> This recourse to emotive politicking represents a form of
> grovelling to the more reactionary elements in the party's
> membership. It does not allow the party a constructive
> role in the debate. And it seemingly locks the party into
> debating irrelevant side-issues rather than the matters of
> substance.[6]

Hewson's conversion to monarchism reached its apotheosis when the Report of the Republic Advisory Committee was released on 5 October. The Report was almost universally praised by the press, especially the serious newspapers, and the *Sydney Morning Herald* went so far as to describe it as 'scrupulously fair'. Hewson said:

> The release today of the Republic Advisory Committee's report has little bearing on the central issue to be addressed by the Australian people. The real question is not how we achieve change, but whether such change is either warranted or desirable.

This, of course, represented the complete reversal of his position in April where he urged that the public be informed of the proposals.

The effort to keep the debate bipartisan was not assisted by a story in the *Australian Financial Review* in late July which attributed to me a series of quite abusive remarks about the Liberal Party. As I wrote in the *Sydney Morning Herald* a few days later, I am too old to imagine that much is served by complaining about the treatment meted out by the press, but the attributed remarks — which included adverse reflections on the intelligence of the parliamentary Liberal Party — were not uttered by me but constituted, I imagine, the journalist's own 'synthesis' of a very long and thoughtful discussion about the role of ideas in conservative politics. Nonetheless the *Australian Financial Review* story did give opponents of the republic, as well as some newspaper leader writers, the opportunity to criticise me for adding to the partisan nature of the debate.

That particular episode was a useful reminder of how dangerous it is to speak to newspaper reporters at all. Few of them nowadays are able to take shorthand and as a result most of the 'quotes' in the press are in fact the journalist's own view of what he or she thinks the subject of the interview meant. The journalist may succeed in accurately encapsulating the subject's point of view, but they rarely bother to quote what was actually said. It is notable that while I have given hundreds of speeches and radio and television interviews I have only ever been embarrassed by remarks attributed to me in the press. Invariably these synthesised quotes are more inflammatory and less considered than anything I have said in public.

One aspect of the *Australian Financial Review* story was, however, reasonably accurate. I made the point that opponents of the republic should not imagine that republicans would fail to employ electoral tactics to promote their cause. This was not to suggest that the Australian Republican Movement would run its own candidates or that it would oppose one party and support another, but rather, like the Women's Electoral Lobby, the Australian Republican Movement was entitled to urge its supporters to vote for parliamentary candidates who favoured a republic and against those who do not. This observation also outraged many in the Liberal Party, although when I subsequently explained this position at a series of Liberal Party gatherings I think many Liberals came to understand that the Australian Republican Movement was just as entitled as any other pressure group to promote its cause in an electoral context. Nobody blinks an eye if the environmentalists oppose a candidate who supports logging rain forests or if the Right to Life movement oppose a candidate who supports abortion on demand. Does anyone imagine that Australians for Constitutional Monarchy will not be hounding republican candidates of all parties?

Many Liberals have justified their reluctance to 'come out of the republican closet' by reference to the fact that the Liberal Party's membership is older and more conservative than the electorate at large. But given that members of the Liberal Party, and elderly conservatives generally, are unlikely to vote Labor, why should a mainstream political party run the risk of alienating the younger sections of the electorate which overwhelmingly support a republic?

A recent opinion poll — commissioned by the Australian Youth Institute — polled 3000 young people between the ages of 14 and 24. The results were 51 per cent supporting the republic, 21 per cent opposed, 27 per cent undecided. Recognising this, the Young Liberals have advocated the

Australian republic for some time. Summing up the difficulties of taking a progressive position within the ranks of the Liberal Party, Trent Zimmerman, National Young Liberals President, said: 'Within some segments of the party it would be easier to argue a change to the Ten Commandments than the change to the republic.'[7]

Among other younger Liberals within the federal parliamentary party, the comments have been mixed. In the first month or so after the election, some of them joined Hewson in his move towards republicanism. The new deputy leader of the party, 36-year-old Victorian MP Michael Wooldridge, said: 'I have no disrespect for the Queen, who is a remarkable person. Nonetheless, as Queen of Australia she is not as relevant to me personally as she is to previous generations.'[8] Even Tony Abbott reflected his party's and his own sour grapes at the election result by saying, 'We are not against a republic, but we are dead against Keating's republic'.[9] This was a particularly revealing statement from the future Executive Director of Australians for Constitutional Monarchy!

The Liberal Party's support for the republic is critical for the success of the referendum — at least if it is to be held within the next few years. The republic is also critical for the future of the Liberal Party. One of the features of Australian politics in the 1990s is the lack of any real ideological difference between the parties. The Labor Party and the Liberal Party are both committed to the market economy. Labor has abandoned any semblance of being socialist. In economic terms the Hawke and Keating Governments have been more 'free enterprise' oriented than the last Liberal Government led by Malcolm Fraser. Indeed, Mr Fraser has frequently criticised the Labor Government for going too far in the direction of deregulation.

Political humorists like Michael Hodgman still encourage Liberals to struggle against 'Keating and his band of socialists in Canberra', but nobody with the slightest familiarity with Australian politics could sensibly describe Keating or his Government as being a socialist one.

Instead of fighting Labor for the middle ground of politics, the Liberal Party sought to differentiate itself from

Labor at the last election by advocating policies which were seen as being radical shifts to the right, at least in Australian terms. Now, in the wake of the March election defeat, the Liberal Party is trying to establish points of difference with Labor that do not place it outside of the centre ground of politics. So we have Liberals like Alexander Downer advocating a more caring approach to politics and less of the doctrinaire economics apparently favoured by Dr Hewson. It is far too early to say what this Liberal rethinking will produce and whether it will be successful.

But just as the Liberals must seek to differentiate themselves from a Labor Party which has embraced market economics, so the Labor Party seeks to find issues which enable it to differentiate itself from the Liberals without leading it back into the discredited doctrines of the socialist left. The republic is the ideal issue for the Labor Party. Already it is seen to have majority support, and overwhelming support among the younger age groups. The trend towards a republic is irresistible, at least in the long term. Looking a little further down the track, it is clear that while there is considerable affection for the Queen, there is very little, for the Prince of Wales. Were the Queen to abdicate or die, support for an Australian republic would become, instantly, almost unanimous.

The republic is a nationalistic cause. It allows its proponents to wrap themselves in the rhetoric of patriotism. And what other rhetoric is appropriate, after all? The republic is an unashamedly patriotic or nationalistic goal. If it cannot be justified as an affirmation of national identity, it cannot be justified at all. So, inevitably, the advocates of the monarchy are left trying to justify why an English woman should be Australia's Head of State.

If the republic is still an issue at the next election, there will inevitably be some Liberal voters who believe strongly enough in a republic to vote Labor as a protest against the Liberal Party's adherence to the monarchy. Liberal Party leaders need to recognise that the Labor Party is no longer seen as a threat to the vested interests of the business community or the middle class. In a political environment where there is so little difference in economic policy between Labor and Liberal, traditional Liberal voters know that they can responsibly vote Labor, because of its support for a republic, without creating a risk of a massive expansion in the public sector at the expense of business of the kind Liberal voters had been taught to expect from Labor in the 1960s and 1970s. This risk to the Liberals will be particularly acute if, by the time of the next election, there has been a recovery in the economy and a reduction in unemployment.

On the other hand, some thoughtful Liberals believe that Liberal-voting republicans are much less likely to switch support than Labor-voting monarchists. John Howard recently compared this feature of the debate with the role of the gun lobby in the 1988 New South Wales state election. In that election the Labor Government of Barry Unsworth had introduced tough gun laws as a reaction to a series of murders in Sydney. Many Labor voters in country electorates, particularly in the Hunter Valley, appeared to switch to the Liberals as a protest against the gun laws. However, the Liberal voters in the city who favoured tight laws stayed with their traditional party. If this analogy is correct (and I do not believe it is), then it may be smart politics for the Liberals to stick with the monarchy even though a majority of Australians favour a change.

While most referendums attract little interest and are forgotten after they have been dealt with by the electorate, the republic referendum will be of great interest and a defeat will not make the republican movement go away. The campaign will continue with increased passion and the Liberal Party will find its most visible point of difference with the Labor Party being its support of the monarchy. Unlike the referendums that were soundly defeated in 1988, the referendum on the republic will have had a long lead time, many more people are acquainted with the issues and perhaps most importantly, by any estimation, people are more passionate about this issue than they will ever be about four-year parliamentary terms or the recognition of local government in the Constitution.

In this respect, it is in the republican movement's interest for there to be an early resolution between the major parties, but it is in the Labor Party's interest for the debate to run and run. As long as Labor perceives the republic as being more popular than the ALP, it is desirable that the issue be kept alive. The only way the issue will be put to rest is by effecting the change. From that moment on the republic is of historical interest only.

Our parliamentary system of government depends upon there being an Opposition which is capable of winning office. It may well be so that the rank-and-file membership of the Liberal Party is very conservative and that the majority of these branch members are opposed to a republic. But just as the British Labour Party allowed its extreme left-wing membership to make it an unelectable party, so could the Liberal Party of Australia allow its conservative membership to do the same.

The loudest Liberal defenders of the monarchy are Bronwyn Bishop and John Howard. They both come from New South Wales, the State in which the Liberal Party has been particularly unsuccessful — holding only eight out of 50 House of Representatives seats. New South Wales is the State with the strongest support for a republic and the State where there is most support for a new non-Labor party. If Senator Bishop and Mr Howard are able to continue to represent the Liberal Party as being dead against the republic, they may imperil not merely the success, but the very survival, of the Liberal Party in Australia's largest State.

As former NSW Premier Nick Greiner said in a prepared paper on the Liberal Party and the republic presented to the Federal Council of the Liberal Party:

> We have no option but to participate [in the debate].
> Leaving it to our opponents is a recipe for irrelevance ...
> I believe the rational and politically astute thing for
> Liberals to do is find a way to participate in producing
> the most acceptable (or least unacceptable) proposal for
> the creation of an Australian republic.

Notwithstanding the passionate monarchism of Howard and Bishop, at a state level, New South Wales has a high number of committed republican Liberals. Back in 1988, New South Wales Premier Nick Greiner precipitated the Australia-wide end of knighthoods and other imperial honours by announcing, upon coming into government, that he would no longer distribute these British honours. In addition to the republican Premier John Fahey, the Attorney-General John Hannaford has stated he is a republican and the Treasurer and Minister for the Arts, Peter Collins, is an ardent supporter of a republic. Indeed a majority of New South Wales Liberal Party parliamentarians support a republic, according to Mr Collins.

Mr Collins spoke, in August 1993, at the opening of an exhibition on 'Australia and the Monarchy' at the Powerhouse Museum:

> What our proclamation as a republic will do is very basic but, like many of life's simpler things, important and fundamental in its simplicity.
>
> It is the most long-awaited core statement we as Australians can make about ourselves.
>
> It says that as Australians we enjoy total sovereignty and independence without reference, however qualified, to any foreign government or Head of State. Many have observed that in a practical (if not formal) sense that has been the situation for a few decades.
>
> The issue now therefore is whether we have the self-confidence and the belief in ourselves to formalise that reality.
>
> The idea that we are neither ready nor capable of taking this modest, crucial step, is utterly repugnant and self-effacing to a degree that the rest of the modern world must find bizarre.

The New South Wales Young Liberal Movement, at its annual convention on the weekend of 14 and 15 August 1993, moved a motion which urged that the parliamentary party reconsider its position and support the republic.

The New South Wales Young Liberal President, Mr John Brogden, said that:

> Young Liberals, as young Australians, see our nation's future as a republic. Our Constitution must recognise Australia's identity into the 21st century and beyond.[10]

And finally, this year, nine years after *Advance Australia Fair* was officially proclaimed the national anthem, members of the NSW State Council of the Liberal Party voted over-whelmingly to stop singing *God Save the Queen* at all future meetings.

Shrewd Liberals would recognise that the republican issue will not go away. If Mr Keating lost interest in a repub-lic, that would not diminish the commitment of the Aus-tralian Republican Movement. We were advocating a republic well before Mr Keating made any public reference to it at all. If the Liberal Party wants to avoid the republic being an election issue, they should participate in the process of drafting the appropriate republican amendments and supporting a referendum to amend the Constitution to be held prior to the next election. The republic will cease to be a political issue at the very moment those amendments are carried.

Speaking at a Liberal Party gathering in August 1993 I said:

> Those in the Liberal Party who take the view that a republic is inevitable, or even desirable, but nonetheless believe it should be opposed because to support it would give Mr Keating a win should think very carefully about that choice. 'Not invented here' is the worst possible reason to oppose a good idea. I have heard other Liberals say that they are concerned that by supporting the republic they would give Mr Keating the aura of 'Father of the Republic' and that this would be politically advantageous to him. Still others have said to me they do not want to give Mr Keating 'a free kick'. In my view Mr

Keating is being given a 'free kick' and will continue to be given one so long as Liberals are seen to oppose the republic, for the very simple reason that the republic is more popular than both Mr Keating and the ALP. By wrongly characterising the republic as a Labor cause you help Mr Keating. You may hurt the republic; not by much in my view. But you undoubtedly assist Mr Keating.

If the republic is supported by the Liberal Party it will not be Mr Keating's republic. More practically perhaps, auras do not count for much in politics. Within weeks of defeating Hitler, Mr Churchill was cast aside by the British electorate. The day after the republic is achieved it will cease to be a political issue.

An early republican referendum, carried with bipartisan support, is the best solution for the Liberal Party. It is in Labor's interest for the debate to continue indefinitely. The longer the Liberal Party is seen as being the monarchist party, the easier it will be for the Labor Party to represent itself as the party of the new, nationalistic Australia of the future.

This is one of the key difficulties facing the monarchists in the Liberal Party. They are supporting an institution which is disappearing from our consciousness. As John Hirst put it in a *Quadrant* article as far back as September 1991: 'the Queen in Australia has lost her civic personality'. Thirty years ago, thing were different. Now she is rarely toasted at private or even public functions. Hospitals, office blocks and parks are no longer named after obscure members of the royal family and there are few portraits of her to be found in schools and public buildings.

On 27 April the new Attorney-General, Michael Lavarch, took an oath of office which for the first time pledged an Australian cabinet minister's commitment to the 'Australian people and our institutions' instead of to 'Her Majesty Queen Elizabeth, Her Heirs and Successors'. In mid-July Sydney Councils began voting with their feet. Portraits of the Queen were removed from Marrickville and South Sydney council chambers. Then on 19 July 1993 Sydney City

Council voted to remove the Queen's portrait from the Sydney Town Hall — barely 15 months after she had been invited to celebrate the sesquicentenary of that Council's existence. If any further reinforcement of 'civic death' of the Queen was required, at the end of July 1993 the Government announced that it would no longer endorse any future applications for the 'royal' prefix by Australian organisations.

In the course of all of the republican and monarchist rhetoric of 1993, I found myself engaged in what became an exhaustive and exhausting analysis of what an Australian republic would really entail. On 28 April the Prime Minister addressed the annual Evatt Foundation dinner at the Regent Hotel in Sydney.

In a speech which had as its theme 'reform' and ranged over *Mabo* and Aboriginal reconciliation, Australia's transformation into a 'competitive export manufacturing country' and industrial relations, the Prime Minister suggested — about two years after the foundation of the Australian Republican Movement! — that:

> ... we should start now on the journey to the creation of an Australian Republic.
>
> I would like to see the Australian people demonstrate our social and political maturity by voting at a referendum for the establishment of a republic ... I am an advocate of what has become known as the minimalist approach.
>
> My view is that the Constitution should be changed sufficiently to replace the hereditary monarchy with a non-hereditary, Australian Head of State. But I do not know what the detail of such changes would be, and what range of options might exist within this minimalist approach.
>
> I have invited Malcolm Turnbull to chair the Republic Advisory Committee and he has accepted. The other members of the Committee are: Mr Nick Greiner, Ms Mary Kostakidis, Ms Lois O'Donoghue, Ms Susan Ryan, Dr John Hirst and Professor George Winterton.

Despite my urgings and those of a number of friends, and editorials in most of the nation's dailies, John Hewson did not appoint a representative to the Committee as he was invited to do by the Prime Minister. The State nominees were Glyn Davis from Queensland and Namoi Dougall from New South Wales. There was much speculation at the time that Professor Geoffrey Blainey, the nominee of the Victorian Government, was somehow 'prevented' by the Prime Minister or by me from participating. This is far from the truth. It was John Fahey, the NSW Premier, who effectively vetoed the Professor's nomination.

Our opponents were quick to attack the Committee as being a 'stacked deck', as all members of the Committee were regarded as being broadly sympathetic to the republican cause.

Nick Greiner responded to this criticism at the first meeting of the committee:

> It would be a nonsense to have an avowed monarchist, because this committee is about the development of republican options ... all we've been asked to do is answer the question, what is a republic?[11]

Within three weeks of the Committee being established I had drafted, settled with the Committee and then released a 5000-word 'Issues Paper' which stated at the outset the Committee's brief:

> The essential objective, therefore, of the Committee's task is to examine the means of introducing into our successful system of representative parliamentary democracy an entirely Australian office of the Head of State which will enhance our national democratic institutions without diminishing the authority or legitimacy of our Parliament, or the Government which is responsible to it.

The Issues Paper went on briefly to describe our way of government, the Constitution and the conventions, and gave background information on the Committee's terms of reference. In the course of the next three months, more than 20 000 copies of the Issues Paper and the Australian Constitution were distributed via public meetings and a '008' number. This was probably the highest readership the Constitution has had since it was framed in the 1890s. The 'hidden agenda' behind the issues paper was to attempt, once and for all, to clarify what was meant by the term 'minimalism'.

The term 'minimalism' had gained some currency during 1992 when both the ARM platform and then George Winterton's Republican Constitution, which was reprinted in the *Independent Monthly*, were described by a host of commentators as 'minimalist'. Donald Horne, in an article which appeared in the *Sydney Morning Herald* in early May 1993, claimed for himself the title of coining the term 'minimalist', and the Prime Minister gave it a substantial boost during his Evatt Foundation speech by saying 'I am an advocate of what has become known as the minimalist approach'. But whoever it was, it was never intended to mean taking a bottle of Tipp-Ex® to the Constitution, whiting out 'Governor-General' and 'Queen' and replacing them with 'President'.

Minimalism simply meant replacing the British monarch with an Australian as our Head of State and not changing the general principles and conventions that currently regulate our system of government. To be more explicit, becoming a republic does not entail changing the flag, changing the powers of the Senate, entrenching a Bill of Rights in the Constitution or altering federal–state relations. While all of these may or may not be admirable goals they deserve to be debated on their merits and not piled on top of the republican proposal.

In an effort to overcome some of these misunderstandings, the Committee was determined to attempt to access as many people as possible within the short time frame allowed to it. The Prime Minister had also invited the Committee to seek expert advice and consult 'widely' in the course of the preparation of the final report.

While the 21 capital cities and regional centres visited by

Committee members was by no means a complete coverage of all population centres in Australia, it was certainly a genuine attempt to cover as much of all the States and Territories as was possible in the limited time available. I chaired more than half of the 22 public meetings. Within three weeks I travelled from the Pilgrims' Hall in Launceston in the south to the Cairns Public Library in the north and the Railway Institute at Bunbury in the west. While our opponents were quick to emphasise the low turnouts in Geelong, Whyalla and Brisbane, they failed to note that in one day in Perth a total of 600 people attended three different meetings and the last week of public hearings saw a total of more than 500 at venues in Sydney, Canberra and Wollongong. We met every State Governor except for Roma Mitchell (the South Australian Governor), talked to the last three Governors-General, spoke with every Premier except Mr Groom in Tasmania, with most State Solicitors-General and with a comprehensive range of ordinary Australians who came to the meetings or contacted me and other Committee members directly.

This was not mass participation by any stretch of the imagination, but it was certainly a vast improvement on the traditional constitutional discourse between academics and political elites and it would be wrong to assume that ordinary people are not interested in this issue. Everywhere I go people stop me to offer words of encouragement or, more rarely, to suggest with great Australian directness that things are OK as they are. There has been enough popular interest to supply countless radio stations with a talkback subject for almost three years — and that is not to mention the columns of newsprint, news stories, press conferences and speeches relating to the Constitution and the republic released over the same time frame.

I must confess to having had some fleeting concern about public participation in the Republic Advisory Committee process when, at one of the first meetings of the Republic Advisory Committee in Cairns, a gentleman stood up and said: 'You and the Prime Minister are just agents of the

Vatican conspiracy in its efforts to establish a one world government.' Anxious to fulfil my duty of public consultation thoroughly, I inquired as to the role of the Masonic Order in this context. 'Don't you know?' the man replied, every word dripping with utter contempt for one so naive as I, 'the Masonic Order is run by the Vatican'. Before I had time to note this down, he called out, 'And do you know who runs the Vatican?' We asked him to tell us; indeed we were on the edge of our seats. 'The international Jewish banking conspiracy, of course.'

From early May until early September I worked virtually full-time on the republic issue. The Government picked up my airfares and accommodation costs but I declined to accept any sitting fees or other payment.

The net cost to the Government of the Republic Advisory Committee was only about $364 000. This was certainly a far cry from the $600 000 claimed by our opponents, and less than one-third of the cost of bringing the Queen and her entourage to Australia in 1992. And this is, of course, not including the intangible benefits associated with a greater understanding of the way our country is governed and the very tangible return on whatever sales the report makes the Australian Government Publishing Service.

The report was officially delivered to the Prime Minister on Tuesday 6 October 1993. It constitutes the most extensive investigation to date of the republican options available to Australians. Perhaps most importantly, it clearly demonstrates that it is possible to move to a republican system of government without affecting any of our much-cherished democratic principles and traditions.

The *Australian* editorial following the report's publication stated that, 'The Republic Advisory Committee has made a necessary and valuable contribution to informed debate', and P. P. McGuinness, traditionally not one of our strongest supporters, said, 'The Republic Advisory Committee has done its work well. Its report is a well-argued, well-documented examination of the issues … Whatever the outcome of the argument, this report will have to be added to the lengthening list of serious officially sponsored textbooks on the Australian Constitution'.

The *Sydney Morning Herald* described the report as 'scrupulously fair', the *Australian Financial Review* said 'it should help focus the debate on the important practical questions', and Peter Cole-Adams in the *Canberra Times* described it as a 'deftly argued review of the issues and options'.

Not surprisingly the report was roundly condemned by members of the Coalition and Australians for Constitutional Monarchy. The most pathetic response was that of Queensland National Party Senator, Bill O'Chee, who predicted that the adoption of any of the report's recommendations would lead to the same bloodshed and violence recently seen in Russia. Senator Bronwyn Bishop dismissed the report as 'a yawn' and 'not warranting public consideration' because it was too long!

Lloyd Waddy QC found it all too complicated to understand, prompting me to observe on radio that if a 150-page report on the options for a republic is too difficult for a QC like Waddy to grasp, then you would seriously consider whether you would give him responsibility for defending you on a parking charge. Mr Waddy even went so far as to say that Australia would remain a monarchy long after Britain became a republic, an interesting point of view, given that section 2 of the *Constitution Act* decrees that our monarch is to be Queen Victoria 'and Her Heirs and Successors in the sovereignty of the United Kingdom'. It follows that unless we amend our Constitution to establish our own laws of succession the moment the Queen of the United Kingdom ceased to be sovereign of the United Kingdom she would similarly cease to be our monarch.

The Liberal Party put up Peter Reith as its public spokesperson in response to the report. Among his criticisms were that Australians shouldn't consider the republic because the report detailed 'a constitutional leap into the unknown', a 'power grab by the Prime Minister involving a significant shift in the power balance between the Executive and the Head of State ... for the benefit of the Executive' and was an attack on one of 'the fundamental guarantees of our freedom, which is to have an independent Head of State who can be a last bulwark against the excesses of the Prime Minister' — and that cutting down on the powers of the Senate was 'a time bomb ticking away in this report'.

As Mike Steketee pointed out,[12] the report actually said that it is both legally and practically possible to amend the Constitution to achieve a republic without making changes which will in any way detract from the fundamental principles on which our system is based. Furthermore, most of the options suggested by the Committee enhance the authority of the Head of State over the executive. The two most popular models, direct election by the people and a two-thirds majority of both Houses of Parliament, must give the Head of State more security of tenure and independence than the current method in which that person is effectively appointed and can be dismissed by the Prime Minister of the day. As to the Senate, only one of the four options suggested to resolve the issue of 1975 involved a reduction in the Senate's powers.

Mike Steketee continued:

In short, the report says pretty well the opposite of what Reith was attributing to it ... Get ready for much more of Peter Reith looking you in the eye through the camera lens and arguing that black is white.

At the official launch of the report at a speech to the National Press Club I attempted to put reluctant republicans on notice by stating that the republican goal is something that must be worked hard for.

Australia is already a republic by any reasonable test — a State in which sovereignty is derived from the people. The one element in the Constitution not consistent with a republic is the Crown, which is hereditary, British and Anglican.

The monarchy is not a sacred silken thread in that great

Australian garment which, if tugged, would bring the whole fabric down in tatters.

Questions of national identity and our Constitution, which are as important as this, should not become footballs in the team game of politics.

The most important element in what goes ahead is that the debate be conducted in a non-partisan way. This is not a party-political cause: there are Liberals who are in favour of a republic, there are Liberals who are against, Labor people for, Labor people against.

The republic debate should be the vehicle for Australians to gain a wider understanding of their Constitution. I have little doubt that more Australians have an understanding of the American Constitution via Hollywood than they do of their own Constitution. But the republic debate — whether you agree with it or not — allows the Australian community perhaps its first chance in 100 years not only to influence a profound constitutional change, but to understand the Constitution itself.

No-one would argue that Australia would not be a republic by the year 2101. If it is to occur by 2001, its supporters will have to fight hard.

Republicans should not assume that a republic will simply fall in their lap like an overripe fruit.

The Report of the Republic Advisory Committee was designed to provide a sound and objective resource of information about the republic so the debate could proceed on a more informed and intelligent basis. However, in my view, the most important achievement of the report is its complete codification of the reserve powers, which is set out and discussed in Chapter 8. The reserve powers have always been regarded as excessively mysterious by constitutional lawyers and a few attempts at codification have been made. It is interesting to note that in the month between publication of the report and writing these lines there has been no outcry or criticism of the codification as misconceived or fundamentally flawed. Drafting, of course, is an art and not a science and I have very little doubt that the Committee's proposed provisions will be improved and honed by draftsmen and women more skilled than I. But we have succeeded in bursting the bubble of impossibility. The reserve powers are not a mystery. They are a set of rules and like all rules can be written down in a language ordinary Australians can understand.

CHAPTER TWELVE

Australia Unbound

The cause of the republic will not be won without struggle. Only rotten fruit falls from the bough unplucked. The opponents of the republic have powerful weapons in their armoury. They cannot appeal to love of country — at least not this country. But they can and will enlist sectarianism and racism and (as it is their most effective weapon) they will continue to promote ignorance and the fear of the unknown that is its inevitable companion.

Australia is a nation; it is our home, and we have no other. Australia is not a simple geographic expression. It is not a giant caravan park into which we have pulled our vans to stay a while, or perhaps for a long time, but always as transients, harking back to other lands and other homes.

Australia is our place. It is our homeland. It is as dear to us who came here yesterday or two centuries ago as it is to those who walked across the land bridge from Asia 40 000 years ago and, as Australia's first settlers, settled in this old land: a land more ancient than any of its inhabitants.

The republican movement, in two-and-a-half years, has ignited a spark. It has set a wheel of tempered steel clattering down the cobblestones of our history. As it rolls, it strikes sparks: sparks which ignite ideas and dreams. Those sparks illuminate our reality and our future. They remind us that we are building today a unique nation composed of many cultures, many faiths and many races. All of us, in our splendid variety, will see different ways to freedom and happiness. We are diverse, and so we are divided.

But in our diversity, in our divisions, we are able to share and experience so much more than those who live in more conventionally homogeneous societies. We Australians are the inheritors of all the cultures and all the history of the world. Children of migrants from China and Greece will inherit Chaucer and Shakespeare as confidently as my children will inherit the thoughts of Confucius and Cavafy.

Many of our forebears came to build a British nation in the South Seas. Their children are building an Australian nation in Australia. We cannot allow our republic, which is no more than a symbol of Australia, to become a political football cynically exploited by those who measure their aspirations in weeks instead of centuries.

The republican movement must now become a people's movement. We must, in the years that follow, develop a mass membership. We must demonstrate that our cause springs from the people. For just as the move to Federation foundered in the hands of politicians and was rescued by thousands of Australians in citizens' movements, so too must the people carry the republican goal to its completion.

When the politicians see that the number of Australians wanting a republic exceeds the number supporting their own parties, and when our leaders — who have been too busy, or perhaps too cynical, to trouble themselves with matters of the spirit — recognise that Australians are possessed of more nerves than those of the hip pocket, then we will have our republic.

But we will need patience, and we will need to be tireless. We need more, and different, advocates of the republic. We need to see many more women describing the Australian citizen they want as Head of State. We need to see many more Aboriginal Australians expressing their vision of a nation whose leaders are unfailingly responsible to the people of that nation. We need to see many more Australians from non-English-speaking backgrounds demanding that their Head of State represent the values all Australians hold dear, rather than those of the first new settlers in this land.

As Australia seeks to resolve critical questions of identity, as we seek to understand our history and our relationship with our indigenous people and as we seek to establish more tangible and commercial regional relationships, the republic will act as a unifying symbol of the new era we are entering.

We have no need, as our opponents do, to stir up fear and prejudice. We do not seek to impose a Head of State who will affront the values of any citizen or group of citizens. Our Head of State will symbolise our Australian, democratic, tolerant and diverse society. We do not have to frighten the elderly or the ill-informed.

While our opponents urge the people not to read about the Constitution and its history, we will urge them to read as much as they can, because we have no fear of knowledge. While our often well-educated opponents refuse to discuss the substance of our Constitution, we must continue to do so. We must endeavour to maintain an intelligent debate even in the face of opponents determined not to think about the issues.

Australia's destiny is in the hands of its people — and it is to the Australian people we must commit the cause of the republic.

APPENDICES

APPENDIX ONE

PROPOSED AMENDMENTS TO THE CONSTITUTION

The text reproduced below is the Australian Constitution in full, showing proposed amendments to make the change to a republic.

WHEREAS the people of New South Wales, Victoria, South Australia, Queensland, ~~and~~ Tasmania *and Western Australia*, humbly relying on the blessing of Almighty God, ~~have~~ agreed to unite in one indissoluble Federal Commonwealth under the Crown of the United Kingdom of Great Britain and Ireland, and under the Constitution hereby established:

~~And whereas it is expedient to provide for the admission into the Commonwealth of other Australasian Colonies and possessions of the Queen:~~

And whereas that Federal Commonwealth, the Commonwealth

of Australia, evolved into an independent nation under the Crown of Australia:

We, the people of Australia, united in an indissoluble Commonwealth of States, acknowledging the equality of all under the law regardless of colour, race, sex or creed, declaring ourselves to be free, sovereign and independent, agree to be bound by these principles of equality and by the provisions of this Constitution.

~~Be it therefore enacted by the Queen's Most Excellent Majesty, by and with the advice and consent of the Lords Spiritual and Temporal, and Commons, in this present Parliament assembled, and by the authority of the same, as follows: —~~

1. This Act may be cited as the Commonwealth of Australia Constitution Act.

2. ~~The provisions of this Act referring to the Queen shall extend to Her Majesty's heirs and successors in the sovereignty of the United Kingdom.~~

3. ~~It shall be lawful for the Queen, with the advice of the Privy Council, to declare by proclamation that, on and after a day therein appointed, not being later than one year after the passing of this Act, the people of New South Wales, Victoria, South Australia, Queensland, and Tasmania, and also, if Her Majesty is satisfied that the people of Western Australia have agreed thereto, of Western Australia, shall be united in a Federal Commonwealth under the name of the Commonwealth of Australia. But the Queen may, at any time after the proclamation, appoint a Governor General for the Commonwealth.~~

4. The Commonwealth shall be established, and the Constitution of the Commonwealth shall take effect, on and after *the first day of January, 1901.* ~~the day so appointed. But the Parliaments of the several colonies may at any time after the passing of this Act make any such laws, to come into operation on the day so appointed, as they might have made if the Constitution had taken effect at the passing of this Act.~~

5. This Act, and all laws made by the Parliament of the Commonwealth under the Constitution, shall be

binding on the courts, judges, and people of every State and of every part of the Commonwealth, notwithstanding anything in the laws of any State; ~~and the laws of the Commonwealth shall be in force on all British ships, the Queen's ships of war excepted, whose first port of clearance and whose port of destination are in the Commonwealth.~~

6. 'The Commonwealth' shall mean the Commonwealth of Australia as established under this Act.

'The States' shall mean such of ~~the colonies of~~ New South Wales, New Zealand, Queensland, Tasmania, Victoria, Western Australia, and South Australia, including the northern territory of South Australia, as for the time being are parts of the Commonwealth, and such ~~colonies or~~ territories as may be admitted into or established by the Commonwealth as States; and each of such parts of the Commonwealth shall be called 'a State'.

'Original States' shall mean such States as are parts of the Commonwealth at its establishment.

7. ~~The Federal Council of Australasia Act, 1885, is hereby repealed, but so as not to affect any laws passed by the Federal Council of Australasia and in force at the establishment of the Commonwealth.~~

~~Any such law may be repealed as to any State by the Parliament of the Commonwealth, or as to any colony not being a State by the Parliament thereof.~~

8. ~~After the passing of this Act the Colonial Boundaries Act, 1895, shall not apply to any colony which becomes a State of the Commonwealth; but the Commonwealth shall be taken to be a self governing colony for the purposes of that Act.~~

9. The Constitution of the Commonwealth shall be as follows: —

THE CONSTITUTION

This Constitution is divided as follows: —

CHAPTER I. — THE PARLIAMENT.

PART I. — GENERAL.

1.   The legislative power of the Commonwealth shall be vested in a Federal Parliament, which shall consist of the ~~Queen~~, *President*, a Senate, and a House of Representatives, and which is herein-after called 'The Parliament,' or 'The Parliament of the Commonwealth.'

2.   ~~A Governor-General appointed by the Queen shall be Her Majesty's representative in the Commonwealth, and shall have and may exercise in the Commonwealth during the Queen's pleasure, but subject to this Constitution, such powers and functions of the Queen as Her Majesty may be pleased to assign to him.~~

(a)   *The Head of State of the Commonwealth shall be the President of the Commonwealth who shall exercise his or her powers in accordance with this Constitution.*

(b)   *The first President of the Commonwealth shall be the person occupying the position of Governor-General at the date of the enactment of this clause. As soon as practicable thereafter, and in any event not later than 90 days, the Prime Minister shall, after consulting the leaders of the other parties represented in the Parliament, propose the name of a person to fill the position of President. Upon the House of Representatives and the Senate voting together in a joint sitting to approve, by a two-thirds majority, the appointment of such person he or she shall be deemed appointed President of the Commonwealth and shall hold that office until the expiry of five years from the date of his or her appointment or his or her death, resignation or removal in accordance with this section.*

(c)   *During any vacancy in the office of the President of the Commonwealth or during the absence from Australia of the President of the Commonwealth, the duties and functions of the President shall be undertaken by the most senior State Governor, or in the event of his or her disability or inability to act, the next most senior State Governor. The seniority of a State Governor is determined by the length of his or her service as State Governor. In the event of more than three States abolishing the office of Governor, the Parliament shall be empowered to enact legislation for the purpose of providing for the appointment of a person to fill the office of President in the event of a vacancy, provided that no such person shall fill the office of President for more than 120 days.*

(d)   *The President must be a citizen of the Commonwealth of Australia entitled to vote for the election of members of the House of Representatives.*

(e)   *Upon the passage, by a two-thirds majority, of a resolution to remove the President by a joint sitting of the House of Representatives and the Senate, the President shall cease to hold the office of President and a casual vacancy in the Presidency shall be created.*

(f)   *The House of Representatives and the Senate shall appoint a President in accordance with this clause within 90 days of the position of President becoming vacant for whatever reason. When the Houses meet to elect a President, the Parliament shall not be prorogued, nor shall the joint sitting be adjourned for a period extending beyond five days after the first attempted election until a President has been elected.*

(g)   *The President shall enter upon the office by making and subscribing publicly the following declaration: 'I, A.B., do solemnly and sincerely promise and declare that I will maintain the Constitution and uphold the laws of the Commonwealth and that I will fulfil my duties faithfully and conscientiously in accordance with the Constitution and the law, and that I will dedicate my abilities to the service and welfare of the people of Australia.'*

(h)   *The President may resign his or her office by writing addressed to the President of the Senate, or the Speaker if there is no President of the Senate or if the President of the Senate is absent from the Commonwealth. Such resignation shall take effect at the time specified therein.*

3.   ~~There shall be payable to the Queen out of the Consolidated Revenue fund of the Commonwealth, for the salary of the Governor General, an annual sum which, until the Parliament otherwise provides, shall be ten thousand pounds.~~

        ~~The salary of a Governor General shall not be altered during his continuance in office.~~

3.   *The salary of the President shall be provided for by Parliament and shall not be altered during the President's term of office.*

4.   ~~The provisions of this Constitution relating to the President Governor General extend and apply to the Governor General for the time being, or such person as the Queen may appoint to administer the Government of the Commonwealth; but no such person shall be entitled to receive any salary from the Commonwealth in respect of any other office during his administration of the Government of the Commonwealth.~~

4A Executive power of the Commonwealth

(i.)   *The executive power of the Commonwealth is vested in the President and is exercisable either directly or through Ministers of State (including the Prime Minister) or persons acting with their authority.*

(ii.) *The executive power of the Commonwealth extends to the execution and maintenance of the Constitution, and of the laws of the Commonwealth.*

(iii.) *The President shall exercise his or her powers and functions in accordance with the advice tendered to him or her by the Federal Executive Council, the Prime Minister or such other Ministers of State as are authorised to do so by the Prime Minister.*

(iv.) *Subsection (iii.) does not apply in relation to the exercise of the powers or functions of the President under sections 4B, 4C(v.), 4D, 4E and 4G.*

4B Appointment of the Prime Minister

(i.) *The President shall appoint a person, to be known as the Prime Minister, to be the Head of the Government of the Commonwealth.*

(ii.) *Subject to subsection 4C(iv.), whenever it is necessary for the President to appoint a Prime Minister, the President shall appoint that person who commands the support of the House of Representatives expressed through a resolution of the House, and in the absence of such a resolution, the person who, in his or her judgment, is most likely to command the support of that House.*

(iii.) *The Prime Minister shall not hold office for a longer period than 90 days unless he or she is or becomes a member of the House of Representatives.*

(iv.) *The Prime Minister shall be a member of the Federal Executive Council and shall be one of the Ministers of State for the Commonwealth.*

(v.) *The Prime Minister shall hold office, subject to this Constitution, until he or she dies or resigns or the President terminates his or her appointment.*

(vi.) *The exercise of a power of the President under subsection (ii.) shall not be examined in any court.*

4C Other Ministers

(i.) *Ministers of State shall be appointed by the President acting in accordance with the advice of the Prime Minister.*

(ii.) One of the Ministers of State may be nominated Deputy Prime Minister.

(iii.) Subject to this section, the President shall only remove a Minister from office in accordance with the advice of the Prime Minister.

(iv.) Upon the death of the Prime Minister, the President shall appoint the Deputy Prime Minister or, if there is no Deputy Prime Minister, the Minister most senior in rank, to be the Prime Minister.

(v.) In this section, 'Minister' does not include the Prime Minister.

4D Dismissal of the Prime Minister: no-confidence resolutions[1]

(i.) If the House of Representatives, by an absolute majority of its members, passes a resolution of confidence in a named person as Prime Minister (other than a person already holding office as Prime Minister), and the Prime Minister does not forthwith resign from office, the President shall remove him or her from office.

(ii.) If the House of Representatives passes, other than by an absolute majority of its members, a resolution of confidence in a named person as Prime Minister (other than a person already holding office as Prime Minister), and the Prime Minister does not within three days resign from office or secure a reversal of that resolution, the President shall remove him or her from office.

(iii.) If the House of Representatives passes a resolution of no-confidence in the Prime Minister or the Government by an absolute majority of its members and does not name another person in whom it does have confidence, and the Prime Minister does not, within three days of the passing of that resolution, either resign from office, secure a reversal of that resolution or advise the President to dissolve the Parliament, the President shall remove him or her from the office of Prime Minister.

(iv.) *If the House of Representatives passes a resolution of no confidence in the Prime Minister or the Government other than by an absolute majority of its members and does not name another person in whom it does have confidence, and the Prime Minister does not, within seven days of the passing of that resolution, either resign from office, secure a reversal of that resolution or advise the President to dissolve the Parliament, the President shall remove him or her from the office of Prime Minister.*

4E Dismissal of the Prime Minister: constitutional contravention

(i.) *If the President believes that the Government of the Commonwealth is contravening a fundamental provision of this Constitution or is not complying with an order of a court, the President may request the Prime Minister to demonstrate that no contravention is occurring or that the Government is complying with the order.*

(ii.) *If, after giving the Prime Minister that opportunity, the President still believes that such a contravention or non-compliance is occurring, the President may apply to the High Court for relief.*

(iii.) *If, on application by the President, the High Court is satisfied that the Government of the Commonwealth is contravening a provision of this Constitution or not complying with the order of a court, the High Court may grant such relief as it sees fit including a declaration to that effect. The High Court shall not decline to hear such application on the ground that it raises non-justiciable issues.*

(iv.) *If on an application by the President, the High Court declares that the Government of the Commonwealth is contravening this Constitution or not complying with the order of a court and the Prime Minister fails to take all reasonable steps to end the contravention or to comply with the order, the President may dissolve the House of Representatives.*

(v.)   *If the President dissolves the House of Representatives under this section, he or she may also terminate the Prime Minister's commission and appoint as Prime Minister such other person as the President believes will take all reasonable steps to end the contravention and who will maintain the administration of the Commonwealth pending the outcome of the general election following the dissolution referred to in subsection (iv) above.*

(vi.)   *The exercise of the powers of the President under this section shall not be examined by any court.*

4F Refusal of dissolution

The President shall not dissolve the House of Representatives —

(i.)   *on the advice of a Prime Minister in whom, or in whose Government, the House of Representatives has passed a resolution of no-confidence, if the House has, by an absolute majority of its members, also expressed confidence in another named person as Prime Minister;*

(ii.)   *on the advice of a Prime Minister in whom, or in whose Government, the House of Representatives has passed a resolution of no-confidence, if the House has, other than by an absolute majority of its members, also expressed confidence in another named person as Prime Minister unless the House has reversed the resolution;*

(iii.)   *while a motion of no-confidence in the Prime Minister or the Government is pending; or*

(iv.)   *before the House of Representatives has met after a general election and considered whether it has confidence in the Prime Minister or the Government, unless the House of Representatives has met and is unable to elect a Speaker.*

For the purpose of subsection (iii.), a 'motion of no-confidence' is one which expresses confidence in another named person as Prime Minister and is to come before the House of Representatives within eight days.

5.   The ~~Governor General~~ *President* may appoint such times for holding the sessions of the Parliament as he *or she* thinks fit, and may also from time to time, by Proclamation or otherwise, prorogue the Parliament, and may in like manner dissolve the House of Representatives.

After any general election the Parliament shall be summoned to meet not later than thirty days after the day appointed for the return of the writs.

~~The Parliament shall be summoned to meet not later than six months after the establishment of the Commonwealth.~~ *(Spent)*

6.   There shall be a session of the Parliament once at least in every year, so that twelve months shall not intervene between the last sitting of the Parliament in one session and its first sitting in the next session.

PART II. — THE SENATE.

7.   The Senate shall be composed of senators for each State, directly chosen by the people of the State, voting, until the Parliament otherwise provides, as one electorate.

~~But until the Parliament of the Commonwealth otherwise provides, the Parliament of the State of Queensland, if that State be an Original State, may make laws dividing the State into divisions and determining the number of senators to be chosen for each division, and in the absence of such provision the State shall be one electorate.~~ *(Spent)*

Until the Parliament otherwise provides there shall be six senators for each Original State. The Parliament may make laws increasing or diminishing the number of senators for each State, but so that equal representation of the several Original States shall be maintained and that no Original State shall have less than six senators.

The senators shall be chosen for a term of six years, and the names of the senators chosen for each State shall be certified by the Governor to the ~~Governor-General~~. *President.*

8. The qualification of electors of senators shall be in each State that which is prescribed by this Constitution, or by the Parliament, as the qualification for electors of members of the House of Representatives; but in the choosing of senators each elector shall vote only once.

9. The Parliament of the Commonwealth may make laws prescribing the method of choosing senators, but so that the method shall be uniform for all the States. Subject to any such law, the Parliament of each State may make laws prescribing the method of choosing the senators for that State.

   The Parliament of a State may make laws for determining the times and places for elections of senators for that State.

10. Until the Parliament otherwise provides, but subject to this Constitution, the laws in force in each State, for the time being, relating to elections for the more numerous House of the Parliament of the State shall, as nearly as practicable, apply to elections of senators for the State.

11. The Senate may proceed to the despatch of business, notwithstanding the failure of any State to provide for its representation in the Senate.

12. The Governor of any State may cause writs to be issued for elections of senators for the State. In case of the dissolution of the Senate the writs shall be issued within ten days from the proclamation of such dissolution.

13. As soon as may be after the Senate first meets, and after each first meeting of the Senate following a dissolution thereof, the Senate shall divide the senators chosen for each State into two classes, as nearly equal in number as practicable; and the places of the senators of the first class shall become vacant at the expiration of three years and the places of those of the

second class at the expiration of six years, from the beginning of their term of service; and afterwards the places of senators shall become vacant at the expiration of six years from the beginning of their term of service.

The election to fill vacant places shall be made within one year before the places are to become vacant.

For the purposes of this section the term of service of a senator shall be taken to begin on the first day of July following the day of his *or her* election, except in the cases of the first election and of the election next after any dissolution of the Senate, when it shall be taken to begin on the first day of July preceding the day of his *or her* election.

14. Whenever the number of senators for a State is increased or diminished, the Parliament of the Commonwealth may make such provision for the vacating of the places of senators for the State as it deems necessary to maintain regularity in the rotation.

15. If the place of a senator becomes vacant before the expiration of his *or her* term of service, the Houses of Parliament of the State for which he *or she* was chosen, sitting and voting together, or, if there is only one House of that Parliament, that House, shall choose a person to hold the place until the expiration of the term. But if the Parliament of the State is not in session when the vacancy is notified, the Governor of the State, with the advice of the Executive Council thereof, may appoint a person to hold the place until the expiration of fourteen days from the beginning of the next session of the Parliament of the State or the expiration of the term, whichever first happens.

Where a vacancy has at any time occurred in the place of a senator chosen by the people of a State and, at the time when he *or she* was so chosen, he *or she* was publicly recognized by a particular political party as being an endorsed candidate of that party and publicly represented himself *or herself* to be such a candidate, a person chosen or appointed under this section in consequence of that vacancy, shall, unless there is no member of that party available to be chosen or appointed, be a member of that party.

Where —

(a) in accordance with the last preceding paragraph, a member of a particular political party is chosen or appointed to hold the place of a senator whose place has become vacant; and

(b) before taking his seat he *or she* ceases to be a member of that party (otherwise than by reason of the party having ceased to exist),

he *or she* shall be deemed not to have been so chosen or appointed and the vacancy shall be again notified in accordance with section twenty-one of this Constitution.

The name of any senator chosen or appointed under this section shall be certified by the Governor of the State to the ~~Governor-General~~. *President*.

~~If the place of a senator chosen by the people of a State at the election of senators last held before the commencement of the *Constitution Alteration (Senate Casual Vacancies)* 1977 became vacant before that commencement and, at that commencement, no person chosen by the House or Houses of Parliament of the State, or appointed by the Governor of the State, in consequence of that vacancy, or in consequence of that vacancy and a subsequent vacancy or vacancies, held office, this section applies as if the place of the senator chosen by the people of the State had become vacant after that commencement.~~

~~A senator holding office at the commencement of the *Constitution Alteration (Senate Casual Vacancies)* 1977, being a senator appointed by the Governor of a State in consequence of a vacancy that had at any time occurred in the place of a senator chosen by the people of the State, shall be deemed to have been appointed to hold the place until the expiration of~~

fourteen days after the beginning of the next session of the Parliament of the State that commenced or commences after he was appointed and further action under this section shall be taken as if the vacancy in the place of the senator chosen by the people of the State had occurred after that commencement.

Subject to the next succeeding paragraph, a senator holding office at the commencement of the *Constitution Alteration (Senate Casual Vacancies)* 1977 who was chosen by the House or Houses of Parliament of a State in consequence of a vacancy that had at any time occurred in the place of a senator chosen by the people of the State shall be deemed to have been chosen to hold office until the expiration of the term of service of the senator elected by the people of the State.

If, at or before the commencement of the *Constitution Alteration (Senate Casual Vacancies)* 1977, a law to alter the Constitution entitled '*Constitution Alteration (Simultaneous Elections)* 1977' came into operation, a senator holding office at the commencement of that law who was chosen by the House or Houses of Parliament of a State in consequence of a vacancy that had at any time occurred in the place of a senator chosen by the people of the State shall be deemed to have been chosen to hold office —

(a)   if the senator elected by the people of the State had a term of service expiring on the thirtieth day of June, One thousand nine hundred and seventy-eight — until the expiration or dissolution of the first House of Representatives to expire or be dissolved after that law come into operation; or

(b)   if the senator elected by the people of the State had a term of service expiring on the thirtieth day of June, One thousand nine hundred and eighty-one — until *the expiration or dissolution of the second House of Representatives to expire or be dissolved after that law came into operation or, if*

~~there is an earlier dissolution of the Senate, until that dissolution.~~ *(Spent)*

16. The qualifications of a senator shall be the same as those of a member of the House of Representatives.

17. The Senate shall, before proceeding to the despatch of any other business, choose a senator to be the President of the Senate; and as often as the office of the President *of the Senate* becomes vacant the Senate shall again choose a senator to be the President *of the Senate.*

    The President *of the Senate* shall cease to hold his *or her* office if he *or she* ceases to be a senator. He *or she* may be removed from office by a vote of the Senate, or he *or she* may resign his office or his seat by writing addressed to the ~~Governor-General.~~ *President.*

18. Before or during any absence of the President *of the Senate,* the Senate may choose a senator to perform his *or her* duties in his *or her* absence.

19. A senator may, by writing addressed to the President *of the Senate,* or to the ~~Governor-General~~ *President* if there is no President *of the Senate* or if the President *of the Senate* is absent from the Commonwealth, resign his *or her* place, which thereupon shall become vacant.

20. The place of a senator shall become vacant if for two consecutive months of any session of the Parliament he *or she,* without the permission of the Senate, fails to attend the Senate.

21. Whenever a vacancy happens in the Senate, the President *of the Senate,* or if there is no President *of the Senate* or if the President *of the Senate* is absent from the Commonwealth the ~~Governor-General,~~ *President,* shall notify the same to the Governor of the State in the representation of which the vacancy has happened.

22. Until the Parliament otherwise provides, the presence of at least one-third of the whole number of the senators shall be necessary to constitute a meeting of the Senate for the exercise of its powers.

23. Questions arising in the Senate shall be determined by a majority of votes, and each senator shall have one

vote. The President *of the Senate* shall in all cases be entitled to vote; and when the votes are equal the question shall pass in the negative.

PART III. — THE HOUSE OF REPRESENTATIVES.

24. The House of Representatives shall be composed of members directly chosen by the people of the Commonwealth, and the number of such members shall be, as nearly as practicable, twice the number of senators.

   The number of members chosen in the several States shall be in proportion to the respective numbers of their people, and shall, until the Parliament otherwise provides, be determined, wherever necessary, in the following manner:—

   (i.) A quota shall be ascertained by dividing the number of the people of the Commonwealth, as shown by the latest statistics of the Commonwealth, by twice the number of the senators:

   (ii.) The number of members to be chosen in each State shall be determined by dividing the number of the people of the State, as shown by the latest statistics of the Commonwealth, by the quota; and if on such division there is a remainder greater than one-half of the quota, one more member shall be chosen in the State.

   But notwithstanding anything in this section, five members at least shall be chosen in each Original State.

25. For the purposes of the last section, if by the law of any State all persons of any race are disqualified from voting at elections for the more numerous House of the Parliament of the State, then, in reckoning the number of the people of the State or of the Commonwealth, persons of that race resident in that State shall not be counted. *(Spent)*

26. Notwithstanding anything in section twenty-four, the number of members to be chosen in each State at the first election shall be as follows: —

~~New South Wales ... twenty-three;~~
~~Victoria—twenty;~~
~~Queensland—nine;~~
~~South Australia—six;~~
~~Tasmania—five;~~
~~Provided that if Western Australia is an Original State, the~~
~~numbers shall be as follows: —~~
~~New South Wales ... twenty-six;~~
~~Victoria—twenty-three;~~
~~Queensland—nine;~~
~~South Australia—seven;~~
~~Western Australia—five;~~
~~Tasmania—five.~~ *(Spent)*

27.   Subject to this Constitution, the Parliament may make laws for increasing or diminishing the number of the members of the House of Representatives.

28.   Every House of Representatives shall continue for three years from the first meeting of the House, and no longer, but may be sooner dissolved by the ~~Governor-General~~ *President*.

29.   Until the Parliament of the Commonwealth otherwise provides, the Parliament of any State may make laws for determining the divisions in each State for which members of the House of Representatives may be chosen, and the number of members to be chosen for each division. A division shall not be formed out of parts of different States.

       In the absence of other provision, each State shall be one electorate.

30.   Until the Parliament otherwise provides, the qualification of electors of members of the House of Representatives shall be in each State that which is prescribed by the law of the State as the qualification of electors of the more numerous House of Parliament of the State; but in the choosing of members each elector shall vote only once.

31.   Until the Parliament otherwise provides, but subject to this Constitution, the laws in force in each State for

the time being relating to elections for the more numerous House of the Parliament of the State shall, as nearly as practicable, apply to elections in the State of members of the House of Representatives.

32. The ~~Governor-General~~ *President* in Council may cause writs to be issued for general elections of members of the House of Representatives.

After the first general election, the writs shall be issued within ten days from the expiry of a House of Representatives or from the proclamation of a dissolution thereof.

33. Whenever a vacancy happens in the House of Representatives, the Speaker shall issue his *or her* writ for the election of a new member, or if there is no Speaker or if he *or she* is absent from the Commonwealth the ~~Governor-General~~ *President* in Council may issue the writ.

34. Until the Parliament otherwise provides, the qualifications of a member of the House of Representatives shall be as follows:—

   (i.) He *or she* must be *eighteen* ~~of the full age of twenty-one~~ years, and must be an elector entitled to vote at the election of members of the House of Representatives, or a person qualified to become such elector, and must have been for three years at the least a resident within the limits of the Commonwealth as existing at the time when he *or she* is chosen:

   (ii.) He *or she* must be ~~a subject of the Queen, either natural-born or for at least five years naturalized under a law of the United Kingdom, or of a Colony which has become or becomes a State, or of the Commonwealth, or of a State.~~ *an Australian citizen.*

35. The House of Representatives shall, before proceeding to the despatch of any other business, choose a member to be the Speaker of the House, and as often as the office of Speaker becomes vacant the House shall

again choose a member to be the Speaker.

The Speaker shall cease to hold his office if he *or she* ceases to be a member. He *or she* may be removed from office by a vote of the House, or he *or she* may resign his *or her* office or his *or her* seat by writing addressed to the ~~Governor-General.~~ *President.*

36. Before or during any absence of the Speaker, the House of Representatives may choose a member to perform his *or her* duties in his *or her* absence.

37. A member may by writing addressed to the Speaker, or to the ~~Governor-General~~ *President* if there is no Speaker or if the Speaker is absent from the Commonwealth, resign his *or her* place, which thereupon shall become vacant.

38. The place of a member shall become vacant if for two consecutive months of any session of the Parliament he *or she*, without the permission of the House, fails to attend the House.

39. Until the Parliament otherwise provides, the presence of at least one-third of the whole number of the members of the House of Representatives shall be necessary to constitute a meeting of the House for the exercise of its powers.

40. Questions arising in the House of Representatives shall be determined by a majority of votes other than that of the Speaker. The Speaker shall not vote unless the numbers are equal, and then he *or she* shall have a casting vote.

PART IV. — BOTH HOUSES OF THE PARLIAMENT.

41. No adult person who has or acquires a right to vote at elections for the more numerous House of the Parliament of a State shall, while the right continues, be prevented by any law of the Commonwealth from voting at elections for either House of the Parliament of the Commonwealth.

42. Every senator and every member of the House of Representatives shall before taking his *or her* seat make and subscribe before the ~~Governor-General~~ *President*

or some person authorized by him *or her*, an oath or affirmation of allegiance in the form set forth in the schedule to this Constitution.

43.   A member of either House of the Parliament shall be incapable of being chosen or of sitting as a member of the other House.

44.   Any person who —

(i.)   Is under any acknowledgement of allegiance, obedience, or adherence to a foreign power, or is a subject or a citizen or entitled to the rights or privileges of a subject or a citizen of a foreign power: or

(ii.)   Is attainted of treason, or has been convicted and is under sentence, or subject to be sentenced, for any offence punishable under the law of the Commonwealth or of a State by imprisonment for one year or longer: or

(iii.)   Is an undischarged bankrupt or insolvent: or

(iv.)   Holds any office of profit under the *executive government of the Commonwealth or a State or Territory of the Commonwealth* Crown, or any pension payable during the pleasure of the *Commonwealth or a State or Territory of the Commonwealth* Crown out of any of the revenues of the Commonwealth: or

(v.)   Has any direct or indirect pecuniary interest in any agreement with the Public Service of the Commonwealth otherwise than as a member and in common with the other members of an incorporated company consisting of more than twenty-five persons:

shall be incapable of being chosen or of sitting as a senator or a member of the House of Representatives.

But sub-section (iv.) does not apply to the office of any of the Queen's Ministers of State for the Commonwealth, or of any of the Queen's Ministers for a State, or to the receipt of pay, half pay, or a pension, by any person as an officer or member of the Queen's

~~navy or army~~ *defence forces of the Commonwealth*, or to the receipt of pay as an officer or member of the ~~naval or military~~ *defence* forces of the Commonwealth by any person whose services are not wholly employed by the Commonwealth.

45. If a senator or member of the House of Representatives —

    (i.) Becomes subject to any of the disabilities mentioned in the last preceding section: or

    (ii.) Takes the benefit, whether by assignment, composition, or otherwise, of any law relating to bankrupt or insolvent debtors: or

    (iii.) Directly or indirectly takes or agrees to take any fee or honorarium for services rendered to the Commonwealth, or for services rendered in the Parliament to any person or State:

    his *or her* place shall thereupon become vacant.

46. Until the Parliament otherwise provides, any person declared by this Constitution to be incapable of sitting as a senator or as a member of the House of Representatives shall, for every day on which he *or she* so sits, be liable to pay the sum of ~~one hundred pounds~~ *two hundred dollars* to any person who sues for it in any court of competent jurisdiction.

47. Until the Parliament otherwise provides, any question respecting the qualification of a senator or of a member of the House of Representatives, or respecting a vacancy in either House of the Parliament, and any question of a disputed election to either House, shall be determined by the House in which the question arises.

48. ~~Until the Parliament otherwise provides,~~ Each senator and each member of the House of Representatives shall receive *such remuneration as the Parliament may provide by law.* ~~an allowance of four hundred pounds a year, to be reckoned from the day on which he takes his seat.~~

49. The powers, privileges, and immunities of the Senate and of the House of Representatives, and of the mem-

bers and the committees of each House, shall be such as are declared by the Parliament, and until declared shall be those of the Commons House of Parliament of the United Kingdom, and of its members and committees, at the establishment of the Commonwealth.

50. Each House of the Parliament may make rules and orders with respect to —

(i.) The mode in which its powers, privileges, and immunities may be exercised and upheld:

(ii.) The order and conduct of its business and proceedings either separately or jointly with the other House.

PART V. — POWERS OF THE PARLIAMENT.

51. The Parliament shall, subject to this Constitution, have power to make laws for the peace, order and good government of the Commonwealth with respect to:—

(i.) Trade and commerce with other countries, and among the States:

(ii.) Taxation; but so as not to discriminate between States or parts of States:

(iii.) Bounties on the production or export of goods, but so that such bounties shall be uniform throughout the Commonwealth:

(iv.) Borrowing money on the public credit of the Commonwealth:

(v.) Postal, telegraphic, telephonic, and other like services:

(vi.) The naval and military defence of the Commonwealth and of the several States, and the control of the forces to execute and maintain the laws of the Commonwealth:

(vii.) Lighthouses, lightships, beacons and buoys:

(viii.) Astronomical and meteorological observations:

(ix.) Quarantine:

(x.) Fisheries in Australian waters beyond territorial limits:

(xi.) Census and statistics:

(xii.) Currency, coinage, and legal tender:

(xiii.) Banking, other than State banking; also State banking extending beyond the limits of the State concerned, the incorporation of banks, and the issue of paper money:

(xiv.) Insurance, other than State insurance; also State insurance extending beyond the limits of the State concerned:

(xv.) Weights and measures:

(xvi.) Bills of exchange and promissory notes:

(xvii.) Bankruptcy and insolvency:

(xviii.) Copyrights, patents of inventions and designs, and trade marks:

(xix.) Naturalisation and aliens:

(xx.) Foreign corporations, and trading or financial corporations formed within the limits of the Commonwealth:

(xxi.) Marriage:

(xxii.) Divorce and matrimonial causes; and in relation thereto, parental rights, and the custody and guardianship of infants:

(xxiii.) Invalid and old-age pensions:

(xxiiia.) The provision of maternity allowances, widows' pensions, child endowment, unemployment, pharmaceutical, sickness and hospital benefits, medical and dental services (but not so as to authorize any form of civil conscription), benefits to students and family allowances:

(xxiv.) The service and execution throughout the Commonwealth of the civil and criminal process and the judgments of the courts of the States:

(xxv.) The recognition throughout the Commonwealth of the laws, the public Acts and records, and the judicial proceedings of the States:

(xxvi.) The people of any race for whom it is deemed necessary to make special laws:

(xxvii.) Immigration and emigration:

(xxviii.) The influx of criminals:

(xxix.) External affairs:

(xxx.) The relations of the Commonwealth with the islands of the Pacific:

(xxxi.) The acquisition of property on just terms from any State or person for any purpose in respect of which the Parliament has power to make laws:

(xxxii.) The control of railways with respect to transport for the naval and military purposes of the Commonwealth:

(xxxiii.) The acquisition, with the consent of a State, of any railways of the State on terms arranged between the Commonwealth and the State:

(xxxiv.) Railway construction and extension in any State with the consent of that State:

(xxxv.) Conciliation and arbitration for the prevention and settlement of industrial disputes extending beyond the limits of any one State:

(xxxvi.) Matters in respect of which this Constitution makes provision until the Parliament otherwise provides:

(xxxvii.) Matters referred to the Parliament of the Commonwealth by the Parliament or Parliaments of any State or States, but so that the law shall extend only to States by whose Parliaments the matter is referred, or which afterwards adopt the law:

(xxxviii.) The exercise within the Commonwealth, at the request or with the concurrence of the Parliaments of all States directly concerned, of any power which can at the establishment of this Constitution be exercised only by the Parliament of the United Kingdom or by the Federal Council of Australasia:

(xxxix.) Matters incidental to the execution of any power vested by this Constitution in the Parliament or in either House thereof, or in the Government of the Commonwealth, or in the Federal Judicature, or in any department or officer of the Commonwealth.

52.　The Parliament shall, subject to this Constitution, have exclusive power to make laws for the peace, order and good government of the Commonwealth with respect to —

(i.)　The seat of government of the Commonwealth, and all places acquired by the Commonwealth for public purposes:

(ii.)　Matters relating to any department of the public service the control of which is by this Constitution transferred to the Executive Government of the Commonwealth:

(iii.)　Other matters declared by this Constitution to be within the exclusive power of the Parliament.

53.　Proposed laws appropriating revenue or moneys, or imposing taxation, shall not originate in the Senate. But a proposed law shall not be taken to appropriate revenue or moneys, or to impose taxation, by reason only of its containing provisions for the imposition or appropriation of fines or other pecuniary penalties, or for the demand or payment or appropriation of fees for licences, or fees for services under the proposed law.

The Senate may not amend proposed laws imposing taxation, or proposed laws appropriating revenue or moneys for the ordinary annual services of the Government.

The Senate may not amend any proposed law so as to increase any proposed charge or burden on the people.

The Senate may at any stage return to the House of Representatives any proposed law which the Senate may not amend, requesting, by message, the omission or amendment of any items or provisions therein. And the House of Representatives may, if it thinks fit, make any of such omissions or amendments, with or without modifications.

Except as provided in this section, the Senate shall have equal power with the House of Representatives in respect of all proposed laws.

54. The proposed law which appropriates revenue or moneys for the ordinary annual services of the Government shall deal only with such appropriation.

55. Laws imposing taxation shall deal only with the imposition of taxation, and any provision therein dealing with any other matter shall be of no effect.

    Laws imposing taxation, except laws imposing duties of customs or of excise, shall deal with one subject of taxation only; but laws imposing duties of customs shall deal with duties of customs only, and laws imposing duties of excise shall deal with duties of excise only.

56. A vote, resolution, or proposed law for the appropriation of revenue or moneys shall not be passed unless the purpose of the appropriation has in the same session been recommended by message of the ~~Governor-General~~ *President* to the House in which the proposal originated.

57. If the House of Representatives passes any proposed law, and the Senate rejects or fails to pass it, or passes it with amendments to which the House of Representatives will not agree, and if after an interval of three months the House of Representatives, in the same or the next session, again passes the proposed law with or without any amendments which have been made, suggested, or agreed to by the Senate, and the Senate rejects or fails to pass it, or passes it with amendments to which the House of Representatives will not agree, the ~~Governor-General~~ *President* may dissolve the Senate and the House of Representatives simultaneously. But such dissolution shall not take place within six months before the date of the expiry of the House of Representatives by effluxion of time.

    If after such dissolution the House of Representatives again passes the proposed law, with or without any amendments which have been made, suggested, or agreed to by the Senate, and the Senate rejects or fails to pass it, or passes it with amendments to which the House of Representatives will not agree, the ~~Gov-~~

~~ernor General~~ *President in Council* may convene a joint sitting of the members of the Senate and of the House of Representatives.

The members present at the joint sitting may deliberate and shall vote together upon the proposed law as last proposed by the House of Representatives, and upon amendments, if any, which have been made therein by one House and not agreed to by the other, and any such amendments which are affirmed by an absolute majority of the total number of the members of the Senate and House of Representatives shall be taken to have been carried, and if the proposed law, with the amendments, if any, so carried is affirmed by an absolute majority of the total number of the members of the Senate and House of Representatives, it shall be taken to have been duly passed by both Houses of the Parliament, and shall be presented to the ~~Governor General~~ *President* for ~~the Queen's~~ assent.

58.(*i.*) Subject only to sub-section (ii.), when a proposed law passed by both Houses of the Parliament is presented to the ~~Governor General~~ *President* for ~~the Queen's~~ assent, he *or she* shall ~~declare, according to his discretion, but subject to this Constitution, that he assents in the Queen's name, or that he withholds assent, or that he reserves the law for the Queen's pleasure.~~ *assent to it if so advised by the Federal Executive Council.*

(*ii.*) The ~~Governor General~~ *President in Council* may return to the House in which it originated any proposed law so presented to him *or her*, and may transmit therewith any amendments which ~~he~~ *the President in Council* may recommend, and the Houses may deal with the recommendation.

59. ~~The Queen may disallow any law within one year from the Governor General 's assent, and such disallowance on being made known by the Governor General by speech or message to each of the Houses of the Parliament, or by Proclamation, shall annul the law from the day when the disallowance is made known.~~ *(Obsolete)*

60. ~~A proposed law reserved for the Queen's pleasure shall not have any force unless and until within two years from the day on which it was presented to the Governor General for the Queen's assent the Governor General makes known, by speech or message to each of the Houses of the Parliament, or by Proclamation, that it has received the Queen's assent.~~ *(Obsolete)*

CHAPTER II. — THE EXECUTIVE GOVERNMENT.

61. The executive power of the Commonwealth is vested in the ~~Queen~~ *President* and is exerciseable ~~by the Governor General as the Queen's representative~~ *on the advice of the Federal Executive Council,* and extends to the execution and maintenance of this Constitution, and of the laws of the Commonwealth.

62. There shall be a Federal Executive Council to advise the ~~Governor General~~ *President* in the government of the Commonwealth, and the members of the Council shall be chosen and summoned by the ~~Governor General~~ *President in accordance with the advice of the Prime Minister* and sworn as Executive Councillors, and shall hold office ~~during his pleasure~~ *until such time as the President is advised by the Prime Minister to terminate such office.*

63. The provisions of this Constitution referring to the ~~Governor General~~ *President* in Council shall be construed as referring to the ~~Governor General~~ *President* acting with the advice of the Federal Executive Council.

64. The ~~Governor General~~ *President acting on the advice of the Prime Minister* may appoint officers to administer such departments of State of the Commonwealth as the ~~Governor General~~ *President* in Council may establish.

~~Such officers shall hold office during the pleasure of the Governor General. They shall be members of the Federal Executive Council, and shall be the Queen's Ministers of State for the Commonwealth.~~

65. ~~Until the Parliament otherwise provides, the Ministers of State shall not exceed seven in number, and shall~~

~~hold such offices as the Parliament prescribes, or, in the absence of provision, as the Governor General directs.~~

66. There shall be payable, ~~to the Queen,~~ out of the Consolidated Revenue Fund of the Commonwealth, ~~for~~ the salaries of the Ministers of State, an annual sum ~~which, until~~ *fixed by* the Parliament. ~~otherwise provides, shall not exceed twelve thousand pounds a year.~~

67. Until the Parliament otherwise provides, the appointment and removal of all other officers of the Executive Government of the Commonwealth shall be vested in the ~~Governor-General~~ *President* in Council, unless the appointment is delegated by the ~~Governor-General~~ *President* in Council or by a law of the Commonwealth to some other authority.

68. The command in chief of the ~~naval and military~~ *defence* forces of the Commonwealth is vested in the ~~Governor-General as the Queen's representative~~ *President acting with the advice of the Executive Council.*

~~69.~~ ~~On a date or dates to be proclaimed by the Governor-General after the establishment of the Commonwealth the following departments of the public service in each State shall become transferred to the Commonwealth: —~~
~~Posts, telegraphs, and telephones:~~
~~Naval and military defence:~~
~~Lighthouses, lightships, beacons, and buoys:~~
~~Quarantine.~~
~~But the departments of customs and of excise in each State shall become transferred to the Commonwealth on its establishment.~~ *(Spent)*

70. In respect of matters which, under this Constitution, pass to the Executive Government of the Commonwealth, all powers and functions which at the establishment of the Commonwealth are vested in the Governor of a Colony, or in the Governor of a Colony with the advice of his Executive Council, or in any

authority of a Colony, shall vest in the ~~Governor General~~ *President*, or in the ~~Governor General~~ *President* in Council, or in the authority exercising similar powers under the Commonwealth, as the case requires.

CHAPTER III. — THE JUDICATURE.

71. The judicial power of the Commonwealth shall be vested in a Federal Supreme Court, to be called the High Court of Australia, and in such other federal courts as the Parliament creates, and in such other courts as it invests with federal jurisdiction. The High Court shall consist of a Chief Justice, and so many other Justices, not less than two, as the Parliament prescribes.

72. The Justices of the High Court and of the other courts created by the Parliament —

   (i.) Shall be appointed by the ~~Governor General~~ *President* in Council:

   (ii.) Shall not be removed except by the ~~Governor General~~ *President* in Council, on an address from both Houses of the Parliament in the same session, praying for such removal on the ground of proved misbehaviour or incapacity:

   (iii.) Shall receive such remuneration as the Parliament may fix; but the remuneration shall not be diminished during their continuance in office.

The appointment of a Justice of the High Court shall be for a term expiring upon his *or her* attaining the age of seventy years, and a person shall not be appointed as a Justice of the High Court if he *or she* has attained that age.

The appointment of a Justice of a court created by the Parliament shall be for a term expiring upon his *or her* attaining the age that is, at the time of his *or her* appointment, the age for Justices of that court and a person shall not be appointed as a Justice of such a court if he *or she* has attained the age that is for the time being the maximum age for Justices of that court.

Subject to this section, the maximum age for

Justices of any court created by the Parliament is seventy years.

The Parliament may make a law fixing an age that is less than seventy years as the maximum age for Justices of a court created by the Parliament and may at any time repeal or amend such a law, but any such repeal or amendment does not affect the term of office of a Justice under an appointment made before the repeal or amendment.

A Justice of the High Court or of a court created by the Parliament may resign his office by writing under his *or her* hand delivered to the ~~Governor General~~ *President*.

Nothing in the provisions added to this section by the *Constitution Alteration (Retirement of Judges)* 1977 affects the continuance of a person in office as a Justice of a court under an appointment made before the commencement of those provisions.

A reference in this section to the appointment of a Justice of the High Court or of a court created by the Parliament shall be read as including a reference to the appointment of a person who holds office as a Justice of the High Court or of a court created by the Parliament to another office of Justice of the same court having a different status or designation.

73.   The High Court shall have jurisdiction, with such exceptions and subject to such regulations as the Parliament prescribes, to hear and determine appeals from all judgments, decrees, orders and sentences:

    (i.)   Of any Justice or Justices exercising the original jurisdiction of the High Court:

    (ii.)   Of any other federal court, or court exercising federal jurisdiction; or of the Supreme Court of any State, or of any other court of any State from which at the establishment of the Commonwealth an appeal lies to the Queen in Council:

    (iii.)   Of the Inter-State Commission, but as to questions of law only:

and the judgment of the High Court in all such cases

shall be final and conclusive.

But no exception or regulation prescribed by the Parliament shall prevent the High Court from hearing and determining any appeal from the Supreme Court of a State in any matter in which at the establishment of the Commonwealth an appeal lies from such Supreme Court to the Queen in Council.

~~Until the Parliament otherwise provides, the conditions of and restrictions on appeals to the Queen in Council from the Supreme Courts of the several States shall be applicable to appeals from them to the High Court.~~

74. ~~No appeal shall be permitted to the Queen in Council from a decision of the High Court upon any question, howsoever arising, as to the limits inter se of the Constitutional powers of the Commonwealth and those of any State or States, or as to the limits inter se of the Constitutional powers of any two or more States, unless the High Court shall certify that the question is one which ought to be determined by Her Majesty in Council.~~

~~The High Court may so certify if satisfied that for any special reason the certificate should be granted, and thereupon an appeal shall lie to Her Majesty in Council on the question without further leave.~~

~~Except as provided in this section, the Constitution shall not impair any right which the Queen may be pleased to exercise by virtue of Her Royal prerogative to grant special leave of appeal from the High Court to Her Majesty in Council. The Parliament may make laws limiting the matters in which such leave may be asked, but proposed laws containing any such limitation shall be reserved by the Governor General for Her Majesty's pleasure.~~ *(Spent)*

75. In all matters —
    (i.) Arising under any treaty:
    (ii.) Affecting consuls or other representatives of other countries:
    (iii.) In which the Commonwealth, or a person suing

or being sued on behalf of the Commonwealth, is a party:

(iv.) Between States, or between residents of different States, or between a State and a resident of another State:

(v.) In which a writ of Mandamus or prohibition or an injunction is sought against an officer of the Commonwealth:

the High Court shall have original jurisdiction.

76. The Parliament may make laws conferring original jurisdiction on the High Court in any matter —

(i.) Arising under this Constitution, or involving its interpretation:

(ii.) Arising under any laws made by the Parliament:

(iii.) Of Admiralty and maritime jurisdiction:

(iv.) Relating to the same subject-matter claimed under the laws of different States.

77. With respect to any of the matters mentioned in the last two sections the Parliament may make laws —

(i.) Defining the jurisdiction of any federal court other than the High Court:

(ii.) Defining the extent to which the jurisdiction of any federal court shall be exclusive of that which belongs to or is invested in the courts of the States:

(iii.) Investing any court of a State with federal jurisdiction.

78. The Parliament may make laws conferring rights to proceed against the Commonwealth or a State in respect of matters within the limits of the judicial power.

79. The federal jurisdiction of any court may be exercised by such number of judges as the Parliament prescribes.

80. The trial on indictment of any offence against any law of the Commonwealth shall be by jury, and every such trial shall be held in the State where the offence was

committed, and if the offence was not committed within any State the trial shall be held at such place or places as the Parliament prescribes.

CHAPTER IV. — FINANCE AND TRADE.

81. All revenues or moneys raised or received by the Executive Government of the Commonwealth shall form one Consolidated Revenue Fund, to be appropriated for the purposes of the Commonwealth in the manner and subject to the charges and liabilities imposed by this Constitution.

82. The costs, charges, and expenses incident to the collection, management, and receipt of the Consolidated Revenue Fund shall form the first charge thereon; and the revenue of the Commonwealth shall in the first instance be applied to the payment of the expenditure of the Commonwealth.

83. No money shall be drawn from the Treasury of the Commonwealth except under appropriation made by law.

~~But until the expiration of one month after the first meeting of the Parliament the Governor-General in Council may draw from the Treasury and expend such moneys as may be necessary for the maintenance of any department transferred to the Commonwealth and for the holding of the first elections for the Parliament.~~ *(Spent)*

84. When any department of the public service of a State becomes transferred to the Commonwealth, all officers of the department shall become subject to the control of the Executive Government of the Commonwealth.

Any such officer who is not retained in the service of the Commonwealth shall, unless he *or she* is appointed to some other office of equal emolument in the public service of the State, be entitled to receive from the State any pension, gratuity, or other compensation, payable under the law of the State on the abolition of his *or her* office.

Any such officer who is retained in the service of the Commonwealth shall preserve all his *or her* existing and accruing rights, and shall be entitled to retire from office at the time, and on the pension or retiring allowance, which would be permitted by the law of the State if his *or her* service with the Commonwealth were a continuation of his *or her* service with the State. Such pension or retiring allowance shall be paid to him *or her* by the Commonwealth; but the State shall pay to the Commonwealth a part thereof, to be calculated on the proportion which his *or her* term of service with the State bears to his *or her* whole term of service, and for the purpose of the calculation his *or her* salary shall be taken to be that paid to him *or her* by the State at the time of the transfer.

~~Any officer who is, at the establishment of the Commonwealth, in the public service of a State, and who is, by consent of the Governor of the State with the advice of the Executive Council thereof, transferred to the public service of the Commonwealth, shall have the same rights as if he had been an officer of a department transferred to the Commonwealth and were retained in the service of the Commonwealth.~~ *(Spent)*

85. When any department of the public service of a State is transferred to the Commonwealth —

    (i.) All property of the State of any kind, used exclusively in connexion with the department, shall become vested in the Commonwealth; ~~but, in the case of the departments controlling customs and excise and bounties, for such time only as the Governor General in Council may declare to be necessary:~~

    (ii.) The Commonwealth may acquire any property of the State, of any kind used, but not exclusively used in connexion with the department; the value thereof shall, if no agreement can be made, be ascertained in, as nearly as may be, the manner in which the value of land, or of an interest in land, taken by the State for public purposes is ascertained under the law of the State in force at the establishment of the Commonwealth:

(iii.) The Commonwealth shall compensate the State for the value of any property passing to the Commonwealth under this section; if no agreement can be made as to the mode of compensation, it shall be determined under laws to be made by the Parliament:

(iv.) The Commonwealth shall, at the date of the transfer, assume the current obligations of the State in respect of the department transferred.

86. ~~On the establishment of the Commonwealth, the collection and control of duties of customs and of excise, and the control of the payment of bounties, shall pass to the Executive Government of the Commonwealth.~~ *(Spent)*

87. ~~During a period of ten years after the establishment of the Commonwealth and thereafter until the Parliament otherwise provides, of the net revenue of the Commonwealth from duties of customs and of excise not more than one-fourth shall be applied annually by the Commonwealth towards its expenditure.~~ *(Spent)*

~~The balance shall, in accordance with this Constitution, be paid to the several States, or applied towards the payment of interest on debts of the several States taken over by the Commonwealth.~~ *(Spent)*

88. Uniform duties of customs shall be imposed within two years after the establishment of the Commonwealth.

89. ~~Until the imposition of uniform duties of customs —~~

~~(i.) The Commonwealth shall credit to each State the revenues collected therein by the Commonwealth.~~

~~(ii.) The Commonwealth shall debit to each State: —~~

~~(a) The expenditure therein of the Commonwealth incurred solely for the maintenance or~~

~~continuance, as at the time of transfer, of any department transferred from the State to the Commonwealth:~~

~~(b) The proportion of the State, according to the number of its people, in the other expenditure of the Commonwealth.~~

~~(iii.) The Commonwealth shall pay to each State month by month the balance (if any) in favour of the State.~~ *(Spent)*

90. On the imposition of uniform duties of customs the power of the Parliament to impose duties of customs and of excise, and to grant bounties on the production or export of goods, shall become exclusive.

~~On the imposition of uniform duties of customs all laws of the several States imposing duties of customs or of excise, or offering bounties on the production or export of goods, shall cease to have effect, but any grant of or agreement for any such bounty lawfully made by or under the authority of the Government of any State shall be taken to be good if made before the thirtieth day of June, one thousand eight hundred and ninety-eight, and not otherwise.~~ *(Spent)*

91. Nothing in this Constitution prohibits a State from granting any aid to or bounty on mining for gold, silver, or other metals, nor from granting, with the consent of both Houses of the Parliament of the Commonwealth expressed by resolution, any aid to or bounty on the production or export of goods.

92. On the imposition of uniform duties of customs, trade, commerce, and intercourse among the States, whether by means of internal carriage or ocean navigation, shall be absolutely free.

~~But notwithstanding anything in this Constitution, goods imported before the imposition of uniform duties of customs into any State, or into any Colony which, whilst the goods remain therein, becomes a State, shall, on thence passing into another State within two years after the imposition of such duties, be~~

~~liable to any duty chargeable on the importation of
such goods into the Commonwealth, less any duty
paid in respect of the goods on their importation.~~
(Spent)

~~93.~~ ~~During the first five years after the imposition of uniform duties of customs, and thereafter until the Parliament otherwise provides —~~

  ~~(i.)~~ ~~The duties of customs chargeable on goods
imported into a State and afterwards passing
into another State for consumption, and the
duties of excise paid on goods produced or
manufactured in a State and afterwards passing
into another State for consumption, shall be
taken to have been collected not in the former
but in the latter State:~~

  ~~(ii.)~~ ~~Subject to the last subsection, the Commonwealth shall credit revenue, debit expenditure,
and pay balances to the several States as prescribed for the period preceding the imposition
of uniform duties of customs.~~ *(Spent)*

94. After five years from the imposition of uniform duties
of customs, the Parliament may provide, on such basis
as it deems fair, for the monthly payment to the several States of all surplus revenue of the Commonwealth.

~~95.~~ ~~Notwithstanding anything in this Constitution, the
Parliament of the State of Western Australia, if that
State be an Original State, may, during the first five
years after the imposition of uniform duties of customs, impose duties of customs on goods passing into
that State and not originally imported from beyond
the limits of the Commonwealth; and such duties
shall be collected by the Commonwealth.~~

  ~~But any duty so imposed on any goods shall not
exceed during the first of such years the duty chargeable on the goods under the law of Western Australia
in force at the imposition of uniform duties, and shall
not exceed during the second, third, fourth, and fifth
of such years respectively, four fifths, three fifths,~~

~~two fifths, and one fifth of such latter duty, and all duties imposed under this section shall cease at the expiration of the fifth year after the imposition of uniform duties.~~

~~If at any time during the five years the duty on any goods under this section is higher than the duty imposed by the Commonwealth on the importation of the like goods, then such higher duty shall be collected on the goods when imported into Western Australia from beyond the limits of the Commonwealth.~~ *(Spent)*

96. ~~During a period of ten years after the establishment of the Commonwealth and thereafter until the Parliament otherwise provides,~~ The Parliament may grant financial assistance to any State on such terms and conditions as the Parliament thinks fit.

97. ~~Until the Parliament otherwise provides, the laws in force in any Colony which has become or becomes a State with respect to the receipt of revenue and the expenditure of money on account of the Government of the Colony, and the revenue and audit of such receipt and expenditure, shall apply to the receipt of revenue and the expenditure of money on account of the Commonwealth in the State in the same manner as if the Commonwealth, or the Government or an officer of the Commonwealth, were mentioned whenever the Colony, or the Government or an officer of the Colony, is mentioned.~~ *(Spent)*

98. The power of the Parliament to make laws in respect to trade and commerce extends to navigation and shipping, and to railways the property of any State.

99. The Commonwealth shall not, by any law or regulation of trade, commerce, or revenue, give preference to one State or any part thereof over another State or any part thereof.

100. The Commonwealth shall not, by any law or regulation of trade or commerce, abridge the right of a State or of the residents therein to the reasonable use of the waters of rivers for conservation or irrigation.

101. There shall be an Inter-State Commission, with such powers of adjudication and administration as the Parliament deems necessary for the execution and maintenance, within the Commonwealth, of the provisions of this Constitution relating to trade and commerce, and of all laws made thereunder.

102. The Parliament may by any law with respect to trade or commerce forbid, as to railways, any preference or discrimination by any State, or by any authority constituted under a State, if such preference or discrimination is undue and unreasonable, or unjust to any State; due regard being had to the financial responsibilities incurred by any State in connexion with the construction and maintenance of its railways. But no preference or discrimination shall, within the meaning of this section, be taken to be undue and unreasonable, or unjust to any State, unless so adjudged by the Inter-State Commission.

103. The members of the Inter-State Commission —

   (i.) Shall be appointed by the ~~Governor-General~~ *President* in Council:

   (ii.) Shall hold office for seven years, but may be removed within that time by the ~~Governor-General~~ *President* in Council, on an address from both Houses of the Parliament in the same session praying for such removal on the ground of proved misbehaviour or incapacity:

   (iii.) Shall receive such remuneration as the Parliament may fix; but such remuneration shall not be diminished during their continuance in office.

104. Nothing in this Constitution shall render unlawful any rate for the carriage of goods upon a railway, the property of a State, if the rate is deemed by the Inter-State Commission to be necessary for the development of the territory of the State, and if the rate applies equally to goods within the State and to goods passing into the State from other States.

105. The Parliament may take over from the States their

public debts or a proportion thereof according to the respective numbers of their people as shown by the latest statistics of the Commonwealth, and may convert, renew, or consolidate such debts, or any part thereof; and the States shall indemnify the Commonwealth in respect of the debts taken over, and thereafter the interest payable in respect of the debts shall be deducted and retained from the portions of the surplus revenue of the Commonwealth payable to the several States, or if such surplus is insufficient, or if there is no surplus, then the deficiency or the whole amount shall be paid by the several States.

105A.(1) The Commonwealth may make agreements with the States with respect to the public debts of the States, including —

    (a)   the taking over of such debts by the Commonwealth;

    (b)   the management of such debts;

    (c)   the payment of interest and the provision and management of sinking funds in respect of such debts;

    (d)   the consolidation, renewal, conversion and redemption of such debts;

    (e)   the indemnification of the Commonwealth by the States in respect of debts taken over by the Commonwealth; and

    (f)   the borrowing of money by the States or by the Commonwealth, or by the Commonwealth for the States.

(2) The Parliament may make laws for validating any such agreement made before the commencement of this section.

(3) The Parliament may make laws for the carrying out by the parties thereto of any such agreement.

(4) Any such agreement may be varied or rescinded by the parties thereto.

(5) Every such agreement and any such variation thereof shall be binding upon the Common-

wealth and the States parties thereto notwithstanding anything contained in this Constitution or the Constitution of the several States or in any law of the Parliament of the Commonwealth or of any State.

(6) The powers conferred by this section shall not be construed as being limited in any way by the provisions of section one hundred and five of this Constitution.

CHAPTER V.— THE STATES.

106. The Constitution of each State of the Commonwealth shall, subject to this Constitution, continue as at the establishment of the Commonwealth, or as at the admission or establishment of the State, as the case may be, until altered in accordance with the Constitution of the State.

107. Every power of the Parliament of a Colony which has become or becomes a State, shall, unless it is by this Constitution exclusively vested in the Parliament of the Commonwealth or withdrawn from the Parliament of the State, continue as at the establishment of the Commonwealth, or as at the admission or establishment of the State, as the case may be.

108. Every law in force in a Colony which has become or becomes a State, and relating to any matter within the powers of the Parliament of the Commonwealth, shall, subject to this Constitution, continue in force in the State; and until provision is made in that behalf by the Parliament of the Commonwealth, the Parliament of the State shall have such powers of alteration and of repeal in respect of any such law as the Parliament of the Colony had until the Colony became a State.

109. When a law of a State is inconsistent with a law of the Commonwealth, the latter shall prevail, and the former shall, to the extent of the inconsistency, be invalid.

110.(i.) The provisions of this Constitution relating to the Governor of a State extend and apply to the Governor for the time being of the State, or other chief executive officer or administrator of the Government of the State.

(ii.) *Subject to this Constitution, including this section, the manner in which a State Governor is appointed and removed, and the tenure, powers, functions and all other matters relating to the office of Governor shall be such as are prescribed by the law of the State.*

(iii.) *The Governor of a State shall be the Head of State of that State and no State Governor shall represent or be appointed by any person who is the Head of State of another country or is an officer in the Government of another country.*

(iv.) *The Commonwealth Parliament shall, subject to this Constitution, have the power to make laws which enact and implement the provisions of this Section.*

111. The Parliament of a State may surrender any part of the State to the Commonwealth; and upon such surrender, and the acceptance thereof by the Commonwealth, such part of the State shall become subject to the exclusive jurisdiction of the Commonwealth.

112. After uniform duties of customs have been imposed, a State may levy on imports or exports, or on goods passing into or out of the State, such charges as may be necessary for executing the inspection laws of the State; but the net produce of all charges so levied shall be for the use of the Commonwealth; and any such inspection laws may be annulled by the Parliament of the Commonwealth.

113. All fermented, distilled, or other intoxicating liquids passing into any State or remaining therein for use, consumption, sale, or storage, shall be subject to the laws of the State as if such liquids had been produced in the State.

114. A State shall not, without the consent of the Parliament of the Commonwealth, raise or maintain any naval or military force, or impose any tax on property of any kind belonging to the Commonwealth, nor shall the Commonwealth impose any tax

on property of any kind belonging to a State.

115. A State shall not coin money, nor make anything but gold and silver coin a legal tender in payment of debts.

116. The Commonwealth shall not make any law for establishing any religion, or for imposing any religious observance, or for prohibiting the free exercise of any religion, and no religious test shall be required as a qualification for any office or public trust under the Commonwealth.

117. ~~A subject of the Queen,~~ *An Australian citizen*, resident in any State, shall not be subject in any other State to any disability or discrimination which would not be equally applicable to him *or her* if he *or she* were ~~a sub-ject of the Queen~~ *an Australian citizen* resident in such other State.

118. Full faith and credit shall be given, throughout the Commonwealth, to the laws, the public Acts and records, and the judicial proceedings of every State.

119. The Commonwealth shall protect every State against invasion and, on the application of the Executive Government of the State, against domestic violence.

120. Every State shall make provision for the detention in its prisons of persons accused or convicted of offences against the laws of the Commonwealth, and for the punishment of persons convicted of such offences, and the Parliament of the Commonwealth may make laws to give effect to this provision.

CHAPTER VI. — NEW STATES.

121. The Parliament may admit to the Commonwealth or establish new States, and may upon such admission or establishment make or impose such terms and conditions, including the extent of representation in either House of the Parliament, as it thinks fit.

122. The Parliament may make laws for the government of any territory surrendered by any State to and accepted by the Commonwealth, ~~or of any territory placed by the Queen under the authority of and~~

~~accepted by the Commonwealth,~~ or otherwise acquired by the Commonwealth, and may allow the representation of such territory in either House of the Parliament to the extent and on the terms which it thinks fit.

123. The Parliament of the Commonwealth may, with the consent of the Parliament of a State, and the approval of the majority of the electors of the State voting upon the question, increase, diminish, or otherwise alter the limits of the State, upon such terms and conditions as may be agreed on, and may, with the like consent, make provision respecting the effect and operation of any increase or diminution or alteration of territory in relation to any State affected.

124. A new State may be formed by separation of territory from a State, but only with the consent of the Parliament thereof, and a new State may be formed by the union of two or more States or parts of States, but only with the consent of the Parliaments of the States affected.

CHAPTER VII. — MISCELLANEOUS.

125. The seat of Government of the Commonwealth shall be determined by the Parliament, and shall be within territory which shall have been granted to or acquired by the Commonwealth, and shall be vested in and belong to the Commonwealth, and shall be in the State of New South Wales, and be distant not less than one hundred miles from Sydney.

Such territory shall contain an area of not less than one hundred square miles, and such portion thereof as shall consist of Crown lands shall be granted to the Commonwealth without any payment therefor.

~~The Parliament shall sit at Melbourne until it meets at the seat of Government.~~

126. The ~~Queen~~ *President with the advice of the Executive Council* may ~~authorize the Governor-General to~~ appoint any person, or any persons jointly or severally, to be his *or her* deputy or deputies within any part of

the Commonwealth, and in that capacity to exercise ~~during the pleasure of the Governor General~~ such powers and functions of the ~~Governor General as he thinks fit to assign to such deputy or deputies, subject to any limitations expressed or directions given by the Queen~~ *President as are assigned to the deputy or deputies aforesaid;* but the appointment of such deputy or deputies shall not affect the exercise by the ~~Governor General~~ *President* himself *or herself* of any power or function.

CHAPTER VIII. — ALTERATION OF THE CONSTITUTION.

128. This Constitution shall not be altered except in the following manner —

The proposed law for the alteration thereof must be passed by an absolute majority of each House of the Parliament, and not less than two nor more than six months after its passage through both Houses the proposed law shall be submitted in each State and Territory to the electors qualified to vote for the election of members of the House of Representatives.

But if either House passes any such proposed law by an absolute majority, and the other House rejects or fails to pass it, or passes it with any amendment to which the first-mentioned House will not agree, and if after an interval of three months the first-mentioned House in the same or the next session again passes the proposed law by an absolute majority with or without any amendment which has been made or agreed to by the other House, and such other House rejects or fails to pass it or passes it with any amendment to which the first-mentioned House will not agree, the ~~Governor General~~ *President in Council* may submit the proposed law as last proposed by the first-mentioned House, and either with or without any amendments subsequently agreed to by both Houses, to the electors in each State and Territory qualified to vote for the election of the House of Representatives.

When a proposed law is submitted to the electors the vote shall be taken in such manner as the Parliament prescribes. But until the qualification of electors of members of the House of Representatives becomes uniform throughout the Commonwealth, only one-half the electors voting for and against the proposed law shall be counted in any State in which adult suffrage prevails.

And if in a majority of the States a majority of the electors voting approve the proposed law, and if a majority of all the electors voting also approve the proposed law, it shall be presented to the ~~Governor-General for the Queen's assent.~~ *President who shall assent to it.*

No alteration diminishing the proportionate representation of any State in either House of the Parliament, or the minimum number of representatives of a State in the House of Representatives, or increasing, diminishing, or otherwise altering the limits of the State, or in any manner affecting the provisions of the Constitution in relation thereto, shall become law unless the majority of the electors voting in that State approve the proposed law.

In this section 'Territory' means any territory referred to in section one hundred and twenty-two of this Constitution in respect of which there is in force a law allowing its representation in the House of Representatives.

SCHEDULE.

OATH

I, A.B., do swear that I ~~will be faithful and bear true allegiance to Her Majesty Queen Victoria, Her Heirs and Successors according to law.~~ *pledge my loyalty to Australia and its people whose democratic beliefs I share whose rights and liberties I respect and whose Constitution and laws I will uphold and obey.* SO HELP ME GOD!

AFFIRMATION

I, A.B., do solemnly and sincerely affirm and declare that I ~~will be faithful and bear true allegiance to Her Majesty~~

~~Queen Victoria, Her heirs and successors according to law.~~
*pledge my loyalty to Australia and its people whose democratic
beliefs I share whose rights and liberties I respect and whose Constitution and laws I will uphold and obey.*

~~(NOTE. The name of the King or Queen of the United Kingdom
of Great Britain and Ireland for the time being is to be substituted
from time to time.)~~

APPENDIX TWO[2]

MEMBERS OF THE COMMONWEALTH OF NATIONS

Governors–General[1]	Monarchies	Republics[4]
Antigua and Barbuda (1981)	Brunei (Sultanate)	Bangladesh (1971) (NEP)[5]
Australia[2]	Lesotho	Botswana (1965, 1966) (EP)[6]
The Bahamas (1973)	Malaysia	Cyprus (1960) (EP)
Barbados (1966)	Swaziland	Dominica (1978) (NEP)
Belize (1981)	Tonga	The Gambia (1965, 1970) (EP)
Canada[2]	Western Samoa	Ghana (1957, 1960) (EP)
Grenada (1974)	(Paramount Chief)[3]	Guyana (1960, 1970) (EP)
Jamaica (1962)	United Kingdom	India (1947, 1950) (NEP)
New Zealand[2]		Kenya (1963, 1964) (EP)
Papua New Guinea (1975)		Kiribati (1979) (EP)
St. Christopher & Nevis (1983)		Malawi (1964, 1966) (EP)
St. Lucia (1979)		Maldives (1965) (EP)
St. Vincent & The Grenadines (1979)		Malta (1964, 1974) (NEP)
Solomon Islands (1978)		Mauritius (1968, 1992) (NEP)
Tuvalu (1978)		Namibia (1990) (EP)
		Nauru (1968) (EP)
		Nigeria (1960, 1963) (EP)
		Pakistan (1947, 1956) (NEP)
		Seychelles (1961, 1966) (EP)
		Sierra Leone (1961, 1971) (EP)
		Singapore (1965) (NEP)
		Sri Lanka (1948, 1972) (EP)
		Tanzania (1964) (EP)
		(Tanganyika 1961, 1962; Zanzibar 1963, 1964)
		Trinidad and Tobago (1962, 1976) (NEP)
		Uganda (1962, 1967) (EP)
		Vanuatu (1980) (NEP)
		Zambia (1964) (EP)
		Zimbabwe (1980) (EP)

APPENDIX TWO — *continued*

[1] Year in brackets refers to the year in which independence was gained.

[2] Opinions differ about the year, or the respective years, in which Australia, Canada and New Zealand became independent.

[3] His Highness Malietoa Tanumafili II is the sole Head of State for life. However, there is provision in the 1962 Western Samoa Constitution for a head of state to be elected by the Legislative Assembly for a five-year term.

[4] Years in brackets refer to the year in which independence was gained, then the year in which the country became a republic.

[5] (NEP) – non-executive presidency.

[6] (EP) – executive presidency.

APPENDIX THREE[3]

COMPARATIVE TABLES ON APPOINTMENT OF HEADS OF STATE

COMMONWEALTH COUNTRIES – NON–EXECUTIVE PRESIDENCIES

Country	Method of Election of President	Minimum age	Term of office	Re-election	Removal of President	Vice-President
Bangladesh*	Parliament	35 years	5 years	Only once	By 2/3 absolute majority of Parliament on the grounds of violating the Constitution or grave misconduct, or by 2/3 absolute majority of Parliament on the grounds of physical or mental incapacity after a report by a medical board.	No
India**	Electoral college of members of both Houses of the Parliament and members of Legislative Assemblies of the States	35 years	5 years	Yes	By 2/3 absolute majority of either house of the Parliament on impeachment, on a charge preferred by the other House by 2/3 absolute majority, on the grounds of violation of the Constitution.	Yes
Malta*	Parliament	–	5 years	Yes	By resolution of Parliament on the grounds of inability to perform the functions of President or of misbehaviour.	No
Mauritius*	Parliament	40 years	5 years	Yes	By Parliament on a motion by the Prime Minister after report by Tribunal on grounds of violation of Constitution or other serious misconduct, or inability to perform functions.	Yes
Singapore*	Popular election after screening of candidates by pre-selection committee	45 years	6 years		By 3/4 of the Parliament after report of tribunal appointed by Chief Justice (after reference by Parliament on absolute majority vote) on grounds of intentional violation of Constitution, treason, misconduct or corruption, or an offence involving fraud, dishonesty or moral turpitude.	No

APPENDIX THREE — *continued*

Trinidad and Tobago**	Electoral college consisting of all members of both Houses of Parliament after nomination by at least 12 members of House of Representatives	35 years	5 years	Yes	By vote of 2/3 of combined membership of both Houses of Parliament voting together after considering report of judicial tribunal (after reference by a motion signed by 1/3 of the members of the House of Representatives) on the grounds of wilful violation of the Constitution, acting in a way to bring the office into hatred, ridicule or contempt, or endangering the State, or inability to perform the functions of the office because of physical or mental incapacity.	No
Vanuatu*	Electoral college consisting of Parliament and Presidents of Regional Councils by 2/3 majority of members	25 years	5 years	Yes	By 2/3 of members of electoral college on motion introduced by at least 1/3 of members, on the grounds of gross misconduct or incapacity.	No

*   Parliament is unicameral.
** Parliament is bicameral.

APPENDIX THREE — *continued*

NON-COMMONWEALTH COUNTRIES – NON-EXECUTIVE PRESIDENCIES

Country	Method of election	Minimum age	Term of office	Re-election	Removal	Vice Pres
Austria**	Popular election with a second election between the 2 leading candidates if no candidate gets more than half the votes in the first ballot. The ballot is in the form of a referendum if there is only one candidate.	35 years	6 years	Only once	1. By the federal constitutional court on a finding that the President has breached the Constitution (on application of both Houses of Parliament in a joint sitting). 2. By popular referendum on the application of 2/3 majority of the Parliament (confirmed by simple majority of both Houses sitting jointly). 3. On the recording of a criminal conviction (after waiver of immunity by both Houses of Parliament sitting jointly).	No
Germany**	Special Federal Convention (*Bundesversammlung*) composed of members of the National Assembly (*Bundestag*) and an equal number of members chosen by the state legislatures.	40 years	5 years	Only once	Either House of the federal Parliament may impeach the President before the Federal Constitutional Court for wilful violation of the Basic Law or any other federal law. The motion must be brought forward by 1/4 of the members of lower or upper House and the decision to impeach requires a 2/3 majority of the lower or upper House.	No
Greece*	Secret ballot in Parliament by an exhaustive process initially requiring 2/3 majority; if a result is not obtained, then a 3/5 majority; a dissolution of Parliament; then if a result is not obtained, an absolute majority; then simple majority.	40 years	5 years	Only once	By special court after vote of 2/3 majority of members of Parliament on the grounds of high treason or intended violation of the Constitution.	No
Iceland**	Popular election on nomination by between 1,500 and 3,000 voters.	35 years	4 years	Yes	By referendum called by 3/4 majority of members of both Houses of Parliament acting jointly.	No

APPENDIX THREE — *continued*

Ireland**	Popular election on the nomination of 20 members of Parliament, 4 County Councils or self-nomination by former or retiring President. There is no election unless there is more than one candidate.	35 years	7 years	Only once	By 2/3 absolute majority of either House of Parliament on impeachment by 2/3 majority of other House for stated misbehaviour, or on the grounds of permanent incapacity to the satisfaction of the Supreme Court.	No
Israel*	By the Knesset on the nomination of 10 or more members	–	5 years	Only once	By Knesset (following complaint by at least 20 members) by 3/4 majority on the grounds of unworthiness 'owing to conduct unbecoming his status as President'.	No
Italy**	Electoral college (parliament sitting jointly with delegates of Regional Assemblies) with 2/3 majority (after 3rd ballot, by an absolute majority).	50 years	7 years	Yes	By constitutional court on impeachment.	No
Portugal*	Popular election nominated by between 7,500 and 15,000 voters.	35 years	5 years	Only once consecutively	Following conviction by a court for an offence committed in the course of Presidential duties in proceedings initiated by Parliament after a 2/3 majority vote of members.	No

*   Parliament is unicameral.
** Parliament is bicameral.

APPENDIX FOUR[4]

COMPARATIVE TABLE ON POWERS OF HEADS OF STATES

COMMONWEALTH COUNTRIES – CONSTITUTIONAL MONARCHIES

Country	Appointment of Prime Minister	Dismissal of Prime Minister	Dissolution of Parliament
Antigua and Barbuda	The Governor–General acts on ministerial advice except where he is required to act 'in his discretion'. Article 80. The Governor–General appoints a member of the House of Assembly who leads the political party that commands the support of the majority of members, or who is most likely to command the support of the majority of members. Article 69.	The Governor–General **shall** revoke the appointment of the Prime Minister where the House of Assembly has passed a vote of no-confidence and the Prime Minister has not within 7 days resigned or advised a dissolution of Parliament. Article 73.	The Governor–General dissolves Parliament on ministerial advice, except that the Governor–General **may** in his discretion dissolve Parliament where the House passes a resolution of no-confidence in the Government and the Prime Minister has not within 7 days either resigned or advised a dissolution of Parliament. Article 60.
Australia	By convention, the Governor–General acts on ministerial advice, except in relation to the exercise of the 'reserve' powers. The Governor–General appoints Ministers, one of whom is the Prime Minister. Section 64.	Ministers hold office 'at the Governor–General's pleasure'. Section 64.	The Governor–General dissolves Parliament. Section 5.

APPENDIX FOUR — *continued*

Bahamas	The Governor–General acts on ministerial advice but acts in 'his own deliberate judgment' in appointing the Prime Minister and in dissolving Parliament. Article 79. The Governor–General appoints the member of the House of Assembly who leads the party which commands the support of the majority of the members, or who is most likely to command the support of the majority of members. Article 73	The Governor–General **must** dismiss the Prime Minister where the House of Assembly has passed a vote of no confidence and the Prime Minister has not within 7 days resigned or advised a dissolution of Parliament. Article 74.	The Governor–General dissolves Parliament on ministerial advice, except that the Governor–General **may** dissolve Parliament otherwise than on advice where the office of the Prime Minister is vacant and the Governor–General considers that there is no prospect of being able to make an appointment within a reasonable time. Article 66.
Barbados	The Governor–General acts in accordance with ministerial advice except where expressly required to act 'in his discretion'. Article 32 The Governor–General acting in his discretion shall appoint the member of the House of Assembly who in his judgment is best able to command the confidence of a majority of the members. Article 65.	The Governor–General **shall** revoke the appointment of the Prime Minister (otherwise than on advice) where the House of Assembly has voted that a revocation should be made and the Prime Minister has not within 3 days resigned or advised a dissolution of the Assembly. Article 66.	The Governor–General dissolves Parliament on the advice of the Prime Minister, except that the Governor–General **shall** dissolve Parliament (otherwise than on advice) where the office of the Prime Minister is vacant and the Governor–General considers that there is no prospect of being able to make an appointment within a reasonable time. Article 61.

APPENDIX FOUR — *continued*

COMMONWEALTH COUNTRIES – CONSTITUTIONAL MONARCHIES

Country	Appointment of Prime Minister	Dismissal of Prime Minister	Dissolution of Parliament
Belize	The Governor–General acts on ministerial advice except where required to act in his own deliberate judgment. Article 34. The Governor–General (acting in his deliberate judgment) appoints a member of the House of Representatives who leads the political party which commands the support of the majority of the members, or who appears to him likely to command the support of the majority of members. Article 37.	The Governor–General **shall** remove the Prime Minister from office (in his own deliberate judgment) where the House of Representatives has passed a vote of no confidence in the Government and the Prime Minister has not within 7 days resigned or advised a dissolution of the National Assembly. Section 37.	The Governor–General **may** dissolve the National Assembly at any time on the advice of the Prime Minister, except that in his deliberate judgment – • the Governor–General **may refuse** to dissolve if he considers that government can be carried on without a dissolution and it would not be in the interests of the country to dissolve; • the Governor–General **may** dissolve if a resolution of no confidence in the Government is passed by the House of Representatives and the Prime Minister does not within 7 days resign or advise a dissolution; and • the Governor–General **shall** dissolve if the office of the Prime Minister is vacant and the Governor–General considers that there is no prospect of being able to make an appointment to that office within a reasonable time. Article 84.
Canada	By convention, the Governor–General acts on ministerial advice except in relation to the exercise of the 'reserve' powers. The Governor–General appoints Ministers. Section 11/Letters Patent.	The Governor–General may remove Privy Councillors at any time. Section 11/Letters Patent.	The Governor–General dissolves Parliament. Section 49.

APPENDIX FOUR — *continued*

Grenada	The Governor–General acts on ministerial advice except in cases where he is required to act 'in his own deliberate judgment'. Article 62. The Governor–General (acting in his deliberate judgment) appoints a member of the House of Representatives who appears to him likely to command the support of the majority of the members. Article 58.	The Governor–General **may** (acting in his own deliberate judgment) remove the Prime Minister from office if – • a resolution of no confidence in the Government is passed by the House of Representatives and the Prime Minister has not within 3 days resigned or advised a dissolution of Parliament; or • after an election but before the House first meets, the Governor–General considers that as a result of changes in membership of the House resulting from that election, the Prime Minister will not be able to command the support of the majority of members of the House. Article 58.	The Governor–General **may** at any time dissolve Parliament on ministerial advice, except that the Governor–General in his deliberate judgment – • **may** dissolve if the majority of all members of the House of Representatives resolve that they have no confidence in the Government and the Prime Minister does not within 3 days either resign or advise a dissolution; and • **shall** dissolve if the office of the Prime Minister is vacant and the Governor–General considers that there is no prospect of being able to make an appointment within a reasonable time. Article 52.
Jamaica	The Governor–General acts on ministerial advice except where required to act 'in his discretion'. Article 80. The Governor–General acting in his discretion appoints the member of the Assembly who in his judgment is best able to command the confidence of a majority of the members of that House. Article 70.	The Governor–General **shall** revoke the appointment of the Prime Minister where the House of Representatives has voted that the appointment should be revoked and the Prime Minister has not within 3 days requested a dissolution. Article 71.	The Governor–General **may** at any time dissolve Parliament on ministerial advice, except that if the House of Representatives has resolved that it does not have confidence in the Government, the Governor–General **shall** dissolve Parliament. Article 64.
New Zealand	By convention, the Governor–General acts on ministerial advice, except in relation to the 'reserve' powers. The Governor–General appoints the Prime Minister. Letters Patent.	The Prime Minister holds office at the Governor–General's pleasure. Letters Patent.	The Governor–General may dissolve Parliament. Section 18.

APPENDIX FOUR — *continued*

COMMONWEALTH COUNTRIES – CONSTITUTIONAL MONARCHIES

Country	Appointment of Prime Minister	Dismissal of Prime Minister	Dissolution of Parliament
Papua New Guinea	The Governor–General acts on ministerial advice or some other body or authority prescribed for that purpose. Article 86. The Prime Minister is elected by the Parliament. Article 142.	1. Governor–General **must** dismiss the Prime Minister after a vote of no confidence (except in the fifth year from the last election) or where dismissal is recommended by a tribunal for misconduct in office. 2. Governor–General **may** dismiss the Prime Minister acting in accordance with a decision of the Parliament where 2 medical practitioners have advised that the Prime Minister is unfit by reason of physical or mental capacity to carry out his duties. Article 142.	1. Constitution provides for a 5 year term, dissolution within the last 12 months after a loss of confidence, or where the Parliament, by an absolute majority decides. Article 105. 2. The Governor–General fixes the date of polling and return of the writs but only in accordance with the advice of the Electoral Commission. Article 105.
St Christopher & Nevis	The Governor–General acts on ministerial advice except where authorised to act 'in his own deliberate judgment'. Article 56. The Governor–General (acting in his deliberate judgment) appoints a Representative who appears to him likely to command the support of the majority of the Representatives. Article 52.	1. The Governor–General **shall** remove the Prime Minister from office if a resolution of no confidence in the Government is passed by the National Assembly and the Prime Minister has not within 3 days resigned or advised a dissolution of Parliament. 2. The Governor–General **may**, in his deliberate judgment, remove the Prime Minister if, after an election, the Governor–General considers that as a result of the election, the Prime Minister will not be able to command the support of the majority. Article 52.	The Governor–General **may** at any time dissolve Parliament on ministerial advice, except that the Governor–General **shall** dissolve Parliament if the office of the Prime Minister is vacant and the Governor–General, acting in his own deliberate judgment, considers that there is no prospect of being able to make an appointment to that office within a reasonable time. Article 47.

APPENDIX FOUR — *continued*

St. Lucia	The Governor–General acts on ministerial advice except where required to act 'in his own deliberate judgment'. Article 64. The Governor–General (acting in his deliberate judgment) appoints a member of the House who appears to him likely to command the support of the majority of the members of the House. Article 60.	1. The Governor–General **shall** remove the Prime Minister if a resolution of no confidence in the Government is passed by the House and the Prime Minister does not within 3 days either resign or advise a dissolution of Parliament. 2. The Governor–General **may**, acting in his deliberate judgment, remove the Prime Minister from office if after a general election, the Governor–General considers that as a result the election, the Prime Minister will not be able to command the support of the majority. Article 60.	The Governor–General **may** at any time dissolve the Parliament acting in accordance with advice of the Prime Minister, except in his deliberate judgment – • the Governor–General **may** refuse to dissolve if he considers that government can be carried on without a dissolution and it would not be in the interests of the country to dissolve; • the Governor–General **may** dissolve if a resolution of no confidence in the Government is passed by the House and the Prime Minister does not within 3 days either resign or advise a dissolution, the • the Governor–General **shall** dissolve if the office of the Prime Minister is vacant and the Governor–General considers that there is no prospect of being able to make an appointment to that office within a reasonable time. Article 55.
St. Vincent & The Grenadines	The Governor–General acts on ministerial advice except where authorised to act 'in his own deliberate judgment'. Article 55. The Governor–General (acting in his deliberate judgment) appoints a member of the House of Assembly who appears to him likely to command the support of the majority of the House of Representatives. Article 51.	1. The Governor–General **shall** remove the Prime Minister if a resolution of no confidence in the Government is passed by the House and the Prime Minister has not within 3 days resigned or advised a dissolution of Parliament. In exercising this power, the Governor–General is not required to act in accordance with ministerial advice. 2. The Governor–General may, acting in his own deliberate judgment, remove the Prime Minister from office if after a general election, the Governor–General considers that as a result of the election, the Prime Minister will not be able to command the support of a majority. Article 51.	The Governor–General **may** at any time dissolve the Parliament on ministerial advice of the Prime Minister, except that in his deliberate judgment – • the Governor–General **may** refuse to dissolve if he considers that government can be carried on without a dissolution and it would not be in the interests of the country to dissolve; • the Governor–General **may** dissolve if a resolution of no confidence in the Government is passed by the House and the Prime Minister does not within 3 days either resign or advise a dissolution; • the Governor–General **shall** dissolve if the office of the Prime Minister is vacant and the Governor–General considers that there is no prospect of being able to make an appointment within a reasonable time. Article 48.

APPENDIX FOUR — *continued*

COMMONWEALTH COUNTRIES – CONSTITUTIONAL MONARCHIES

Country	Appointment of Prime Minister	Dismissal of Prime Minister	Dissolution of Parliament
Solomon Islands	The Governor–General acts on ministerial advice except where required to act 'in his deliberate judgment'. Article 31. The Prime Minister is elected by the Parliament. Article 30.	1. The Governor–General **shall** remove the Prime Minister from office where a resolution of no confidence is passed by Parliament. Article 34.	The Governor–General **shall** dissolve Parliament where Parliament by an absolute majority decides. Article 73
Tuvalu	The Governor–General acts on ministerial advice except where required to act 'in his own deliberate judgment (in which case he shall exercise an independent discretion)'. Article 52. The Prime Minister is elected by members of the Parliament. Article 63.	1. The office of the Prime Minister becomes vacant if he resigns or dies; a new election is held; he ceases to be a member of Parliament; or if a motion of no confidence in the Government receives a majority of votes of the total membership of the Parliament. 2. The Governor–General **may**, acting in his own deliberate judgment, remove the Prime Minister from office where after considering a report from medical practitioners the Governor–General is satisfied that it is in the interests of good government to do so. Article 64.	1. The Governor–General, acting in accordance with a resolution of Parliament, **may** at any time dissolve Parliament. 2. The Governor–General **may**, acting in his own deliberate judgment, dissolve Parliament if the office of Prime Minister is vacant and no person has been elected to that office within such period as the Governor–General, acting in his own deliberate judgment, thinks reasonable. Article 118.

APPENDIX FOUR — *continued*

COMMONWEALTH COUNTRIES – NON–EXECUTIVE PRESIDENCIES

Country	Appointment of Prime Minister	Dismissal of Prime Minister	Dissolution of Parliament
Bangladesh	The President acts on ministerial advice except in appointing the Prime Minister. Article 48 The President appoints the member of Parliament who appears to him to command the support of the majority of the members of Parliament. Article 56	If the Prime Minister ceases to retain the support of a majority of members of the Parliament, he shall either resign or advise the President to dissolve Parliament. Article 57.	1. The President shall dissolve the Parliament if advised to by the Prime Minister after a vote of no-confidence if satisfied that no other member of Parliament can command the support of a majority of members of Parliament. Article 57 2. The President shall dissolve Parliament in accordance with the written advice of the Prime Minister. Article 72.
Dominica	The President acts on ministerial advice except where authorised to act 'in his own deliberate judgment'. Article 63. The President acting in his deliberate judgment appoints the member of the House of Representatives who appears to him to command the support of a majority of its elected members. Article 58.	1. The President shall remove the Prime Minister if a resolution of no confidence in the Government is passed and the Prime Minister has not within 3 days resigned or advised a dissolution. 2. The President may in his deliberate judgment remove the Prime Minister from office if, after an election, the President considers that as a result of the election the Prime Minister will not be able to command the support of a majority. Article 58.	The President may at any time dissolve Parliament on the advice of the Prime Minister, except that the President shall dissolve Parliament if the office of the Prime Minister is vacant and the President, acting in his own deliberate judgment, considers that there is no prospect of being able to make an appointment within a reasonable time. Article 54.
India	The President acts on ministerial advice. Article 74. The President appoints the Prime Minister. Article 75.	Ministers hold office during the pleasure of the President. Article 75.	The President may from time to time dissolve the House of the People. Article 85.

APPENDIX FOUR — continued

COMMONWEALTH COUNTRIES – NON-EXECUTIVE PRESIDENCIES

Malta	The President acts on ministerial advice, except he acts 'in accordance with his own deliberate judgment' in dissolving Parliament otherwise than on advice and in appointing and removing the Prime Minister. Article 85.	1. The President dissolves Parliament on ministerial advice, except that the President **may** dissolve Parliament otherwise than on that advice where –
		• within 3 days after a vote of no confidence, the Prime Minister has not resigned or advised a dissolution;
		• the office of the Prime Minister is vacant and the President considers that there is no prospect of being able to make an appointment to the office within a reasonable time.
	The President appoints the member of the House of Representatives who in his judgment is best able to command the support of a majority of the members of that House. Article 80.	2. The President can refuse to dissolve the Parliament if the President believes that government can be carried on without a dissolution and it would not be in the interests of the country to dissolve. Article 76.
	The President **may** remove the Prime Minister if a vote of no confidence in the Government is passed and the Prime Minister has not within 3 days resigned or advised a dissolution of Parliament. Article 81.	
Mauritius	The President acts on ministerial advice except where he is required to act 'in his own deliberate judgment'. Article 64.	The President dissolves Parliament on ministerial advice, except that the President can dissolve Parliament acting in his own deliberate judgment where –
		• if within 3 days of a vote of no confidence, the Prime Minister has not resigned or advised a dissolution of Parliament; or
	The President appoints the member of the Assembly who appears to the President, acting in his own deliberate judgment, best able to command the support of a majority of the Assembly. Article 59.	• where the office of the Prime Minister is vacant and the President considers that there is no prospect of being able to make an appointment to that office within a reasonable time. Article 57.
	1. The President **shall** remove the Prime Minister if a resolution of no confidence in the Government is passed and the Prime Minister has not within 3 days resigned or advised a dissolution of Parliament.	
	2. The President **may** remove the Prime Minister after an election if the President considers acting in his own deliberate judgment that the Prime Minister will not be able to command the support of the Assembly (provided that the opposition has gained a majority of seats). Article 60.	

APPENDIX FOUR — *continued*

Pakistan	The President acts on the advice of the Prime Minister and such advice shall be binding on him. Article 48. The Prime Minister is elected by the National Assembly 30 days after a general election and a new Prime Minister takes office if named as part of a motion of no confidence in the current Prime Minister. Article 91.	1. The Prime Minister ceases to hold office if a vote of no confidence is passed in the Prime Minister in the National Assembly in which a successor is named. Article 96. 2. A Prime Minister who through the President seeks a vote of confidence by means of a popular referendum and loses that referendum is deemed to have tendered his or her resignation. Article 96A.	The President **shall** dissolve the National Assembly if so advised by the Prime Minister, except where – • a resolution of no confidence against the Prime Minister is pending or has been passed; • the Prime Minister has resigned ; or • another Minister is performing the Prime Minister's functions. Article 58.
Singapore	The President acts on ministerial advice, but may act in his discretion in appointing the Prime Minister and withholding consent to a request for a dissolution of Parliament. Article 21. The President appoints as Prime Minister a Member of Parliament who in his judgment is likely to command the confidence of the majority of Members of Parliament. Article 25.	The President declares the office of Prime Minister vacant if – • the Prime Minister resigns; or • the President, acting in his discretion, is satisfied that the Prime Minister has ceased to command the confidence of a majority of the Members of Parliament, except that the President may dissolve Parliament instead of making such a declaration if the Prime Minister requests it. Article 26.	1. The President **may**, acting in his discretion, dissolve Parliament if the office of Prime Minister is vacant and a reasonable period of time has elapsed since the office was last vacated and there is no Member of Parliament likely to command the confidence of a majority of Members. 2. The President **may** at any time dissolve Parliament on the advice of the Prime Minister but is not obliged to do so unless he is satisfied that in tendering that advice, the Prime Minister commands the confidence of a majority of the Members of Parliament. Article 65.

APPENDIX FOUR — *continued*

COMMONWEALTH COUNTRIES – NON–EXECUTIVE PRESIDENCIES

Trinidad & Tobago	The President acts on ministerial advice except in cases where he is required to act 'in his discretion. He acts in his own deliberate judgment' in appointing the Prime Minister. Article 80. The President shall appoint as Prime Minister the member of the House of Representatives who leads the party which commands the support of the majority of members, or who is most likely to command the support of the majority of members. Article 76.	The Prime Minister shall revoke the appointment of the Prime Minister where the House of Representatives passes no confidence motion in the Prime Minister and the Prime Minister has not within 7 days resigned or advised a dissolution. Article 77.	The President, acting in accordance with the advice of the Prime Minister, **may** at any time dissolve Parliament. Article 68.
Vanuatu	The Prime Minister is elected by Parliament. Article 39.	1. The Prime Minister ceases to hold office – • where a motion of no confidence has been passed by an absolute majority of the members; • when, after a general election, Parliament meets to elect a new Prime Minister; • if the Prime Minister ceases to be a member of Parliament for any reason (other than a dissolution of Parliament); or • he is elected as President or Speaker. Articles 41 and 43.	1. The President **may**, on the advice of the Council of Ministers, dissolve Parliament. 2. Parliament **may** at any time decide, by resolution of an absolute majority of members at a special sitting at which 3/4 of members are present, to dissolve itself. Article 26.

APPENDIX FOUR — *continued*

NON–COMMONWEALTH COUNTRIES – NON–EXECUTIVE PRESIDENCIES

Country	Appointment of Prime Minister	Dismissal of Prime Minister	Dissolution of Parliament
Austria	The President appoints the Federal Chancellor, and other ministers on the advice of the Federal Chancellor. Article 69.	1. The President may dismiss the Federal Chancellor. Article 70. 2. The President must dismiss the Federal Chancellor if the National Diet passes a vote of no confidence in the Chancellor. Article 74.	The Federal Chancellor may dismiss the National Diet on the advice of the Federal Council of Ministers. Article 29.
Germany	The President appoints the person elected by the majority of members of the Bundestag to be Federal Chancellor on a proposal of the President. Article 63.	The President must dismiss the Federal Chancellor at the request of the Bundestag after it has expressed its lack of confidence in the Chancellor and elected a successor. Article 68.	1. Where the Bundestag has not assented to a vote of confidence in the Federal Chancellor, the President may dissolve the Bundestag on the Chancellor's, advice provided that the Bundestag has not elected another Federal Chancellor. Article 67. 2. The President may dissolve the Bundestag if it fails to elect a Federal Chancellor. Article 63.
Republic of Ireland	The President acts on ministerial advice except where required to act in his absolute discretion. Article 13.9. The President appoints on the advice of the Dáil Éireann (lower House). Article 13.1.	The Prime Minister shall resign from office on his ceasing to retain the support of a majority in Dáil Éireann unless on his advice the President dissolves the Dáil Éireann and on its reassembly after the dissolution the Prime Minister secures the support of a majority in the Dáil Éireann. Article 28.10.	1. Dáil Éireann shall be dissolved by the President on the advice of the Prime Minister. 2. The President **may**, in his absolute discretion, refuse to dissolve Dáil Éireann on the advice of a Prime Minister who has ceased to retain the support of a majority in Dáil Éireann. Article 13.2.

APPENDIX FOUR — continued

NON-COMMONWEALTH COUNTRIES – NON-EXECUTIVE PRESIDENCIES

Israel	The President invites a member of the Knesset to form a government which is only constituted when it has received a vote of confidence in the Knesset. Articles 9 and 11.	A Government which receives a vote of no-confidence from the Knesset must tender its resignation to the President.	The President has no role in dissolution of the Knesset.
Italy	The President appoints the Prime Minister. Article 92. The Government must enjoy the confidence of Parliament and must obtain its confidence within 10 days of formation. Article 94.	There is no express provision.	The President may dissolve one or both Chambers after consultation with their Chairmen. Article 88.

APPENDIX FIVE[5]

EXPENDED AND OBSOLETE PROVISIONS IN THE CONSTITUTION – A SURVEY OF PROPOSALS

TABLE 9.1

EXPENDED AND OBSOLETE PROVISIONS IN THE CONSTITUTION – A SURVEY OF PROPOSALS

Section of Constitution	Professor Winterton's Draft[1]	1988 Constitutional Commission[2]	1983 Constitution Alteration Bill[3]	1976 Hobart Constitutional Convention[4]	Comments
s. 3	yes	yes (p. 337)	no	yes	The reference to the Governor–General's salary is outdated. The Hobart Convention recommended that the words 'an annual sum which, until the Parliament otherwise provides, shall be ten thousand pounds' be replaced by 'such annual sum as the Parliament provides'. The Winterton draft and the Constitutional Commission go further and specify that the salary shall not be reduced during the term of the appointment, rather than the current requirement that it not be altered. The Winterton draft, which is a draft republican Constitution, omits the reference to the Queen.
s. 5 (last paragraph)	yes	yes (p. 174)	yes	yes	Expended: transitional provision dealing with summoning of first Parliament.
s. 7 (second paragraph)	yes	yes (p. 980)	no	no	Expended on the basis of the argument that Queensland's power to divide itself into different divisions for Senate elections cannot be revived, even if the Commonwealth (which has 'otherwise provided' in the Commonwealth Electoral Act) were to repeal that legislation.
s. 10	no	yes (p. 215)	no	no	The part of the provision which applies State electoral laws to the election of Senators until Parliament otherwise provides is clearly expended. It ceased to have operation as soon as the Commonwealth Parliament enacted electoral laws. But the conferral of power – via s. 51(xxxvi) – to legislate with respect to Senate elections would need to be retained in any rewording. Similar comments apply to s. 31 of the Constitution which has similar language referring to House of Representatives elections.
s. 15 (paragraphs 5 to 8)	yes	yes (p. 982)	yes	not applicable (inserted in 1977)	Expended: lengthy provisions dealing with transitional issues relevant to Senate casual vacancies in 1977, including if the 1977 referendum on simultaneous elections had proved successful (it wasn't).
s. 25	yes	yes (pp. 155–7)	yes	yes	The argument here is that the provision, which excludes from the census persons of any race who may be disqualified from voting by a State law, is clearly outmoded. But this is a policy judgment, not a legal assessment. While it has no practical operation at present, it is theoretically possible for it to do so, if a State were to introduce a racially discriminatory franchise. Views on the provision differ. Some support it on the basis that it is a constitutional guarantee penalising any State which denies people the franchise on the ground of race (by diminishing its number of House of Representatives seats under the s. 24 formula). Others oppose it on the basis that it is repugnant for openly contemplating the disqualification of persons from voting on the basis of race.[5]

APPENDIX FIVE — *continued*

Section of Constitution	Professor Winterton's Draft	1988 Constitutional Commission	1983 Constitution Alteration Bill	1976 Hobart Constitutional Convention	Comments
s. 26	yes	yes (p. 191)	yes	yes	Expended: transitional provision dealing with representation in the first Parliament.
s. 31	no	yes (p. 215)	no	no	See comments in relation to s. 10.
s. 34	yes, updating provision but leaving in words 'until Parliament otherwise provides'	yes, but substituting a new provision (pp. 274–288)	no	yes, updating provision but leaving in words 'until Parliament otherwise provides'	The provision sets out qualifications for Members of the House of Representatives (and Senators by virtue of s. 16), including being a 'subject of the Queen' and a minimum age of 21 years, which were to apply until Parliament made other provision. Parliament has made other provision, currently found in s. 163 of the *Commonwealth Electoral Act 1918* which, inter alia, requires a Member or Senator to be an Australian citizen of at least 18 years of age. The provision is therefore expended, except to the extent that it confers a power on Parliament to prescribe qualifications for its members. The Constitutional Commission recommended that Australian citizenship and eighteen years of age be made qualifications set out in the Constitution with Parliament able to prescribe a lower minimum age.[6] The Hobart Convention and the Winterton draft modernise the provision, referring to Australian citizenship and a minimum age of 18 years, but leave in the phrase 'until Parliament otherwise provides'. Such changes might be considered superfluous given that Parliament has already made other provision.
s. 41	no	yes (p. 129)	no	'no adult person' to be replaced by 'no person attaining the age of 18 years'	The Constitutional Commission argued[7] that s. 41 is now a dead letter and should be repealed. This is on the basis of the High Court's decision in 1983 in *R v Pearson; Ex parte Sipka*[8] where six of the seven judges took a narrow reading of s. 41, holding that it was a transitional provision which offered protection only to those people who had acquired the right to vote for the lower House in their State by 1902 (when the first uniform Commonwealth franchise was introduced). Three of the judges stated explicitly that 'the practical effect of s. 41 is spent'. The dilemma here is that, in contrast to other provisions, it is not readily apparent from the language of the section itself that it is expended. This raises the issue of whether it can truly be regarded as expended if there is any room for argument that a future High Court may reverse its approach and give the section more room for operation.
s. 48 (part)	yes	yes (pp. 262)	no	yes	Expended: spent parts of the provision dealing with salaries of Senators and Members ('until Parliament otherwise provides' and 'four hundred pounds' etc) would be removed so that the provision reads simply that Parliament sets the amount

APPENDIX FIVE — *continued*

Section of Constitution	Professor Winterton's Draft	1988 Constitutional Commission	1983 Constitution Alteration Bill	1976 Hobart Constitutional Convention	Comments
s. 51(xxxviii) (part)	no	yes (p. 1049)	no	yes	The words 'or by the Federal Council of Australasia' are redundant in view of the fact that the Constitution itself provides for the handing over to the Commonwealth of all the powers that were previously exercised by the Federal Council of Australasia (the Federal Council of Australasia was abolished by clause 7 of the *Commonwealth of Australia Constitution Act 1901*). In the words of the mover of the motion at the 1975 Melbourne meeting of the Australian Constitutional Convention to abolish this section 'It would appear that nobody is quite sure why the founders of the Constitution included those words.'[9]
s. 52 (ii)	no	yes (pp. 362–3)	no	no	The Constitutional Commission argued that it is not necessary to have an express Commonwealth power to legislate with respect to its own departments. It said that the power was unnecessary and anomalous in that it purports to give the Federal Parliament exclusive power to legislate on matters relating to some departments but not others.[10]
s. 58 (part dealing with reservation power), ss. 59, 60	yes	yes (pp. 82–3)	yes	only recommends repeal of s. 59	These provisions for reservation of laws for, and disallowance of laws by, the Queen – which were designed to ensure Imperial surveillance of colonial legislation – would clearly need to be removed under a republican Constitution. In any event, s. 59 is clearly obsolete: as far back as 1930, the Imperial Conference noted that disallowance of Dominion legislation was outmoded and that such provisions were obsolete.[11] In relation to power of reservation in s. 58, it is arguable whether it is expended (there have been 15 bills reserved for the Queen's pleasure since 1901, the most recent occasions being in 1968, 1973 and 1975).[12] The 1983 Adelaide meeting of the Australian Constitutional Convention and the Constitutional Commission recommended that it should be repealed.
s. 64 (part)	yes	yes (p. 322)	yes	yes	The opening words 'After the first general election' in the final paragraph are spent. The Winterton draft places the redrafted paragraph elsewhere.

APPENDIX FIVE — *continued*

Section of Constitution	Professor Winterton's Draft	1988 Constitutional Commission	1983 Constitution Alteration Bill	1976 Hobart Constitutional Convention	Comments
s. 65 (part)	yes	yes (p. 330)	no	yes	The reference to there being a maximum of seven Ministers until Parliament otherwise provides is clearly expended. The Winterton draft and the Constitutional Commission's recommendations both delete s. 65 but preserve elsewhere the power of Parliament to prescribe the maximum number of Ministers. The Hobart Convention recommended that the latter provision be redrafted to enable Parliament to determine the number of Ministers. The latter part of the provision, which states that Ministers 'shall hold such offices as the Parliament prescribes, or, in absence of provision, as the Governor–General directs' is not expended. Ministers' commissions include the statement that the Governor–General has directed them to hold their particular portfolio offices.
s. 66 (part)	yes	yes (p. 332)	no	yes	Expended: spent parts of the provision dealing with salaries of Ministers ('which, until Parliament otherwise provides, shall not exceed twelve thousand pounds a year') would be removed so that, in line with what is suggested for s. 48, the provision reads simply that Parliament sets the amount.
s. 69	yes	yes (pp. 357–8, 363)	no	no	Expended: provision deals with the transfer of State departments.
s. 73 (last paragraph)	yes (last para)	yes, but other parts reworded (pp. 385–8)	no	no	The last paragraph is expended, with Parliament having otherwise made provision in relation to the restrictions on appeals from State Supreme Courts to the High Court (see s. 35 of the *Judiciary Act 1903*). It also contains an outmoded reference to appeals from State Supreme Courts to the Privy Council (see s. 74 comments below). For a republican Constitution, there is the presentational issue of whether any reference to the 'Queen in Council' (referring to the Privy Council) should remain. The Winterton draft deletes the last paragraph but leaves intact two references to the avenue of appeal to the 'Queen in Council' as at the establishment of the Commonwealth (in the previous paragraph and s. 73(ii)). The Constitutional Commission rewords the provision to delete the last paragraph and the two other references to 'Queen in Council'.

APPENDIX FIVE — *continued*

Section of Constitution	Professor Winterton's Draft	1988 Constitutional Commission	1983 Constitution Alteration Bill	1976 Hobart Constitutional Convention	Comments
s. 74	yes	yes (pp. 388–9)	yes, in part (delete last clause of last sentence)	no	The provision is outmoded as appeals no longer lie to the Privy Council from Australian courts. The *Privy Council (Limitation of Appeals) Act 1968* (Cth) and the *Privy Council (Appeals from the High Court) Act 1975* (Cth) abolished all appeals from the High Court to the Privy Council except those where the High Court grants a certificate pursuant to the first paragraph of s. 74. The High Court has subsequently held, in relation to this power to grant a certificate, that 'such limited purpose as it had has long since been spent' and that the provision is obsolete.[13] Appeals to the Privy Council from State courts were abolished by the *Australia Act 1986* (Cth). The Constitutional Commission recommended that, as well as repealing s 74, the words 'and shall not be subject to appeal, by prerogative or otherwise' should be added to the end of s. 73. This would prevent any arguments that repealing s. 74 would revive the prerogative to admit appeals to the Privy Council. As the phrase 'Queen in Council' is used in s. 74 to refer to the Privy Council, there is an argument that, presentationally, a move to a republic should encompass repeal of this section.
s. 83 (last paragraph)	yes	yes (p. 831)	yes	yes	Expended: transitional provision allowing the Governor–General in Council to draw and spend money for a short period after federation, in relation to the first election and the transfer of departments to the Commonwealth. Because there is a reference to the Governor–General in Council, there is an argument that a move to a republic should encompass repeal of this section.
s. 84 (last paragraph)	yes	yes, but the whole of the section should be repealed (pp. 357–364)	yes	yes	Expended: provision deals with the rights of State officials transferred to the Commonwealth at the time of federation. The Constitutional Commission took the view that all of s. 84 and s. 85, which deal with rights and obligations which arise when State departments are transferred to the Commonwealth, are expended. The Commission believed that these provisions only applied to the original transfer of departments authorised under s. 69. In doing so it differed with Standing Committee C of the Australian Constitutional Convention which thought that s. 84 and s. 85 had continuing operation, particularly if the States made a reference of power under s. 51(xxxvi).

APPENDIX FIVE — continued

Section of Constitution	Professor Winterton's Draft	1988 Constitutional Commission	1983 Constitution Alteration Bill	1976 Hobart Constitutional Convention	Comments
s. 85 (last part of paragraph (i))	yes	yes, but all of the section should be repealed (pp. 357–364)	yes	yes	Expended: the second phrase of para (i) refers to the possibility of a transfer back to the States of State property transferred at federation to the Commonwealth in relation to departments of customs, excise and bounties. See s. 84 above for views of the Constitutional Commission about abolishing the whole section.
ss. 86, 87, 89, 93 and 95	yes	yes (p. 845)	yes	yes, for all but s. 89	Expended: these sections all deal with the transitional arrangements associated with the Commonwealth taking exclusive control of the power to levy customs duties. It is not clear why Standing Committee C omitted s. 89 from this group of sections to be repealed (the explanatory memorandum for the 1983 Bill to remove expended provisions says it was 'inexplicably left out' of the Hobart resolution) – it is clearly spent as it relates only to the period until uniform customs duties were imposed.
s. 90 (second paragraph)	yes	yes (p. 829)	yes	yes	Expended: provision saves grants or agreements for State bounties made before 30 June 1898.
s. 92 (second paragraph)	yes	yes (p. 803)	yes	yes	Expended: provision enabled duty to be charged by the States until the uniform tariff was imposed.
s. 96 (first phrase)	yes, but together with extra words	yes, but together with extra words (pp. 835, 838)	no	no	It is submitted that the words 'During a period of ten years after the establishment of the Commonwealth and thereafter' are clearly expended, even though the 1983 bill and the Hobart resolution did not seek their repeal. The Constitutional Commission argued for their repeal, but in the context of a wider amendment which included the words following on from this phrase, 'until the Parliament otherwise provides'. The Commission argued that these words serve no purpose as it is unlikely that the Parliament would attempt to terminate its power to grant financial assistance – assuming such to be the result of the opening words.[14] But as Parliament has not otherwise provided' (whatever that might consist of), it is difficult to see that the extra words the Commission seeks to repeal can properly be regarded as expended.

APPENDIX FIVE — *continued*

Section of Constitution	Professor Winterton's Draft	1988 Constitutional Commission	1983 Constitution Alteration Bill	1976 Hobart Constitutional Convention	Comments
s. 97	yes	yes (p. 845)	no	yes, but it needs to be replaced with specific power with respect to audit	Apart from the opening words 'until the Parliament otherwise provides' the provision, which deals with transitional arrangements for auditing, is clearly expended. There is argument whether the opening words are redundant. The Constitutional Commission says that the power to audit that this provision, together with s. 51(xxxvi), appears to give Parliament is redundant as it clearly has power to make laws relating to the auditing of the receipt and expenditure of monies under s. 51 (xxxix) in its relation to s. 61.[15] The Hobart resolution, however, expressed the view that this section is the basis of power for the Audit Act and that it would need to be replaced by a specific power with respect to audit.[16]
s. 117 ('subject of the Queen' replaced by 'Australian citizen')	yes	no – replace with 'person' (p. 68)	no	yes	The expression 'subject of the Queen' is clearly obsolete in a republican Constitution. The Constitutional Commission argues that there is no reason to confine the s. 117 protection to Australian citizens and uses the word 'person' in its recommended reformulation of the section which is designed to give it a wider meaning than that which has resulted from High Court decisions.[17]
s. 122 (part)	yes	yes (p. 990)	no	no	Words 'or of any territory placed by the Queen under the authority of and accepted by the Commonwealth' are clearly obsolete, and would obviously be out of place in a republican Constitution.
s. 125 (last paragraph)	yes	no	yes	yes	Expended: upon the move to Canberra in 1927, the provision, which refers to Parliament sitting in Melbourne until it meets at the 'seat of Government', became expended. It is not clear why the Constitutional Commission did not recommend its repeal.

APPENDIX FIVE — *continued*

Footnotes

1 'Professor Winterton's draft' refers to the draft Constitution proposed by Professor Winterton which appeared in the March 1992 issue of *The Independent Monthly*.

2 '1988 Constitutional Commission' refers to the Constitutional Commission's recommendations on expended and outmoded provisions which are distributed throughout its *Final Report of the Constitutional Commission* ('Final Report'), AGPS, Canberra, 1988. The page numbers in this column are references to the *Final Report*.

3 1983 Constitution Alteration Bill' refers to the Constitution Alteration (Removal of Outmoded and Expended Provisions) Bill 1983 which was introduced into the Senate by the then Attorney–General in October 1983. It did not proceed to referendum.

4 1976 Hobart Constitutional Convention' and 'Hobart Convention' refer to the 1976 Hobart meeting of the Australian Constitutional Convention which adopted unanimously a resolution recommending amendments to the Constitution to remove outmoded and expended provisions (*Proceedings of the Australian Constitutional Convention, Hobart 27–29 October 1976*('Proceedings'), Melbourne, 1977, at pp. 140–4 following an identical resolution at the 1975 Melbourne meeting of the Australian Constitutional Convention which itself followed a 1974 report by the Convention's Standing Committee C. The above table does not include references to the recommendations by the Hobart Convention to amend sections 12, 19 and 37 of the Constitution on the basis that the changes proposed, while relatively minor, could not properly be characterised as removing outmoded or expended provisions.

5 Final Report, op. cit., pp. 156–7.

6 ibid, pp. 274–288.

7 ibid, p. 129.

8 (1983) 152 CLR 254.

9 *Proceedings of the Australian Constitutional Convention, Melbourne, 24–26 September 1975*, Melbourne, p. 114).

10 Final Report, op. cit., p. 363.

11 See *Report of the Advisory Committee on Executive Government of the Constitutional Commission*, Canberra, 1987, pp. 8–9.

12 See AR Browning (ed), *House of Representatives Practice*, (2nd ed), AGPS, Canberra, p. 810.

13 *Kirmani v Captain Cook Cruises Pty Ltd (No 2)* (1985) 159 CLR 461, 465.

14 Final Report, op. cit., p. 835.

15 ibid, p. 845.

16 Proceedings, op. cit., p. 175.

17 Final Report, op. cit., p. 68.

NOTES

Chapter One: *A Republican Roused*

1 Invercargill is a town at the southernmost tip of New Zealand.

Chapter Two: *A Dual Identity*

1 Quick and Garran, *Annotated Constitution of the Commonwealth of Australia*, Sydney, 1901, p. 693.
2 C. M. H. Clark, *A History of Australia*, vol. IV, p. 242.
3 Quoted in Quick and Garran, p. 81.
4 J. D. Lang, *Freedom and Independence for the Golden Lands of Australia*, 1852, p. 193.
5 Quick and Garran, p. 295.
6 Quoted in Stephen Alomes and Catherine Jones (eds), *Australian Nationalism*, Sydney, 1901, p. 33.
7 J. D. Lang, p. 34.

8 J. D. Lang, p. 41.
9 J. D. Lang, p. 64.
10 J. D. Lang, pp. 78–79.
11 J. D. Lang, p. 42.

Chapter Three: *The Reluctant Nation*

1 Quick and Garran, *Annotated Constitution of the Common-wealth of Australia*, Sydney, 1901, p. 117.
2 Quoted by A. W. Martin in *Henry Parkes*, Melbourne University Press, Melbourne, 1980, p. 391.
3 Convention Debates, 9 September 1897, p. 239.
4 Convention Debates, 9 September 1897, p. 240.
5 The delegation consisted of Edmund Barton (NSW), Alfred Deakin (Victoria), J. R. Dickson (Queensland), Charles Kingston (South Australia) and Sir Philip Fysh (Tasmania).
6 Quick and Garran, p. 233.
7 Quick and Garran, p. 235.
8 Original s. 74 quoted by L. F. Crisp in *Federation Fathers*, Melbourne University Press, Melbourne, 1990, p. 349.
9 Quick and Garran, p. 240.
10 See above, and section 60 of the Constitution.
11 Quoted in J. A. La Nauze (ed.), *Federated Australia: Selections from letters to the Morning Post 1900–1910 Alfred Deakin*, Melbourne University Press, Melbourne, 1968, p. 187.
12 Hudson and Sharp, *Australian Independence: Colony to Reluctant Kingdom*, Melbourne 1988, pp. 43–44.
13 Hudson and Sharp, p. 45.
14 Hansard, House of Commons *Debates*, vol. 149, 14 December 1921, col. 30.
15 L. F. Fitzhardinge, *The Little Digger: 1914–1952, a Political Biography of William Morris Hughes*, Sydney, 1979, p. 488.
16 L. F. Fitzhardinge, p. 494.
17 From 'Jim, Who ran away from his Nurse, and was eaten by a Lion', in H. Belloc, *Cautionary Verses*, 1940.
18 Quoted by Prime Minister S. M. Bruce in *Commonwealth*

Parliamentary Debates, House of Representatives, 3 March 1927, pp. 65–66.

19 Hudson and Sharp, p. 99.
20 Hudson and Sharp, p. 100.
21 J. Arnold, P. Spearitt and D. Walker (eds), *Out of Empire,* 1993, p. 23.
22 David Day, *The Great Betrayal,* 1988, p. 15.

Chapter Four: *Menzies and Beyond*

1 R. G. Menzies, *Afternoon Light,* Melbourne, 1967, p. 15.
2 R. G. Menzies, p. 16.
3 R. G. Menzies, p. 42, citing letter from Menzies to Bruce 22 February 1940 CRS M103 January–June 1940 AA.
4 David Day, *The Great Betrayal,* 1988, p. 33.
5 *Commonwealth Parliamentary Papers,* 1910, vol. 2, pp. 85–87.
6 Quoted from Lord Moran's diary in Day, p. 241.
7 Curtin's remarks quoted by K. H. Bailey in 'Attitude to Britain', *Round Table,* vol. 32, no. 127, June 1942, pp. 419–21 and extracted in J. Arnold, P. Spearitt and D. Walker, (eds) *Out of Empire,* 1993, p. 71.
8 J. Arnold, P. Spearitt and D. Walker, p. 72.
9 Quoted in David Day, *Reluctant Nation,* Melbourne, 1992, p. 222.
10 H. V. Evatt's second reading speech, 2 October 1942, quoted in *Foreign Policy of Australia: Speeches by H. V. Evatt,* Sydney 1945, p. 94.
11 Sir Percy Spender, *Politics and a Man,* Sydney, 1972, p. 322.
12 For this discussion of the Suez crisis and Australia's role in it, see W. J. Hudson, *Blind Loyalty: Australia and the Suez Crisis, 1956,* Melbourne University Press, Melbourne, 1989.
13 W. J. Hudson, p. 57.
14 W. J. Hudson, p. 64.
15 W. J. Hudson, p. 103.
16 W. J. Hudson, p. 118.
17 W. J. Hudson, p. 126.

18 Invercargill is a town at the southernmost tip of New Zealand.
19 Quoted in Judith Brett, *Robert Menzies' Forgotten People*, Macmillan, 1992, p. 146.
20 *Commonwealth Parliamentary Debates*, 18 February 1953, p. 55.
21 *Commonwealth Parliamentary Debates*, 18 February 1953, p. 57.
22 *Commonwealth Parliamentary Debates*, 18 February 1953, p. 58.
23 F. A. Mediansky (ed.), *Australia in a Changing World*, 1992, p. 107.
24 *Commonwealth Yearbook*, 1910, p. 114.
25 *Commonwealth Yearbook*, 1954, p. 353.
26 Jonathan Aitken, *Land of Fortune*, 1971, p. 23.
27 *Oteri and Oteri v R* (1976) 11 ALR, p. 142.

Chapter Five: *The Office of the President*

1 The British equivalent of Minister for the Navy.
2 *HMS Pinafore*, Act 1.
3 W. Bagehot, *The English Constitution* (2nd edn), Henry S. King, London, 1872 (reprinted Garland Publishing, New York, 1978), p. 57.
4 Republic Advisory Committee 1993, *An Australian Republic: The Options*, vol. 1, *The Report*, H. J. Law, CGP, Canberra, p. 38.
5 *Far Eastern Economic Review*, 14 October 1993.
6 See *NSW v. Commonwealth (No 1)* (1932) 46 CLR 155.
7 A. S. Morrison, 'Dominions Office Correspondence on NSW Constitutional Crises 1930–32', *Journal of the Royal Australian Historical Society*, (1976) 61, 323, 337.
8 Liberal Premier of Western Australia, 1974–82.
9 Although the High Court subsequently held that one of these Bills had not been rejected by the Senate within the meaning of section 57.
10 Republic Advisory Committee 1993, vol. 1, p. 114.
11 Based on G. Winterton, 'A Constitution for an Australian Republic', *Independent Monthly*, March 1992, section 60A.

Chapter Six: *The Election of the President*

1 See George Winterton's proposed republican constitution published in the *Independent Monthly*, March 1992.

Chapter Seven: *The States, the Commonwealth and Public Opinion*

1 Formerly the Attorney-General; in the Fahey Government, Minister for State Development and the Arts.
2 Quoted in McIntyre, *The Significance of the Commonwealth*, 1991, pp. 246–247.
3 Attributed to Benjamin Disraeli by Mark Twain in his *Autobiography*.

Chapter Eight: *Amending the Constitution*

1 See Constitution of South Africa, s. 7(5), and Constitution of Ceylon, 1945, s. 4(2).
2 Statement by Sir John Kerr, Governor-General, issued 11 November 1975; reproduced in Geoffrey Sawer, *Federalism under Strain*, Melbourne University Press, Melbourne, 1977, p. 210.
3 See the discussion of the events following the disappearance of Prime Minister Holt in Appendix 6 to the Report of the Republic Advisory Committee.
4 This section draws a distinction between resolutions carried by an absolute majority of members of the House of Representatives and those which are not. Where a resolution is carried other than by an absolute majority, it may be that the Opposition has secured a temporary majority because Government members are overseas or otherwise unable to attend. Subsections (2) and (4) therefore give the Prime Minister the opportunity to reverse that resolution.

Chapter Nine: *The Politics of the Republic*

1 Quoted in *Weekend Australian*, 1–2 February 1992, p. 1.

2 Sally Loane, 25 February 1992.
3 The use of the term 'mate' gives a clue to his identity. He must have been from New South Wales.
4 *Australian*, 15 May 1992, p. 3.
5 Opposition immigration spokesman, Philip Ruddock, quoted in the *Sunday Age*, 28 June 1992.
6 *Sydney Morning Herald*, 2 March 1993, p. 13.

Chapter Ten: *The Monarchists*

1 *Australian*, 24 June 1993.
2 Sir David Smith, 'Some Thoughts on the Monarchy/ Republic Debate', given at the first fundraising dinner of Leadership Beyond Politics — Australians for Constitutional Monarchy, Parliament House, Sydney, 10 September 1992, p. 6.
3 At p. 225.
4 *Bulletin*, 5 October 1993.
5 *Sydney Morning Herald*, 18 May 1993.
6 *Age*, 11 May 1993.

Chapter Eleven: *Exploring the Options*

1 Quoted in *Telegraph–Mirror*, 29 March 1993.
2 *Weekend Australian*, 9–10 October 1993.
3 Quoted in *Weekend Australian*, 1–2 May 1993.
4 *Canberra Times*, 15 June 1993.
5 *Sydney Morning Herald*, 10 July 1993.
6 *Sydney Morning Herald*, 12 July 1993.
7 *Sydney Morning Herald*, 2 April 1993.
8 *Weekend Australian*, 1–2 May 1993.
9 *Sunday Telegraph*, 2 May 1993.
10 *Sydney Morning Herald*, 17 August 1993.
11 *Telegraph–Mirror*, 28 May 1993.
12 *Sydney Morning Herald*, 9 October 1993.

Appendices

1 This section draws a distinction between resolutions

carried by an absolute majority of members of the House of Representatives and those which are not. Where a resolution is carried other than by an absolute majority, it may be that the Opposition has secured a temporary majority because Government members are overseas or otherwise unable to attend. Subsections (2) and (4) therefore give the Prime Minister the opportunity to reverse that resolution.

2 Republic Advisory Committee 1993, *An Australian Republic: The Options*, vol. 2, H. J. Law, CGP, Canberra, p. 1

3 Republic Advisory Committee 1993, vol. 2, pp. 2–5.

4 Republic Advisory Committee 1993, vol. 2, pp. 6–18.

5 Republic Advisory Committee 1993, vol. 2, pp. 315–322.

INDEX